Inexcusable

Absence

DATE DUE

NOV 28 2011	
MAY 31 2012	

BRODART, CO.   Cat. No. 23-221-003

Inexcusable

Absence

Why 60 million girls still aren't in school
and what to do about it

Maureen A. Lewis and Marlaine E. Lockheed

Center for Global Development
Washington D.C.

Maureen A. Lewis is an Advisor to the Human Development Vice President of the World Bank and a non-resident fellow at the Center for Global Development. She was formerly Chief Economist of the Human Development Network of the World Bank and prior to that managed a unit in the Bank dedicated to economic policy and human development research and programs in Eastern Europe and Central Asia. Marlaine E. Lockheed is a visiting fellow at the Center for Global Development, having retired from the World Bank in 2004. She served as Director for Education, ad interim, for the World Bank, 2000–01, and managed units responsible for education strategy and lending in the Middle East and North Africa and for evaluating the impact of World Bank learning programs.

Copyright © 2006
CENTER FOR GLOBAL DEVELOPMENT
1776 Massachusetts Avenue, N.W.
Washington, D.C. 20036
www.cgdev.org

Library of Congress Cataloging-in-Publication Data

Lewis, Maureen.
Inexcusable absence : Why 60 million girls still aren't in school and what to do about it / Maureen Lewis and Marlaine Lockheed.
 p. cm.
ISBN 1-933286-14-8
1. Sex discrimination in education. 2. Sex discrimination against women. 3. Girls--Education. I. Lockheed, Marlaine E. II. Title.

LC212.8.L49 2006
371.822--dc22

Printed in the United States of America
Editing, cover design, and typesetting by Communications Development Incorporated, Washington, D.C.
Printed by United Book Press, Baltimore, Maryland

The paper used in this publication meets the minimum requirements of the American National Standard for Information Sciences—Permanence of Paper for Printed Library Materials: ANSI Z39.48-1992.

Center for Global Development

The Center for Global Development is an independent, nonprofit policy research organization dedicated to reducing global poverty and inequality and to making globalization work for the poor. Through a combination of research and strategic outreach, the Center actively engages policymakers and the public to influence the policies of the United States, other rich countries, and such institutions as the World Bank, the IMF, and the World Trade Organization, to improve the economic and social development prospects in poor countries. The Center's Board of Directors bears overall responsibility for the Center and includes distinguished leaders of nongovernmental organizations, former officials, business executives and some of the world's leading scholars of development. The Center receives advice on its research and policy programs from the Board and from an Advisory Committee that comprises respected development specialists and advocates.

The Center's president works with the Board, the Advisory Committee and the Center's senior staff in setting the research and program priorities, and approves all formal publications. The Center is supported by an initial significant financial contribution from Edward W. Scott Jr. and by funding from philanthropic foundations and other organizations.

v

Foreword

My interest in girls' education was sparked when I read *The Breadwinner* to my nine-year-old daughter, Nikki. We were both moved by Deborah Ellis's compelling story about a girl in Afghanistan who is forced to disguise herself as a boy in order to support her family. The book depicts the harsh reality that can confront girls, and the barriers they can face in attempting to receive an education. When we closed the book, Nikki asked me simply: "Mummy, what can we do to help?"

In Canada, first as a business leader involved in my community and now as a politician, I have seen the effect of economic and political forces on people's jobs, livelihoods and on their quality of life. I have worked to help build economic opportunities at the community, national and international levels. When I had the honor to serve as a Cabinet Minister in Canada, the Minister of Human Resources and Social Development, I focused on improving the role that government can play in helping out, and helping up, disadvantaged groups in our society. My term as Minister also spanned the Year of Development, when the challenges of meeting basic needs on a global level rose to the forefront of international attention.

Strong leadership at the highest levels of all governments is essential if the international community is to succeed in ensuring that, over time, all countries can provide essential services to poor and disadvantaged citizens. As Maureen Lewis and Marlaine Lockheed show in *Inexcusable*

Absence, girls' schooling is a neglected issue in too many countries; indeed, throughout the developing world, 60 million girls are still out of school, three quarters of them from excluded minorities. The cost in human and economic terms of this effective educational segregation is simply too high, in terms both of opportunity lost to individual girls and women and of the damage to the health of local communities and entire societies. Education is the golden key to advancement, a global right, and yet an entire group of people is denied the ability to contribute fully.

But there's good news. Effective solutions are not only possible—they have been demonstrated, and there is a growing body of best practices.

This book is a very important step in the right direction—but it is only the first step. It is my hope that the policy solutions proposed in the book will focus the global discussion we need to have on girls' education, and stimulate leadership for an action campaign. This is one of the most important issues in global development today.

To make good decisions, we need good information. So I am delighted to see the Center for Global Development take the lead in providing a credible platform for careful research and creative ideas to help make education possible for the world's girls and young women for whom going to school remains an elusive dream.

The Honourable Belinda Stronach
Member of Parliament of Canada (Newmarket-Aurora, Ontario),
and member of the board of directors, Center for Global Development
www.belindastronach.ca

Contents

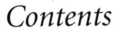

Preface

The images of girls returning to school in Afghanistan after the fall of the Taliban drew attention to the lack of educational opportunities for girls all too common in many developing countries. Girls' education, indisputably crucial to development, has received a lot of attention—but surprisingly little hardheaded analysis to inform practical policy solutions. In *Inexcusable Absence*, Maureen Lewis and Marlaine Lockheed start with an arresting fact: 70 percent of out-of-school girls are "doubly disadvantaged" by their ethnicity, language, or other factors. Remarkable increases in primary schooling over the past decade have brought gender equity to the education systems of many poor countries; yet the problem of these "doubly disadvantaged" girls has yielded little to these advances.

Building on this key point, Lewis and Lockheed propose new strategies for reaching these girls and their parents. Their study is a fine successor to the Center's 2005 contribution to the United Nations Millennium Project series: *Toward Universal Primary Education: Investments, Incentives and Institutions*. Like all of our work at the Center, it aims to provide guidance for donors, activists, and the development community on practical steps to improve the lives of the poor and secure a more prosperous world. In this case, we hope it will also catalyze new thinking and new initiatives on the part of educators and advocates throughout the developing countries.

Getting socially excluded girls into school is not simple. Reaching them is costly, in part because it often requires fresh approaches that may differ from mainstream educational policies. Attempts to change the "culture" of families who are reluctant to send their daughters to school can be controversial. In the classroom, the inclusion of local languages for instruction may make schools more accessible; conversely, limited proficiency in official languages could restrict students' future opportunities in mainstream society. By the same token, gender-segregated schools have the potential to draw more students, but run the risk of establishing a second-class system if sufficient resources are not channeled towards them.

But these problems have been addressed before—in the developed world. Canada, New Zealand and the United States faced challenges in reaching their own excluded groups—indigenous peoples, Maoris, and black Americans and Native Americans, respectively. The authors use these experiences to inform potential strategies to reach the excluded girls in the developing world.

Getting the excluded girls to school is a realistic goal. And giving girls the opportunity of attendance leads to high returns: the book finds that once girls are given access to school, they often overtake boys in the number of years completed and on measures of learning, at least until adolescence. This suggests that lack of opportunity is the single biggest reason that girls' achievement levels lag behind boys'.

Maureen Lewis and Marlaine Lockheed have contributed a much needed understanding both of the complexities of the problem, and of how they can be addressed. *Inexcusable Absence* will be an important tool for policymakers, informing interventions that can make a profound impact on the lives of the 60 million out-of-school girls.

Our decision to undertake the research and analysis that underpin this volume was catalyzed by the keen interests of two of our Board members. Belinda Stronach, then the CEO of Magna International Inc. in Canada and now a Member of Parliament, aware of the barriers girls face in attending school in many parts of the developing world, asked me if the Center had ideas and analysis that could make a difference. And our Board Chair Edward W. Scott, Jr., has not rested in his gentle insistence that we address the problem of discrimination against girls and women all over the world. Preparation and publication of the book was made possible in part by grants from the Nike Foundation, the Jacob and Hilda Blaustein Foundation and the William and Flora Hewlett Foundation, among other sponsors, and by the core support that Ed Scott provides for the Center's work.

Nancy Birdsall
President
Center for Global Development
Washington, D.C.

Acknowledgements

We would like to thank a number of people who contributed to this volume. Nancy Birdsall of the Center for Global Development (CGD) provided the inspiration and impetus for the work and made helpful suggestions throughout, and Elizabeth King (World Bank) initiated our thinking about the issue of gender and ethnicity. Lant Pritchett (World Bank) and Geeta Rao Gupta of the International Center for Research on Women (ICRW) served as peer reviewers and kept us out of trouble. Useful comments were provided by the study group, consisting of Jane Hannaway (The Urban Institute); Sidney Schuler, George Ingram, and Annababette Wils of the Academy for Educational Development (AED); Myra Buvinic, Deon Filmer, and Dominique van der Walle (World Bank); Emily Hannum (University of Pennsylvania); Jennifer Adams (Stanford University); Raquel Gomes (Oxfam); Susan Klein (Feminist Majority); and Kelly Hallman and Cynthia Lloyd (Population Council). Cynthia Lloyd not only participated in the study group but offered constructive comments throughout, and Jacob Meerman—a former World Bank economist and distinguished visiting scholar, Institute of International and Malaysian Studies, National University of Malaysia—provided inputs on social exclusion. Emmanuel Jimenez (World Bank) and Barbara Herz, a former USAID and World Bank official, provided comments on the final draft.

Raquel Gomes, then a post-doctorate fellow at the Center for Global Development, researched and prepared two background papers, one on community schools and one on developed-country education policies toward excluded groups. Lara Iverson, as a consultant to CGD, provided broad support in drafting various topics and developing the anthropological evidence. As research assistant, Bilal Siddiqi of CGD brought spirit and expertise to the team. Bruce Ross-Larson's team at Communications Development edited and produced the book; we thank Elizabeth Collins for her attention to detail in the final stages of production. Lindsay Morgan coordinated production for CGD.

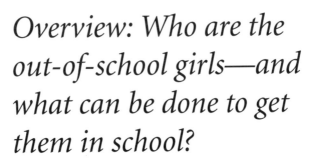

Overview: Who are the out-of-school girls—and what can be done to get them in school?

Impressive strides have been made in bringing girls into primary school over the past 25 years, with many countries achieving universal primary education and gender parity. But considerable disparity exists within and across countries, with intracountry differences stemming largely from the lagging involvement of excluded groups—rural tribes in Pakistan, lower castes in India, Roma in Europe, indigenous peoples in Latin America. Of the 60 million girls not in primary school, almost 70 percent are from excluded groups. If further progress is to be realized, educating these girls must be a priority.

Who are the 60 million girls who remain out of school nearly two decades after the worldwide declaration on Education for All? These are their faces:

Meera, 8, lives with her family on a sidewalk in New Delhi, India. During the day she roams major intersections, her infant sister hanging from her hip, begging drivers for coins in the few words of English she knows. She does not go to school. In a few years she will be married off to a stranger. She will have six children, one of whom will go to school. Or she will die young, possibly immolated in a kitchen fire for having brought with her an insufficient dowry.

Sonia, 10, lives on the outskirts of a capital city in Eastern Europe. Like her siblings, all of whom speak only Romani, she does not attend school. Instead, Sonia spends her days

1

committing petty theft to support her family. Adults in the town spit at her and warn visitors to watch their purses when they see her.

Lia, 12, went to school for a few years in her remote hill village in Thailand. Then her family sent her to the capital to earn a respectable living in a factory, but she was sold into the sex trade instead. She lives in a brothel and services dozens of clients a day. She will die young, most likely from HIV/AIDs.

Wambui, 14, goes to boarding school because no secondary school is available in her Kenyan village. But she will soon be expelled from school because she is pregnant, having been raped at school by boy students from another tribe, who considered it a mere prank.

Many developing countries have achieved gender equity in education, with near-universal girls' participation converging with that of boys:

Indrani, 10, is the daughter of illiterate parents living in rural Bangladesh. She goes to school. Her older sister is finishing secondary school and plans to work in the garment factory in the market center. While her mother was betrothed at 12, her parents have decided that their daughters must finish school before marrying.

Monique, 12, is excelling in secondary school in Tunisia. She and her siblings have finished primary school, with the exception of her eldest sister, whose arranged marriage interrupted her schooling. She expects to work before she marries and plans to have two children.

Are excluded girls simply the daughters of the poor, or are other, more subtle factors at work? Why do some countries make better progress? School participation figures from six low- and middle-income countries offer some clues:

- In Laos, a low-income country, Lao-Tai girls living in rural communities complete five years of school, whereas hill tribe girls living in comparable communities complete fewer than two years of school.
- In Bangladesh, a low-income country, 86 percent of primary school-age girls attend school and 69 percent complete primary school. There is no significant difference between girls living in urban and rural communities.
- In Guatemala, a lower middle-income country, 62 percent of Spanish-speaking girls but only 26 percent of indigenous, non-Spanish-speaking girls complete primary school.
- In Tunisia, a lower middle-income country, 95 percent of all girls complete primary school and 68 percent are enrolled in secondary school.
- In the Slovak Republic, an upper middle-income country, 54 percent of Slovak girls but only 9 percent of minority girls attend secondary school.

- In Botswana, an upper middle-income country, 95 percent of all girls complete primary school and 57 percent attend secondary school.

Sources, forms, and levels of exclusion

What accounts for these differences? Most obvious is the presence or absence of significant subgroups. Bangladesh, Botswana, and Tunisia are largely homogeneous, while Guatemala, Laos, and the Slovak Republic have excluded subgroups.[1] In homogeneous countries higher shares of girls complete primary school, enroll in secondary school, and see higher achievement than those in heterogeneous countries (figure 1).

Excluded subgroups are based on tribal, ethnic, linguistic, or traditional occupational classifications, such as the "untouchable" occupations of the lowest caste groups in India. But ethnic or linguistic diversity within a country does not necessarily lead to a failure to educate girls—the Basques in Spain, for example, are linguistically diverse but have high levels of female education. It is diversity accompanied by derogation and discrimination that leads to exclusion. The main driver of the remaining gender inequalities in education is the existence of subgroups within countries, accompanied by social stratification and cultural norms that seclude women. This driver operates both culturally and structurally to exclude girls from school. It is thus a particularly pernicious barrier.

Exclusion can take many forms—the more severe, the greater its effect on school opportunities (table 1). At one end are extreme forms of exclusion leading to genocide. Only somewhat less severe is the exclusion associated with ethnically based slavery (not slavery as an outcome of conflict), where education is denied to children of slaves, as was the case for African slaves in the southern United States or Brazil in the 1800s. The shunning of a group, such as the Dalits in India or the Roma in Europe, is less severe. It can result in lack of schools, inaccessible schools, segregated or "special" schools, corporal punishment of students, teacher absenteeism, and generally poor-quality schools. Moderate exclusion can result in schooling that is poorly matched with the needs of students. Consider the conditions faced by Berber children in Morocco before 2005 (see box 3.2): teaching and school materials were not in their mother tongue, mild corporal punishment and ability tracking were used, and early qualifying exams excluded poorly performing children from further education.

A mild form of exclusion is that associated with individual social preferences, whereby teachers may overlook students from excluded groups or children from a minority group may not be included in social events. Exclusion can also result in decreased demand for education or for autonomy in the provision of education.

---

1. The excluded subgroups are: indigenous peoples in Guatemala, hill tribes in Laos, and Roma in the Slovak Republic.

Figure 1. Homogeneous countries have stronger education outcomes than comparable heterogeneous countries

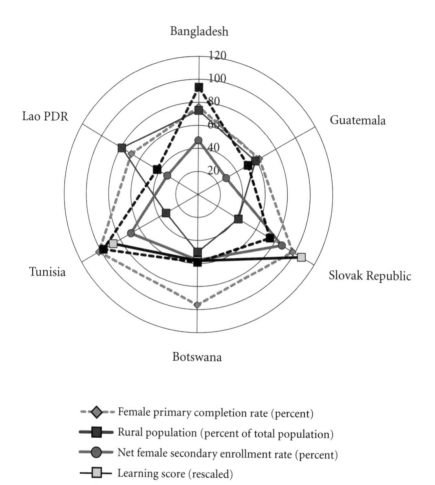

- ◇ Female primary completion rate (percent)
- ■ Rural population (percent of total population)
- ● Net female secondary enrollment rate (percent)
- □ Learning score (rescaled)
- ■ Ethnic homogeneity

Source: World Bank 2005b; Alesina and others 2003; Martin and others 2004; Crouch and Fasih 2004.

Severe exclusion has structural consequences: schools are not built, curricular materials are not supplied, roads to schools are not paved, and teachers are often absent. Milder exclusion is cultural. It can affect the behavior of teachers and schoolmates, making teachers insensitive to excluded students' needs.

Language and ethnicity are only two of the sources of exclusion. Children living in remote rural communities face structural barriers to education due to distance, and these barriers are most pronounced for girls. Poor children face barriers to education due to the direct and indirect costs of education. Because the poor in developing countries often show a strong preference for sons, education investments are biased toward boys. Residential segregation often results in access to poorer quality schools.

The cultures of subgroups can differ with respect to the status and roles accorded to women. Where women are secluded, or expected to work long hours performing domestic chores or agricultural labors, cultural beliefs and norms limit girls' educational opportunities. Girls face special cultural barriers associated with their roles in the home and as future wives. As a result, social exclusion from these multiple sources has severe consequences for girls' education and will require different, more tailored policies to remedy them. The degree and nature of exclusion dictates the approach and scope of interventions; often multiple efforts are needed.

How many girls are excluded?

How many girls are affected by exclusion due to multiple causes? No formal estimates of the numbers of excluded out-of-school girls are available, because most developing countries do not systematically collect or report data on school participation disaggregated by all of the subgroups subject to exclusion. Data from various sources can be used to estimate the figure, however. These data reveal a staggering finding: nearly three-quarters of girls who do not go to school come from excluded groups, while these groups represent only about 20 percent of the developing world's population (table 2).

Most out-of-school girls live in Africa and South Asia, which together account for 78 percent of all girls not in school (UIS 2005). In some large countries a small share of girls are out of school, but the size of the country means that large numbers of girls are affected. In some small countries the share of out-of-school girls is high, which represents a huge national challenge but adds little quantitatively to the global problem. For example, in Guinea-Bissau 55 percent of school-age girls never attend school, but because the total population of the country is little more than 1.2 million, only about 60,000 school-age girls are not in school. By contrast, in India 20 percent of school-age girls are not in school, but with a national population exceeding 1 billion, 27.7 million girls (ages 7–14) are not in school (Census of India 2001).

Data on excluded girls are limited. But recent Indian census data document how multiple exclusions can deter girls' participation in school. Of the nearly 50 million children 7–14 years old not enrolled in school in India, 55 percent are girls. This figure is disproportionately high, with girls representing just 48 percent of all children 7–14 years old. Of the 27.7 million girls 7–14 years old not enrolled in school, 33 percent

Table 1. Levels of social exclusion and their effect on education

Intensity of exclusion	Example of socially excluded groups	School participation indicators
Extreme	• Black Africans in Darfur • Tutsis in Rwanda • Muslims in Bosnia and Kosovo • Tamil in Sri Lanka	• Uneven attendance (even where schools are available)
Severe	• Roma in Eastern Europe • East Asian hill tribes • Dalits and scheduled tribes in India before 1980 • North American indigenous people in nineteenth century • Australian Aboriginals in twentieth century	• Minimal enrollment • Poor attendance • High dropout rate
Moderate	• Berbers in North Africa • Indigenous people in Central America • Maori in New Zealand before 1990 • Scheduled tribes in some states in India • Ethnic minorities in some provinces in China • Tibetans in China	• Low enrollment • Poor attendance • High dropout rate
Mild	• Girls in Yemen and North Africa • Minorities in integrated schools in OECD countries	• Student underperformance • Student rejection of schooling

Demand for schooling and factors reducing demand	Schooling supply and characteristics of schools	Education policy priorities by intensity of exclusion
• Education not a top priority • Formation of separate national entity with its own education system and society	• Inadequate school infrastructure • Destruction of schools • Violence against teachers and communities	• UN Refugee Agency schools • Nongovernmental organizations • Private schools
• Weak demand and reluctance to send children to school • Dissatisfaction with poor or irrelevant schools • Concern about girls' safety and virginity • Low economic returns to education • Discrimination in schools	• Lack or inaccessibility of schools • Language barrier • Segregated or "special" schools • Poor-quality schooling • Corporal punishment • High teacher absenteeism	• Reduce distance to school • Upgrade school infrastructure, improve quality and relevance of schools • Improve outreach to families • Tailor school programs to specific needs • Offer compensatory school programs • Conduct preschool in children's mother tongue; offer bilingual early primary education • Provide distance education
• Low demand • Lagging interest among children • Concern about opportunity cost of time • Low economic returns to education • Discrimination in schools	• Teaching and school materials not in mother tongue • Mild corporal punishment • Ability tracking • Early qualifying exams in language other than mother tongue • Teacher absenteeism	• Provide mother tongue preprimary and bilingual primary school and materials • Provide culturally appropriate teaching and materials • Increase outreach to households and parental involvement in schools • Use interactive radio instruction
• Uneven demand • Alienated and disaffected students • Acceptance of discrimination	• Teachers ignore students • Children from excluded groups may not interact socially with other children	• Address implicit discrimination • Adopt affirmative action • Provide teacher training and incentives for inclusion and tolerance

Table 2. Most primary school-age girls out of school are from excluded groups, 2000

Region	Girls out of school (thousands)	Excluded girls out of school[a] (thousands)	Excluded girls as percent of all girls out of school	Excluded subgroups
Sub-Saharan Africa	23,827	17,870[b]	75	Members of nondominant tribes
South Asia	23,552	15,780[c]	67	Rural people in Afghanistan, scheduled castes and tribes in India, lower castes in Nepal, rural tribes in Pakistan
Middle East and North Africa	5,092	1,680[d]	33	Berbers, rural populations
East Asia and the Pacific	4,870	4,383[e]	90	Hill tribes, Muslim minorities, other ethnic minorities
Eastern Europe and Central Asia, Commonwealth of Independent States	1,583	1,425[f]	90	Roma, rural populations in Turkey
Latin America and the Caribbean	1,497	1,482[e]	99	Indigenous and Afro-Latino populations
Total	60,421	42,620	71	

Note: Data are for girls 7–12-years-old, unless otherwise noted.

a. Estimated. The percentages in column 3 provide the basis for estimating the total number of out-of-school girls by region reported in column 2.

b. Based on the density of heterogeneity and the assumption that most out-of-school children are from minority groups.

c. Based on 2001 census data from India for the number of girls 7–14-years-old from scheduled castes and scheduled tribes, on tribal breakdowns in the Pakistan Integrated Household Survey, a household survey of Nepal, and linguistic and ethnic data from non-urban girls in Afghanistan.

d. Percent of Berbers used to determine the number of out-of-school children.

e. Assumes all children out of school come from excluded groups.

f. Includes Roma and Turkish girls out of school.

Source: UIS 2005; India census 2001; Pakistan household survey 2001–02; Vietnam Living Standard Measurement Survey 1998; Ringold, Orenstein, and Wilkens 2003; Winkler and Cueto 2004.

come from scheduled castes or scheduled tribes.[2] This figure is also disproportionately high, because only 26 percent of girls this age come from scheduled tribes or scheduled castes.

The cost of excluding girls from school is high, and the benefits of inclusion significant, as chapter 1 documents. The social benefits of educating girls have been widely documented, and studies have also found economic benefits from educating girls.

Mild forms of exclusion often affect girls once they enter school, but the evidence suggests that when girls from excluded groups are given the opportunity to go to school, they tend to go—and to succeed—at least through primary school. Their achievement is often comparable to that of girls from nonexcluded groups and equal to or better than that of excluded boys. Given that the quality of primary schools attended by excluded children is often poor, this is remarkable.

A concatenation of sources of exclusion—gender, ethnicity, area of residence—greatly reduces overall achievement by the time girls reach lower secondary school. Designing interventions and proposing solutions thus require assessing the demand for and supply of education and examining the school practices that affect girls and other excluded subgroups. Chapter 2 defines exclusions, analyzes the demand and supply barriers to girls' schooling, and examines key policies.

Lessons from developed countries can guide donors and policymakers in developing countries. But even developed countries grapple with exclusion. In some, failure to establish a level playing field early on has resulted in a backlash that exacerbates rather than mitigates differences. In developing countries, the diversity of subgroups and the specificities of the cultural contexts make building a new body of knowledge essential. The experience of high-income OECD countries is examined in chapter 3, along with discussions of academic performance of excluded groups and girls in both developed and developing countries.

Ensuring that excluded girls go to school is a major challenge, requiring targeted interventions that address both the structural and cultural dimensions of discrimination in education. The costs of failing are tremendous in terms of lives lost and development opportunities missed.

Advancing excluded girls' education

Strategies for advancing excluded girls' education do not apply in all contexts—what works in one country may prove disastrous in another, and "one size does not fit all." Consider busing. In Bulgaria the largely urban and peri-urban Roma community benefited greatly from being bused to better schools. In rural Turkey, busing led parents to

---

2. Scheduled castes are the lowest caste populations in India and include the "untouchables". Scheduled tribes include indigenous people. They are both on a government schedule of disadvantaged groups, hence the name.

pull their daughters out of school over concern for their safety because the new school was in another village. Context is critical. The recommendations proposed in this volume, and elaborated in chapter 4, should thus be options for consideration, not a menu for direct implementation.

Policies to spark progress with the remaining out-of-school populations will require actions on various fronts:

- Altering education policies and addressing discrimination by changing laws and administrative rules.
- Expanding options for educating out-of-school children, especially girls.
- Improving the quality and relevance of schools and classrooms by ensuring that excluded girls receive basic educational inputs and providing professional development to help teachers become agents of change.
- Supporting compensatory preschool and in-school programs that engage and retain excluded children, particularly girls.
- Providing incentives for households to help overcome both the reluctance to send girls to school and the costs of doing so.

Donors could spearhead innovation by:

- Establishing a trust fund for multilateral programs targeted at excluded girls that supports experimentation, innovative programs, alternative schooling options, and the basic inputs for effective schools.
- Expanding the knowledge base about what works to improve the school participation and achievement of excluded girls through a girls' education evaluation fund. The fund could finance a range of evaluations to build the knowledge base for policy. It could also assist more heterogeneous countries in participating in international assessments of learning achievement to monitor change over time.
- Creating demand by financing the compensatory costs associated with reaching excluded children; promoting outreach programs for parents; building partnerships for conditional cash transfers; and providing school meals, scholarships for girls, and school stipend programs for books and supplies.

Altering education policies and addressing discrimination

Changes in policies and rules can help determine the environment in which excluded groups function and increase the credibility of government efforts to reach out-of-school children. Policies alone ensure little, however. Establishing clear mandates against discrimination, a legal system that enforces both entitlements and rights of all citizens, administrative rules that foster the completion of basic education for all children, and an articulated education policy for excluded groups are needed to strengthen the credibility of government, establish a foundation for action, and bring together target populations. These actions also provide a context for engaging donors in advocating for marginalized groups, particularly marginalized girls, and in reaching underserved regions with education programs.

Antidiscrimination laws undergird both legal and policy efforts in fighting exclusion. Clear legal protection offers a beginning in reversing implicit and explicit discrimination against minorities. It has proved critical in Canada, New Zealand, and the United States, where official and public discrimination against minorities was once widespread. South African blacks suffered similarly during apartheid, as did Cuban blacks prior to the revolution of 1958. Unless discrimination is aggressively addressed in the labor market, returns to education will not materialize, reducing the demand for schooling, particularly by girls. Barring trained workers from jobs on the basis of ethnicity, language, or cultural differences has adverse consequences for education because it reduces demand for education by groups that believe the returns will not be positive.

Affirmative action—and the less controversial "preferential" action, which emphasizes bolstering the performance of disadvantaged students while maintaining common standards—has been effective in many countries. Summer math programs and after-school enrichment can strengthen the skills of disadvantaged children. Compensatory programs assume that the minority groups suffer from deficits that can be remedied through tutoring, behavioral guidance, or other compensatory interventions. Brazil, India, Malaysia, South Africa, and Sri Lanka use a combination of affirmative action and compensatory investments to mitigate the effects of discrimination.

Administrative rules often prevent girls from attending schools. In some communities, separate schools for boys and girls are required, which often results in too few schools for girls. Rules preventing children from studying in their mother tongue keep some children who do not speak the language of instruction out of school or make it harder for them to learn. Early ability-based tracking allows schools to provide unequal education programs and produces dropout. Expulsion of pregnant girls from school and lack of flexibility in school hours for young mothers attempting to continue their schooling after giving birth severely limit their educational opportunities. Changes in all of these rules could increase the number of excluded girls attending school.

Donors could expedite integration by fostering alternative forms of positive discrimination and expanding opportunities for girls who would otherwise have no options. The Open Society Institute assisted local nongovernmental organizations and governments in their efforts to initiate laws and regulations to protect the Roma and make schools safe havens for Roma children. Donor initiatives could also help countries analyze the educational regulations in place that act as barriers to girls.

Expanding options for schooling

One of the lessons from the high-income OECD countries is that targeted, tailored programs are essential to complement overall schooling investments in order to reach excluded populations and keep excluded children in school. A first step in improving access is making schools or school equivalents locally available. Increasing the number of local schools typically results in greater access for children who are historically excluded.

One way of increasing the number of locally available schools is to allow communities to establish their own schools. Community schools are formal schools that provide the basic elements of the school curriculum, adapted to local conditions, including variations in language of instruction and hours of operation. They are designed to shape schooling to meet the needs and ensure the involvement of community members. They are the ultimate means of giving parents voice in the running of schools. South Asia pioneered the approach in 1987 with its *Shiksha Karmi* Project in Rajasthan, India, which uses paraprofessional teachers, allows the community to select and supervise teachers, and hires part-time workers to escort girls to school.

Two alternatives to formal schooling are nonformal schools and distance education. Nonformal schools address gaps or compensate for limitations of existing schools, particularly for children who never started school or who dropped out early and are older than primary school students. In some cases nonformal schools provide basic literacy training. In others they serve as preparation for re-entry into mainstream schools. Nonformal schools can be highly important in preparing disadvantaged children academically and in developing appropriate social skills and self-discipline. Such schools have contributed to progress in primary education in Bangladesh, which has recently achieved gender parity in primary school.

When expansion of schooling requires the use of teachers with less education, radio or television can help provide better quality lessons. Primary education programs that combine radio delivery of a high-quality curriculum with local monitoring of children's progress have been rigorously evaluated and found to boost learning. The most widely used are interactive radio instruction programs, which use professionally developed curricula broadcast to children in remote regions. Thirteen countries have successfully applied such programs.

At the secondary level, distance education programs such as Mexico's *Telesecondária* offer a full range of courses, which would be difficult to provide in schools serving small communities. For girls with limited access to information or learning outside the immediate community, such programs vastly increase educational opportunities.

What has not succeeded, though, is providing separate schools for children from ethnic, cultural, and linguistic minorities—often tried in earlier periods, as in the United States, Canada, and New Zealand. Separate schools, for example for the Roma throughout Eastern Europe or blacks in the United States pre-1954, are inherently unequal and suffer from poor quality. Similarly, creating separate schools for girls may fail to improve girls' educational outcomes. Separate schools for girls can also limit their access and, because of poor quality, their performance. Indeed, the lagging performance of Pakistan in girls' education can be attributed in part to the need for double investments in schooling, one for girls, the other for boys. Bangladesh, which has coeducational primary schools, has sped ahead while Pakistan continues to struggle with expanding separate access for both genders.

Lack of funding often prevents experimentation with innovative means of expanding schooling to difficult-to-reach groups or adapting effective programs to new contexts. A trust fund for multilateral programs targeting excluded girls could provide the financial basis for expanding successful efforts of donors and governments.

Donors could also play a catalytic role in devising and financing alternative schooling options, particularly for innovative programs for adolescent girls. Programs such as English language immersion classes or computer training provide an alternative to secondary school that equips girls with marketable skills. Creation of a girls' education evaluation fund to finance bilateral, multilateral, and nongovernmental organization evaluations of new or ongoing programs aimed at reaching girls would help fill a major gap and offer guidance to both policymakers and donors eager to use their resources to promote girls' education.

Improving the quality and relevance of schools and classrooms

Excluded girls often attend schools that lack the basic inputs needed for learning. Failure to provide basic inputs in these schools drives even the poor away from publicly provided schools and lowers achievement of those who remain. In Pakistan, for example, girls have access to fewer single-sex schools than boys, and the schools that are available often lack essential inputs. So parents withdraw their daughters, preferring to send them to private coeducational schools. In Egypt lower quality schools—those with multiple shifts and temporary teachers—increased the likelihood that girls leave school; schools with adequate facilities and in-service teacher training reduced the likelihood of girls dropping out.

Basic inputs are necessary for learning. In Brazil, higher school quality—more educated teachers and better physical facilities—was associated with significantly higher student test scores. In Chile, 10 years of programs providing additional support to improve the quality of the lowest performing schools significantly reduced the gaps in learning achievement between indigenous and nonindigenous students.

Where excluded children do not speak the language of instruction, specific actions are required to bridge the gap. Because girls in remote areas have less experience outside their communities than do boys, they tend to be less familiar with the dominant language and experience greater difficulties adapting to a new language when entering school.

Effective bilingual education programs start with developing the child's reading, writing, and thinking skills in the home language—something that requires teachers who are fluent in that language. At the same time, the target language is taught as a subject. Children who need to transition from a mother tongue to a national language can benefit from programs that "flood" the classroom with storybooks in the national language and train teachers on how to use books to promote literacy. "Book flood" programs have achieved rapid gains in English skills in Fiji, New Zealand, Singapore, South Africa, and Sri Lanka.

Mother tongue-based bilingual education has been found to be particularly effective in breaking down barriers against girls. In Mexico children of monolingual indigenous mothers were more likely to attend school if the school was bilingual. In Guatemala students in bilingual primary schools had higher attendance and promotion rates, lower dropout rates, and higher achievement in all subjects, including Spanish. In Mali bilingual programs led to sharp declines in dropout and repetition rates, and rural children have outperformed urban children on national exams.

Policymakers and donors can support efforts ensuring that basic inputs reach poorly performing schools. Support to finance improvement programs for schools with average learning achievement below national standards has had spillover effects for girls and indigenous children (in Chile, for example) and avoids the potential political problems associated with ethnically or linguistically targeted programs.

Donors could help children transition into mainstream schools by underwriting bilingual programs, adding culturally relevant dimensions to curricula, and financing engaging bilingual storybooks. Use of mother tongue for instruction at school entry and in the early grades boosts both enrollment and retention in school, but effective bilingual programs require fully bilingual teachers, who are often in short supply. The lack of reading materials in many languages spoken at home and the lack of interesting reading materials in the national language are also barriers in many countries.

Teachers can be agents of change and beacons of tolerance, a characteristic of particular importance in ethnically mixed classrooms, where tolerance should be expected. Sensitizing teachers and providing them with tools to cope with and address inevitable gender and ethnic tensions in the classroom could contribute to both learning and the integration of cultures.

Donors could supplement publicly supported programs by financing school improvement grants for the worst performing schools. Such grants could support activities at the school level designed in consultation with local communities and teachers.

Supporting compensatory preschool and in-school programs

The OECD experience demonstrates that simply providing easy access to schools will not necessarily serve the needs of excluded children or ensure their education. Additional initiatives are needed. Five initiatives are preschools for underserved children, compensatory in-school programs, materials and teacher training for transitioning into a national language in upper-primary grades, outreach to parents, and transportation and busing. Middle-income countries such as Brazil, Chile, and Mexico have pioneered means of reaching the excluded, but many countries cannot afford the extra efforts. It therefore falls to donors to pick up the cost of initiatives aimed at ensuring that all girls can go to a good-quality school.

Preschools are one of the most effective means for ensuring later success in school and are particularly important for excluded children, especially girls. Programs for children of excluded groups reduce primary school dropout rates. Preschool programs in Bolivia, Brazil, India, and Turkey have had remarkable impacts on children's subsequent school progress, proving cost-effective in the long run.

In-school programs that compensate for the absence of education reinforcements at home may be critical to retaining children from excluded groups in school. Such programs, often involving tutors and curriculum enrichment, have been effective in Brazil, India, and Spain. They may be necessary to ensure that students keep up with their peers. Compensatory programs offer a major incentive to parents to keep their children in school. After-school supervision and academic support, remedial programs for those behind on entry, and special summer enrichment initiatives have been effective in OECD countries and deserve attention and investment in low-income settings. Children who do not receive reinforcement at home need school-based support to succeed, but like other extras, such support is generally not affordable in developing countries. Simple after-school activities can build social capital among children and ensure that students have a place to complete homework.

Parent outreach is needed to encourage illiterate, disadvantaged parents to support their children. International studies show parent involvement to be a predictor of student achievement. Parent outreach includes engaging parents and communities in the oversight of schools and engaging parents in establishing a supportive environment for learning.

Providing the means to reach a better school may be preferable to or more affordable than upgrading an existing school, especially where geographic divisions segregate schools. Busing can help to integrate minority children and provide them with a sound education. Experience in rural Turkey suggests that busing does not always work, however, especially when primary school children are bused to unfamiliar villages.

Financing transportation for excluded children, possibly separately for girls, could quell the safety concerns parents have about girls traveling to other villages to attend school. Older women could be paid to accompany girls to schools outside their villages.

A logical extension of the transportation issue is construction of basic roads and communication infrastructure. Roads make it easier for teachers, students, and textbooks to reach schools; communication and electrical infrastructure broaden schooling options beyond teachers and textbooks. School buildings, materials, and latrines also require donor financing, especially in the poorest areas.

Creating incentives for households to send girls to school

Cultural taboos, the opportunity cost of labor, low demand for education, and reluctance to allow children, especially girls, to enter mainstream schools contribute to low enrollment, low completion rates, and below-average achievement among excluded groups. Three types of programs—conditional cash transfers, girls' scholarships, and school feeding programs—have shown promise in meeting these challenges.

Conditional cash transfers provide resources to households to defray the costs of sending their children to school. They tie social assistance payments to desirable behaviors, in this case enrolling and keeping children in school. Although challenging to administer, conditional cash transfers provide financial incentives to families and put the onus on them to ensure that children actually go to school, something that school officials often find impossible to do. Robust evaluations have shown that conditional cash transfers increase both school enrollment and retention rates. Excluded groups, who are often more difficult to attract to these programs, have not been identified in these evaluations, so the impact on those groups is not yet known.

Scholarships for girls offer financing for primary and secondary school. They also encourage girls to stay in school. Scholarships compensate families for the direct and indirect costs of education. They are effective when households view cost as the impediment to girls' schooling. Scholarships also provide an additional revenue stream for secondary schools. They have been effective for girls at the secondary level in several countries, notably Bangladesh.

Various types of school feeding programs have been associated with higher attendance, higher enrollment, and, in some cases, lower dropout and higher student achievement. School feeding programs are most effective in meeting school attendance objectives. They are particularly successful where attendance is relatively low at the outset and children come from poor households. A concern, however, is whether school feeding provides additional nutrition or simply substitutes for home meals, particularly for girls; this issue deserves attention.

Governments and multilateral donors have forged partnerships for conditional cash transfers in many countries in Latin America. Expanding those initiatives to other countries and to difficult-to-reach groups could increase the number of excluded girls who attend school. How successful such programs can be in attracting excluded girls, especially adolescent girls, to school remains an open question. Donors could finance and manage household stipend components of conditional cash transfers for low-income countries that lack the managerial capacity and resources to conduct a conditional cash transfer program.

Scholarships for girls have demonstrated enormous promise. Donor initiatives to expand such programs to lower secondary, higher secondary, and tertiary education would increase the number of educated women in low-income countries. Educated women from disadvantaged households could serve as both community leaders and role models for excluded girls.

Stipends could be used to finance uniforms, school supplies, and books for girls—items parents often cannot afford or refuse to pay for because they do not appreciate their value. Providing assistance through stipends avoids the bureaucratic management problems of subsidizing inputs.

Financing school meals can attract children to school. It can also provide employment for adults and help involve parents in school, reinforcing the school as a focus of community life. Such initiatives offer an entry point to help upgrade schools and provide the potential for additional help to children with faltering attendance or performance. School feeding programs have not been tested specifically among excluded groups. Donor funding could help determine whether these programs are effective among excluded children.

1

Progress in girls' education

Progress in getting children into school has been impressive over the past decade, with most of the benefits for girls. The female net primary enrollment rate increased from 74 percent in 1990 to 79 percent in 2000 despite high fertility levels in low-income countries (UNESCO 2003). But much remains to be done.

In 2002 roughly 115 million primary school-age children—53 percent of them girls—were not in school (UIS 2005). Many children do not finish primary school, and too few go on to secondary school. Secondary education brings significant economic and social benefits at the national and household levels. Secondary school enrollment was 71 percent for boys and 66 percent for girls, but significant disparities persist across and within countries (World Bank 2005b).

Female enrollment rates vary greatly throughout the world. In some regions, such as Latin America and the Caribbean, enrollment is near universal. Girls are outpacing boys in enrollment and completion in Brazil, Colombia, and Jamaica. But girls trail boys significantly in the Middle East, South Asia, and Sub-Saharan Africa (except Lesotho and South Africa, where they outpace boys).

Frequently overlooked, social exclusion—based on gender, ethnicity, language, location, and wealth—is a major barrier to universal access and completion. Already excluded because of their gender, many girls face multiple barriers,

19

making it more difficult for them to enroll in and complete primary school and continue on to secondary school.

Reaching excluded groups generally means higher costs and alternative policies and strategies because their needs differ from those of the majority population. Concerted efforts must deal directly with the sources of exclusion. Simply doing more of the same will not be enough.

Girls catching up—global progress in education

After decades of trailing boys in primary and secondary school enrollment and completion, girls are beginning to catch up. In some countries girls have surpassed boys in enrollment and attainment. Expanding access to public schools has contributed to the gains in many countries, though private schools have made inroads in some countries by responding to unmet demand or capitalizing on parental dissatisfaction with public offerings.

Enrollment, attendance, and completion have increased rapidly among both boys and girls. (box 1.1) This marked improvement reinforces evidence that modern education is being embraced by the world at large. Rapid expansion necessarily favors girls because they have been neglected yet are some of the easiest children to reach.

Most developing countries have made significant strides in education in the past 25 years. The poorest countries have done so in the face of the highest fertility rates ever recorded. Despite average fertility rates (roughly the average number of children per woman) as high as six—almost doubling the population of some countries in little more than a decade—many leaders pushed ahead with schooling expansion. Achievements in Africa and South Asia have been particularly noteworthy. Progress in the recent past represents a remarkable achievement and bodes well for meeting the ambitious Millennium Development Goals embraced by the international community.

Progress in primary education

The rate of primary school enrollment across the developing world has been impressive over the past decade. Indeed, some countries' growth in enrollment rates exceeds that of developed countries at similar levels of per capita income. Pressure from parents and the challenges of globalization have no doubt been key elements in public investments, but pressure from the international community and momentum from international forums have also played a role.

Overall primary enrollment and the ratio of female to male gross primary enrollment rose between 1960 and 2000. Overall levels of primary enrollment have remained at 90 percent or higher since the 1960s in Latin America and the Caribbean and Eu-

Box 1.1. School participation measures defined

Gross enrollment rate: The number of pupils enrolled at a given level of education, regardless of age, expressed as a percentage of the population in the relevant official age group. Gross enrollment rates can exceed 100 percent as a result of grade repetition and entry at younger and older ages than are typical. Gross enrollment is the most commonly available measure of schooling success in developing countries, as data on other indicators are often poor. However, gross enrollment rates can be misleading. Countries with poor-quality education may report high gross enrollment rates because many students routinely repeat grades or fail to graduate.

Net enrollment rate: The percentage of children in the official age group for a given level of education enrolled in school. Net enrollment is a better measure of schooling access than gross enrollment, but data are less often available. Some experts criticize the use of the net enrollment rate as a measure of access, because it fails to take late entrants into account.

(Net) attendance: The number of students in the official age group for a given level of education who attend school regularly.

Ever attended school: The number of children in the official age group for a given level of education who have attended school. Attendance data come from national household surveys. In many countries enrollment is notional and attendance better captures whether children regularly go to school.

School completion: The total number of students successfully completing the last year of a given level of education in a given year minus the number of repeaters in that grade divided by the total number of children of official graduation age in the population.

Repetition: Number of repeaters in a given grade in a given school year, expressed as a percentage of enrollment in that grade the previous school year.

Dropout: Percentage of students who drop out from a given grade in a given school year. The dropout rate is the difference between 100 percent and the sum of the promotion and repetition rates. Dropout and repetition rates are indicators of the inefficiency of the education system. They may also indicate poor quality.

Source: World Bank EdStats 2006.

rope and Central Asia. The legacy of the Soviet Union, combined with high overall enrollment rates in Eastern Europe before World War II, puts all the former Soviet republics and the countries of Eastern Europe and Central Asia close to Organisation for Economic Co-operation and Development (OECD) countries in terms of gender performance (figure 1.1).

These figures are encouraging. But they also reflect problems. Many countries' high enrollment rates are due in part to high repetition rates, which artificially swell gross enrollment figures. High gross enrollment can simply reflect a catching up, by

Figure 1.1. Gross primary enrollment surged in many parts of the world between 1960 and 2000

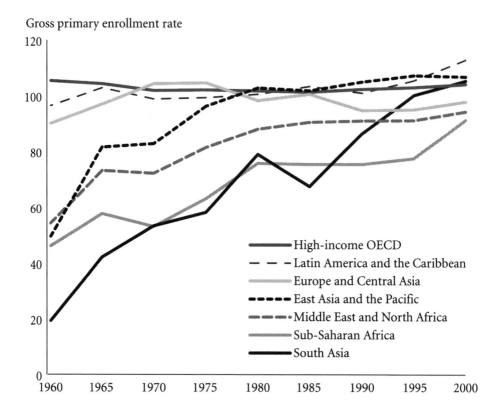

Gross primary enrollment rate

Source: UNESCO Institute of Statistics data.

allowing children of different ages to enroll in school for the first time. Net primary enrollment figures suggest as much. Net enrollment data are incomplete for all years except 2000, so trend data are not available, but net enrollment levels differ markedly across regions. Net enrollment rates in Latin America and the Caribbean were 97 percent, Europe and Central Asia were 94 percent, and East Asia and the Pacific were 93 percent. Net enrollment rates for less well performing countries were much lower, with the Middle East and North Africa at 84 percent, South Asia at 77 percent, and Sub-Saharan Africa at 64 percent—all notches below more successful regions.

East Asia caught up with OECD countries and the best performers by 1980 and has maintained its enrollment levels since then. South Asia bounded upward, posting the most dramatic gains in gross enrollment of any region over the past 40 years. Sub-Saharan Africa began with an enrollment rate that was more than twice that of South

Figure 1.2. Gender parity in primary enrollment rose between 1960 and 2000

Female to male primary enrollment
(percent)

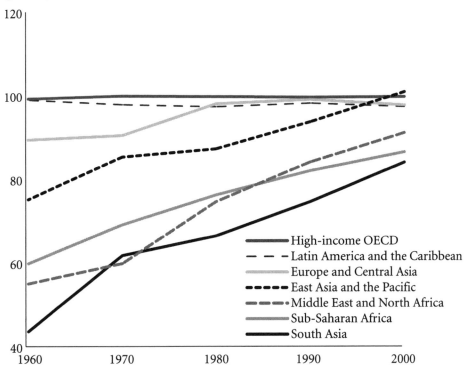

Source: UNESCO Institute of Statistics data.

Asia, but its more modest improvements mean that enrollment there is now well below that in South Asia. Gains in the Middle East were impressive in the early 1960s and the 1970s, but they have tapered off, lagging behind all regions but Sub-Saharan Africa.

Girls have caught up with boys in much of the world, achieving more than 80 percent gender parity globally. The regions with modest enrollment ratios in 1960 demonstrated remarkable progress, with girls' enrollment in South Asia rising from less than 45 percent of boys' in 1960 to almost 85 percent in 2000 (figure 1.2).

Indeed, all regions saw dramatic gains over the past four decades, though some are compensating for ruefully poor ratios before 1960. The data confirm that the world has changed its perceptions of educating girls, implementing policies that increase enrollments.

While difficult to collect and uneven in coverage, primary completion rates,

Table 1.1. Population-weighted gains in primary completion by region, 1990–2000

	Primary completion rate for girls			Primary completion rate for boys		
	1990	2000	Percent change	1990	2000	Percent change
Sub-Saharan Africa	43	46	7	57	56	−2
East Asia and the Pacific	92	98	7	97	98	1
Europe and Central Asia	85	93	9	95	95	0
Latin America and the Caribbean	71	85	20	64	81	27
Middle East and North Africa	71	78	10	84	86	2
South Asia	59	63	7	77	84	9
All developing countries	65	76	17	79	85	8

Source: Bruns, Mingat, and Rakotomalala 2003.

which remove the artificial inflation of overage children in school, offer a far better metric of performance than gross or net enrollments. These rates vary widely across regions (table 1.1). Latin America and the Caribbean made the greatest progress for both boys and girls, but left boys 4 percentage points behind girls by 2000. Indeed, the percentage increase in mean grade attainment in the 1960s and 1970s was zero for boys and 43 percent for girls, who began to outpace boys (Behrman, Duryea, and Szekely 1999). East Asia and the Pacific had the highest percentage of children in school in 1990, and by 2000 girls had caught up to boys, achieving universal primary coverage. Among the lagging regions in primary completion only in South Asia did boys post a higher percentage increase in completion rates than girls. Overall, the girls' completion rate of change was double that of boys.

Progress in secondary education

Secondary education offers the next big challenge as countries close in on primary education goals. Universal enrollment hinges on progress in secondary and tertiary education; no country has reached even 90 percent net primary enrollment without attaining secondary enrollment of about 45 percent (Clemens 2004). The attention to secondary schooling suffered in the drive to ensure that all children entered primary school—efforts to make up for that neglect are needed. For girls, entering secondary school has multiple benefits over and above those of primary school. It also yields

Box 1.2. Educating girls leads to economic growth—and more

Knowledge about the benefits of girls' education spans all disciplines and has held up to scrutiny on multiple levels. Evidence from cross-country studies, household surveys, and anthropological observations provides a sound basis for concluding that educating women provides multiple payoffs for households and societies (World Bank 2001; Herz and Sperling 2004; Lloyd 2005). Development economists have emphasized the importance of girls' educational attainment in reaching overall development goals. Summers (1994) has noted that "investment in girls' education may well be the highest return investment available in the developing world" (p. 1).

The positive association between gender equality in educational attainment and GDP levels is well known. Cross-country studies examining the impact of female education on GDP consistently demonstrate positive effects (Hanushek and Kimko 2000). Increasing female secondary education and reducing gender disparities lead to economic growth (Klasen 1999; World Bank 2001; Hill and King 1995; Dollar and Gatti 1999).

Returns to girls' education in developing countries are largely positive and in some cases exceed those observed in developed countries. Educated women are more likely to enter the formal labor market, where earnings are higher than those of informal or home-based work (Malhotra, Grown, and Pande 2003). And women with secondary schooling see significant returns (Psacharopoulos and Patrinos 2002; Schultz 1993, 2002; Lloyd 2005) In countries with a tradition of dowries or bride prices the perceived value of a potential bride grows with education (Schuler forthcoming; Behrman and others 1999).

Educated female farmers raise productivity (Lockheed, Jamison, and Lau 1980), and their returns can exceed those of men (Quisumbing 1996). Moreover, improvements in women's farming methods can reduce malnutrition (Smith and Haddad 1999).

The social impact of female education is profound. Most prominent is the role of mothers' education in reducing infant and child mortality, lowering fertility, and promoting children's education. On average, infant mortality declines 5–10 percent for each year of girls' education (Schultz 1993). Results for Africa indicate a 40 percent boost in child survival for mothers with five years of primary education (Summers 1994). Cross-country studies by Klasen (1999) and Hill and King (1995) show similar results. Greater control over family finances directly affects children, as women are more likely to spend discretionary resources on investments in human capital—health, education, and food (Thomas 1990; Hoddinott and Haddad 1995; Bruce and Lloyd 1996; Morley and Coady 2003).

Educated girls tend to marry later, and they are more likely to plan their families, improving reproductive health and lowering fertility, which in turn contribute to lower infant mortality rates. Klasen (1999) and Lloyd, Kaufman, and Hewett (2000) show that surges in education almost always precede the transition to lower average fertility. Women with secondary education reduce their fertility by two or more children compared with uneducated mothers (Subbarao and Raney 1995; Schultz 1993).

Parental education shows universally positive impacts on children's schooling. Mothers' education has a strong effect on girls, particularly where girls' enrollment lags behind that of boys (Behrman and Sengupta 2002; Schultz 2002; Alderman and King 1998;

Box 1.2. Educating girls leads to economic growth—and more (continued)

Ridker 1997). Filmer's (2000) study of 14 countries suggests that an additional year of mothers' education raises the likelihood of children's enrollment by 1–6 percentage points.

The scourge of HIV/AIDS disproportionately affects females, particularly teenage girls. In Africa prevalence among girls 15–19 years old is six times that of their male peers. But encouraging evidence suggests that education can help halt transmission of the virus (Herz and Sperling 2004). Educated women are better able to reduce risky behavior by negotiating safe sex with partners (Malhotra, Grown, and Pande 2003).

Education also empowers women to fend off domestic violence. Evidence from Bangladesh and India reveals fewer beatings among women with some education (Purna 1999; Jejeebhoy 1998; Bates, Schuler, and Islam 2004; Schuler forthcoming).

Education leads to higher social standing, more independence, and greater autonomy in women's lives and in the household. With its positive impacts on economic and social development, countries cannot afford to neglect girls' education.

---

significant social and economic returns for society (box 1.2).

Unfortunately, secondary school data before 1990 are too fragmented to be useful. Data for 2000 show gross enrollment rates ranging from 25 percent for girls and 30 percent for boys in Africa, to more than 80 percent for both boys and girls in Latin America and the Caribbean, and to more than 90 percent for both boys and girls in Europe and Central Asia.

The catch-up for girls remains a feature of increases in secondary school enrollment (figure 1.3). Latin America and the Caribbean is closest to parity in male-female gross secondary enrollment. In Europe and Central Asia though girls slipped a bit relative to boys over the decade 1990–2000, female-male gross secondary enrollment is close to parity. In East Asia and the Pacific, the Middle East and North Africa, and South Asia the proportion of girls enrolled in secondary school rose. Improvements were more modest in Sub-Saharan Africa. In all three regions—Asia and the Pacific, the Middle East and North Africa, and South Asia—enrollment grew more rapidly among girls during the 1990s. Girls' enrollment has stalled in South Asia, where it is just 75 percent of boys', and in Sub-Saharan Africa, where it is 80 percent.

Despite improvement, secondary school enrollment of both boys and girls remains low in most regions of the world. Increasing the percentage of children who attend secondary school poses a range of new challenges for families and governments. In much of Africa the supply of secondary schools is limited, forcing children to compete for the few available spots. Demand also limits the number of girls in secondary school. In many countries single-sex secondary schools are required, often meaning fewer schools for girls. The lack of local schools means that girls have to travel outside

Figure 1.3. Secondary school enrollment rose more rapidly among girls than boys in almost every region during the 1990s

Female to male secondary enrollment
(percent)

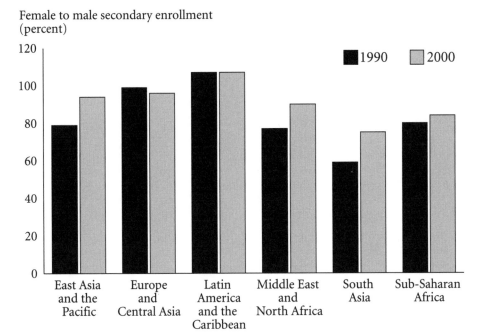

Source: UNESCO Institute of Statistics data.

their villages, something many parents do not allow out of concern for their children's safety. Many countries ban pregnant girls from attending schools or prescribe strict, inconvenient hours, for example, 6–9 at night, for them to complete their schooling. Competition from the labor market and early marriage also keep adolescent girls out of school. Bringing more girls into secondary schools thus requires not simply building and staffing more schools but taking account of social, geographic, and financial barriers as well.

Changes in the gender gap

Data from Demographic and Health Surveys in 49 developing countries show how girls and boys have fared over the past two decades (table 1.2) The trend is clear: children increasingly go to school, and girls are entering school at a faster rate than are boys. Overall, the gender gap narrowed considerably over the past decade in countries at all levels of income. In the poorest countries the percentage of girls ever having attended school rose almost 19.5 percent over the most recent decade, well above the 4.2 percent

Table 1.2. Girls and boys ages 10–14 who ever attended school in 49 countries, by region (percent)

Region	Male	Female	Change in most recent decade		Change of earlier decade	
			Male	Female	Male	Female
Africa						
Eastern and Southern Africa	81	78	−2.7	4.5	2.3	9.0
Western and Middle Africa	74	66	2.4	16.4	11.6	22.4
Asia						
South and Southeast Asia[a]	91	82	5.6	21.7	11.6	23.5
Central Asia[b]	100	100	−0.2	0.2	0.1	−0.2
Latin America and the Caribbean						
Caribbean and Central America	92	92	2.6	7.0	6.2	10.5
South America	98	99	2.7	1.7	1.7	3.5
Middle East and North Africa	93	83	1.2	8.1	8.5	18.5
Total	89	82	3.6	15.1	8.8	16.8

Note: Weighted averages, based on UN population estimates for 2000 (UN 2000).

a. India's Demographic and Health Survey does not include enrollment data for 10- to 14-year-olds.

b. Includes Former Soviet Republics in Asia (Kazakhstan, Kyrgyz Republic, Uzbekistan, Tajikistan, Turkmenistan).

Source: Lloyd and others 2005, based on Demographic and Health Survey data, circa 1980–2003.

increase for boys. In the previous 20 years girls' increases were roughly triple those of boys in low-income countries and double in middle-income countries (Lloyd 2005).

Whatever metric is used, girls' attendance, enrollment, and completion have seen substantial increases over the past 45 years. Across the globe as overall schooling improves girls benefit disproportionately. Parity has been achieved in only some parts of the world, mostly in regions where the female-male differential was already small.

The era of ignoring girls' education appears to be past. But how much more progress is needed? Where is it a priority? And what is a feasible pace of improvement?

Why has there been so much progress—and can it continue?

Identifying the factors behind the recent progress in education is important, because progress has been uneven, both within and across countries, and continued progress cannot be assured. Is progress likely to continue?

Expanding education means replacing informal learning within clans or extended families with formal classroom learning, drawing children into the mainstream of society and the economy. Mass education (education that aims at universal enrollment) began in northern Europe and North America in the late eighteenth century (Meyer, Ramirez, and Soysal 1992). It spread throughout Europe in the nineteenth century and then to other countries and European colonies outside of Sub-Saharan Africa as well as countries such as Japan and Turkey. With decolonization at the end of World War II, mass education increased sharply. Indeed, though education enrollment levels remained around 10–15 percent in European colonies between 1880 and World War II, decolonization after the war led to a sharp increase in school expansion, reaching 72 percent average enrollment by 1960, which limited room for further improvement. By 1985 mass education was compulsory in 80 percent of countries.[1]

Mass education correlates with the spread of nationalism, which required a tool like mass education to bring citizens together for common purposes. Meyer, Ramirez, and Soysal (1992) find that characteristics of states, such as location, religion, and urbanization, have no effect on mass education. Once under way, mass education simply expands toward universality, driven by its own internal momentum and growing demand from policymakers and citizens. The more erratic pattern of expansion of secondary education suggests that it is less important to nation building.

Economic growth, or lack of growth, has in some countries promoted expansion, though often for secondary and higher education. East Asian countries emphasized technical education as an engine for exports and growth, and families and governments invested heavily in schooling. Specific investments to upgrade skills in electronics and related fields coincided with domestic efforts to drive growth by developing high-technology industries. One component of attracting foreign direct investment was the availability of a well educated, productive labor force. Foreign firms in the Republic of Korea, Malaysia, and Taiwan (China), for example, further developed investment and

---

1. China, Japan, the Republic of Korea, Turkey, and parts of Latin America were among the first to attempt mobilization and nation building outside the Western system. Educational expansion was an outgrowth of struggles and efforts to compete nationally and internationally. At independence many former European colonies were so far removed from the nation state that limited enrollment in the early years was to be expected (Meyer, Ramirez, and Soysal 1992). However, limited resources delayed the implementation of mass education.

business skills, leading to successful spin-off firms run by local entrepreneurs (de Ferranti and others 2003; Dahlman and Andersson 2000).

Competition from East Asia and the need to compete in a globalized world drive education priorities, especially in middle-income countries. In looking for a regional production site in Latin America, Intel considered only Chile and Costa Rica, which have larger stocks of educated labor than do other countries in the region. Its search sent a clear signal to the rest of the region about the importance of education for attracting foreign direct investment. Indeed, given the competitive international environment, not investing in education is costly. Cross-country evidence shows a significant correlation between the average number of years of schooling of adults and the level of foreign direct investment, reinforcing the idea that secondary education drives economic growth (Noorbakhsh and Paloni 2001).

Low-income countries benefit from the foreign investment and trade agreements that drive the expansion of the garment and other low-technology industries in some of the world's poorest countries. The greater prospects of employment, particularly for girls and women, make education desirable—and available. A virtuous circle emerges, with education leading to jobs and jobs leading to education.

Across countries school enrollment expansion follows an S-shaped diffusion pattern. In the initial stages growth is low because there are many people to educate and few teachers to teach. Once the supply of teachers increases, enrollment accelerates rapidly before tapering off at the point where roughly 70 percent of children ages 5–14 are in school (Wils, Carrol, and Barrow 2005; Clemens 2004; Meyer, Ramirez, and Soysal 1992). The final 10 percent are particularly difficult and often costly to reach because of their remoteness, poverty, and ethnicity (Wils, Carrol, and Barrow 2005).

For 70 of the world's lowest income countries, it took on average 88 years to move from 10 percent completion to 90 percent (Wils, Carrol, and Barrow 2005). Unless the slowest countries—Brazil, the Democratic Republic of Congo, Guyana, Mexico, and Mongolia—improve their performance, they will need 120 years to reach 90 percent completion.

Closing the gender gap is also of concern. Clemens (2004) estimates the growth trajectory of the gender transition using the ratio of female to male gross enrollment (figure 1.4). For example, a country with a female-male gross enrollment ratio of 0.80 is estimated to take 28 years to reach a ratio of 0.95. Therefore, in countries where fewer than one girl is enrolled for every two boys, it would take substantially longer to reach parity.

Clemens's (2004) examination of the determinants of the differences in the speed of gender transition helps explain the observed patterns. Countries most likely to close the gender gap quickly are those that have higher percentages of educated adults, are not predominantly Muslim or Christian, are predominantly Buddhist, and (counter-

Figure 1.4. Reaching gender parity can take a long time

Female to male gross primary enrollment rate
(percent)

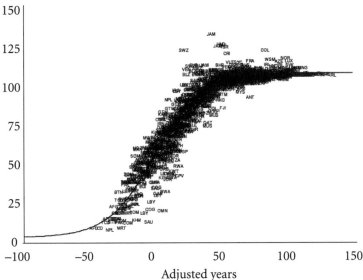

Adjusted years

Note: Gender transition in primary enrollment for all countries 1950–2000. Adjusted years are the elapsed time since girls' gross primary enrollment reached 50 percent of boys'. Data points show country-years in five-year increments.
Source: Clemens 2004.

intuitvely) have high fertility.[2] High female labor force participation carries a positive sign but is insignificant. The cross-country analysis did not confirm a relationship between women's labor force participation and girls' education, but country studies, such as King's (1990) study of Peru, have found such a link.

These results suggest that girls are indeed closing the gender gap at the primary level, but the process is slow and does not necessarily lend itself to policy tools. Moreover, some outliers have shown only modest progress. For the most part, however, countries have made strides in the recent past or are starting to do so. Except in conflict countries, commitments to universal education are being implemented. Given the already rapid escalation in enrollment and the natural limits of change, increasing the rate of change will be difficult.

In addition to gender, income, equity, urbanization, and ethnicity help explain education coverage across countries (Birdsall, Levine, and Ibrahim 2005; Lloyd and

---

2. This finding is consistent with those of Glick and Sahn (2000) and Al-Samarrai and Peasgood (1998) but at odds with those of Lloyd and Gage-Brandon (1994) and others. In contrast to country-level studies, cross-country regressions can be difficult to interpret, particularly when countries are at different stages of development and at varying points in their demographic transition.

Figure 1.5. In most countries urban-rural differentials are greater than male-female differentials in attendance at the primary level

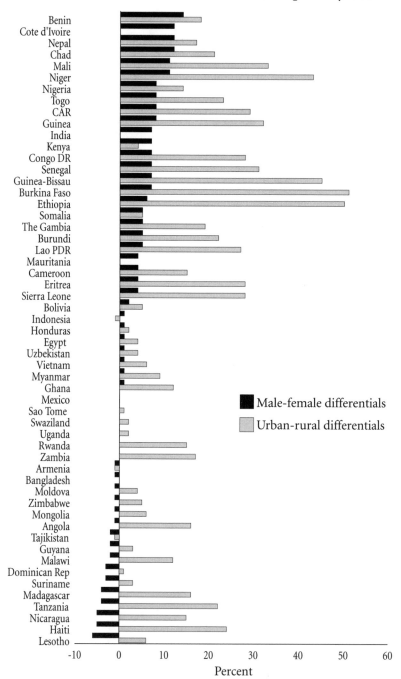

Note: Full parity is represented by a value of zero (no bar).

Source: Wils, Carrol, and Barrow 2005, based on Demographic and Health Survey data.

others 2005; Wils, Carrol, and Barrow 2005). Exploring these determinants requires reliance on household survey data, reducing the number of countries in the sample to a subset of developing countries and transition economies.

Because of the rapid catch-up by girls, in most countries gender does not appear to be as much of a drag on overall completion as location or income. Moreover, gender and other household characteristics often move in tandem. Countries with high primary school attendance rates tend to have minimal urban-rural differences in attendance (Wils, Carrol, and Barrow 2005). Male-female and urban-rural attendance gaps for 57 countries show that in every country urban-rural differences exceed gender differences. In some countries urban-rural gaps are as high as 50 percent (figure 1.5). In many countries small gaps in urban-rural attendance are associated with minimal gender differences. Thus it is likely, as discussed later, that girls are more disadvantaged in countries with inequality in attendance by location.

Children not enrolled in school overwhelmingly come from poor households. Children from wealthier families are more likely to complete both primary and secondary school. Gender disparities are magnified by the wealth gap in education. Using Demographic and Health Survey data for 41 countries, Filmer (2000) and Filmer and Pritchett (1999) analyze the effect of income on education disparities within countries. The largest differences are in India, with a 10-year gap between the average number of years of education of the poor (0) and the rich (10), and in Pakistan, where the gap is 9 years. In Bangladesh the difference was eight years in 1993–94 and six years in 1996–97, a dramatic shift in a three-year period, reflecting increasing equalization of education across the population. By contrast, the average for the low-income countries in East Asia is three years and in Latin America and the Caribbean, three to four years. Africa is less homogeneous, with a two-year gap in Rwanda and a six-year gap in Burkina Faso, Côte d'Ivoire, and Senegal.

How does the distribution of education within countries affect the average level of school attainment? Average years of schooling is negatively correlated with the education Gini coefficient for all countries for which data were available for 1960, 1980, and 2000 (figure 1.6).[3] The momentum of mass education thus appears to increase enrollment and improve coverage of schooling. This finding suggests that equity in education is reached only as educational opportunities open up.

---

3. The education Gini coefficient is calculated in two steps. First, an education Lorenz curve is constructed, based on the proportion of the population with various levels of schooling and the length of each level of schooling. Then the education Gini coefficient is calculated as the ratio of the area between the Lorenz curve and the 45 degree line (perfect equality) to the total area of the triangle (Thomas, Wang, and Fan 2001).

Figure 1.6. The average years of schooling increases as the education Gini coefficient declines

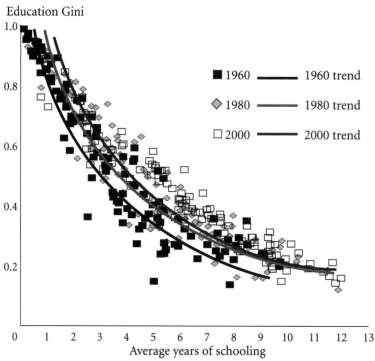

Education Gini

Note: Each country in the world for which data was available is represented.
Source: Barro and Lee 2000; Thomas, Wang, and Fan 2001.

Lagging performance of groups within countries remains a challenge

The overall increase in primary education enrollment masks low enrollment of groups within countries. Minority populations at the subregional level are the last significant pool of children left out of the school system. Children from ethnic minorities, isolated clans, linguistic minorities, and very poor households are most likely to be left behind in the move to mass education. Minority girls, the group of school-age children most discriminated against, are also the most likely to be kept out of school.

To illustrate the circumstances of doubly excluded girls, this section shows the patterns of school enrollment and completion across cohorts for a sample of developing countries. The focus is on school participation (learning and the determinants of schooling are examined in chapter 3).

Education and gender in heterogeneous countries

Comparisons of trends in enrollment and completion across different groups within countries reveal the effects of exclusion. The patterns for a sample of heterogeneous countries and three comparator homogeneous countries show how exclusion keeps girls, and boys, out of school. In most countries as development proceeds gender gaps close first, followed by location gaps, then gaps between nonminority children and children from ethnic and linguistic minority groups. The plight of ethnic girls is particularly worrisome. The largest gender gap is among minorities, while the majority population is reaching parity.

Guatemala and Mexico. In Guatemala Mayan (indigenous) girls are much less likely than Ladinos (of Spanish descent) to have ever enrolled in school, although improvements in recent years suggest that things are starting to change (figure 1.7). Mayan girls start school later and drop out earlier than do Mayan boys and Ladino boys and girls. At age seven, 75 percent of Ladino girls and 71 percent of Mayan boys are enrolled in

Figure 1.7. In Guatemala Mayan girls are left behind in going to and staying in school

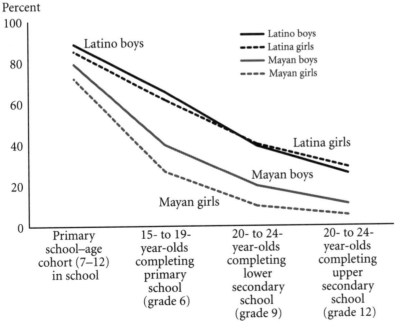

Note: Data are for 2000.
Source: Hallman and Peracca 2006.

school, while only 54 percent of Mayan girls go to school. Mayan girls enroll later, and by age 16 three-quarters have dropped out. In contrast, roughly half of all boys and La-dino girls remain in school. Among Mayan girls the poor fare even worse, with only 20 percent of the poor and 4 percent of the extremely poor still in school at age 16 (Hall-man and Peracca forthcoming). The patterns in Mexico are similar, where Mayan girls are less likely to go to school and more likely to drop out than are Ladino children, lead-ing to a significant, persistent gap between the two groups (Hall and Patrinos 2006).

Laos. Laos faces a major challenge given its uneven progress in enrollment and attain-ment. Among children 6–12, 92 percent of urban Lao-Tai girls, the majority, attend school, but only 52 percent of rural ethnic minority girls do, a 40 percentage point gap. Primary enrollment peaks at ages 9–10, well above the entry level at age 6, and many

Figure 1.8. In Laos rural minority girls are excluded from school

Average years of schooling

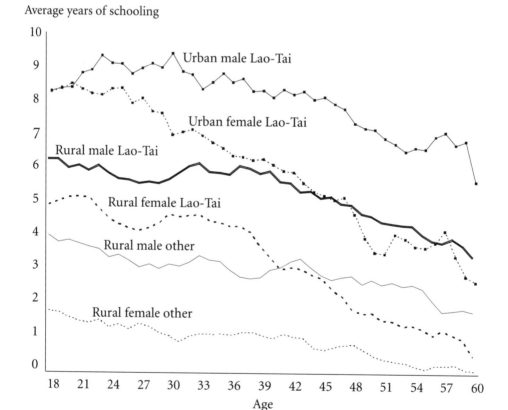

Note: Ages reflect three-year moving averages. Because the number of observations dwindles with age due to mortality, only data for those up to 60 years old are plotted. Data are from 2003.
Source: King and van de Walle (2006).

girls drop out. By age 18 the average urban Lao-Tai girl will have completed more than eight years of schooling, the same as boys in the same group (figure 1.8). In contrast, rural girls from ethno-linguistic minorities complete less than two years—far less than the majority population and less than half as many years as boys in the same group. Literacy disparities are therefore not surprising. Lao-Tai male literacy exceeds 90 percent, but even the youngest cohorts of rural ethnic women reach only 30 percent. The pace of change over age cohorts suggests that the disadvantage of living in a rural area is rapidly being overcome, but ethnic minorities, especially girls, continue to face exclusion in access to schooling (King and van de Walle forthcoming).

India. The Indian caste system complicates efforts to reach universal primary education (figure 1.9). Rural girls from scheduled castes, scheduled tribes and other "backward" castes remain behind urban boys and girls by at least 20 percentage points and behind boys from lower castes or tribes by almost 10 percentage points.

Gender and caste also affect attendance. Among 7- to 14-year-old girls belonging to scheduled castes or scheduled tribes 37 percent do not attend school. Among

Figure 1.9. In India gender, caste, and location affect primary school enrollment

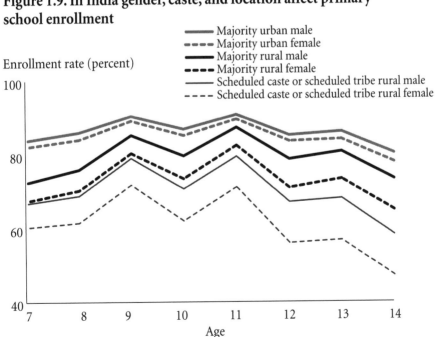

Note: Data are for 2001.
Source: Census of India 2001.

the majority it is 26 percent. This means that 9 million girls from scheduled castes or tribes and 19 million majority girls are not in school. Nonattendance among boys from scheduled castes or tribes is 11 percentage points lower than that for girls of their group, at 26 percent (see Census of India 2001 at www.censusindia.net). Thus it is lower caste or tribal girls who are most likely to drop out.

Pakistan. Enrollment figures for Pakistan showed little change between 1995 and 2001 (figure 1.10). Even among urban girls, fewer than 60 percent complete primary school. Among minority girls from rural areas, fewer than 10 percent do so. Compare that with a 65 percent completion among urban boys, the largest gap of the countries examined here. Enrollment rates follow a similar pattern, with rural girls lagging behind urban boys and girls and rural boys. Gaps in enrollment between the better-off and the poor are even larger (Lloyd, Mete, and Grant forthcoming).

Eastern Europe. There are 6–7 million Roma living across Europe, many of them in Eastern Europe, where they make up a growing segment of the population, reaching 11 percent in Slovakia and FYR Macedonia. With 1.3 million Roma children of school age

Figure 1.10. In Pakistan gender, ethnicity, and location affect primary school completion

Completion rate (percent)

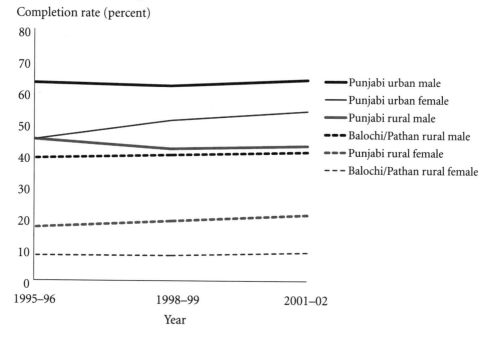

Source: Pakistan Integrated Household Survey 2001–02.

out of school, educational attainment remains low both absolutely and relative to the majority population. Roma completion rates remain well below those of the majority population with close to 15 percent of Roma with no schooling at all. In Bulgaria only 10 percent of Roma go beyond primary. Enrollment rates improved in Hungary over the 1990s, but in Bulgaria Roma primary enrollments were 33 percentagee points lower than the majority population and in Romania 20 percent lower. In Serbia and Montenegro only 9 percent of the Roma population has completed primary and 63 percent have no education, a staggering gap compared with the majority population, of whom 100 percent begin school and roughly 90 percent complete primary.

Girls do particularly poorly, though data remain spotty. In the 2001 Czech Republic census Roma women had 8.2 years of schooling compared to 9.2 for Roma men and 11.8 for all women (Burnett and Lewis 2005). Among Roma primary school age children in Serbia and Montenegro in 2003 only 72 percent were enrolled and two-thirds of them were boys. Net secondary enrollment for Roma is a paltry 17 percent, and boys are more likely to actually attend school (Bodewig and Sethi 2005).

Such statistics put these highly educated populations to shame. Attainment in Bulgaria, Hungary, and Romania exceeds that of most developing countries, but their Roma populations achieve at levels closer to the poorest developing countries (Ringold, Orenstein and Wilkens 2003; Burnett and Lewis 2005).

Figure 1.11. Differences in gender and ethnicity affect years of school in Benin...

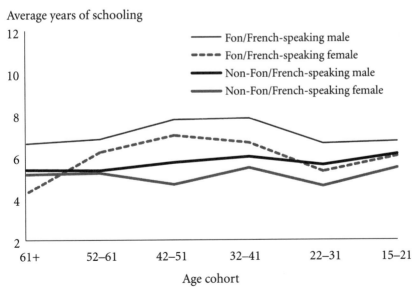

Average years of schooling

Age cohort

Note: Data are for 2001.
Source: Benin Demographic and Health Survey 2001.

Figure 1.12. ...in Ghana...

Average years of schooling

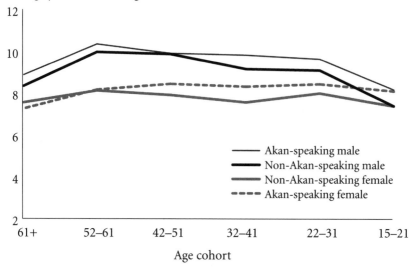

Age cohort

Note: Data are for 2003.
Source: Ghana Demographic and Health Survey 2003.

Figure 1.13. ...and in Malawi

Average years of schooling

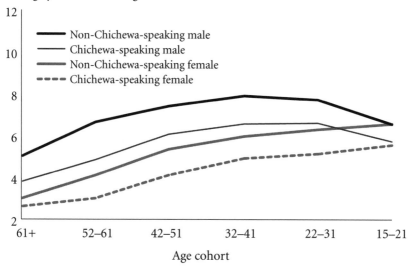

Age cohort

Note: Data are for 2001.
Source: Malawi Demographic and Health Survey 2001.

Benin, Ghana, and Malawi. Benin, Ghana, and Malawi comprise multiple tribes speaking different languages. In Benin linguistic minority males begin to catch up in the 22–31 age cohort, overtaking majority girls. Minority males have outperformed majority girls over time, but the youngest cohort of majority girls has surpassed disadvantaged boys (figure 1.11). In Ghana, until the most recent cohort, males of all tribal groups outpaced girls in school attainment. However, among 15–21-year-olds, girls have caught up with boys in their own tribes, though the non-Akan speakers still lag behind the majority Akan speakers by almost a year of schooling (figure 1.12). In Malawi the dominant tribe and language are actually a minority in the country. Gender differences in school attainment are greater than differences in language group, however (figure 1.13).

The trends toward gender convergence in Latin America, South Asia, and East Asia do not always hold for Africa. African majority populations may be part of an excluded group, reside in rural areas, or live in abject poverty. The legacy of the arbitrary boundaries created during colonization contributes to the highly heterogeneous nature of African countries. Indeed, the continent has the highest concentration of ethnically and linguistically mixed countries (Alesina and others 2003). The lack of relevant data and analytic work on ethnically and linguistically distinct populations makes it difficult to draw meaningful conclusions.

Education and gender in homogeneous countries

In highly homogeneous countries it may make sense to reach all children with a single push for universal access, as the Republic of Korea, Tunisia, and Bangladesh have successfully done.[4] Among the most homogeneous countries in the developing world the pace of education growth has been impressive. All began scaling up education during periods of extreme poverty—the Republic of Korea after World War II, Tunisia in the late 1950s, and Bangladesh in the 1980s.

The Republic of Korea. The speed with which the Republic of Korea increased enrollment between 1945 and 1955 was unprecedented in the twentieth century, with enrollment tripling in 10 years, bringing virtually all children into the primary school system.

Tunisia. In 1960 literacy among adults (15 years and older) in Tunisia was a mere 16 percent. By 1990 the figure reached 59 percent, and by 2006 was 94 percent among 15- to 24-year-olds (Lockheed and Mete forthcoming). In 2004 primary enrollment approached 97 percent due to a sharp increase following specific reforms in the early 1990s, when girls' primary enrollment lagged behind boys' by about 6 percentage points and less than 60 percent of girls completed primary school. Virtually all children in Tunisia, girls and

---

4. See table 2.1 for degree of homogeneity in 120 developing countries.

Figure 1.14. Tunisia has achieved universal primary school completion for both boys and girls, 1988–2003

Children completing school as percent of graduation-age cohort

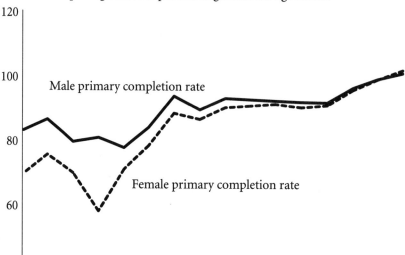

Source: World Bank EdStats 2006.

boys, now complete primary school (figure 1.14). Clear policies, adequate funding, and focused implementation—with explicit efforts to help girls reach parity with boys—led to vast improvements and achievement of universal primary education.

Bangladesh. Bangladesh, a highly homogeneous country in both ethnicity and language, has made stunning progress in girls' education (figure 1.15). Demand for schooling crosses all income groups, with poor families perceiving education as the way out of poverty (Schuler forthcoming). Enrollment in 2005 reached 84.4 percent of children 6–10, with a higher proportion of girls in school, a pattern repeated for adolescents 16–20 and for women 21–24.

Grade attainment among girls exceeds that for boys among both the wealthiest and the poorest children, a reversal of the historical dominance of boys. Convergence across gender and location are virtually identical. But income shows significant disparity, remaining the central factor in keeping children out of school in Bangladesh (Schuler forthcoming).

In homogenous, monolingual countries convergence across gender, location, and income occurs more quickly and evenly than it does in heterogeneous countries. While

**Figure 1.15. Bangladesh has made stunning progress in girls'
education but income is still a significant barrier**

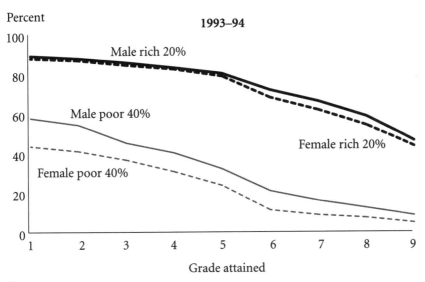

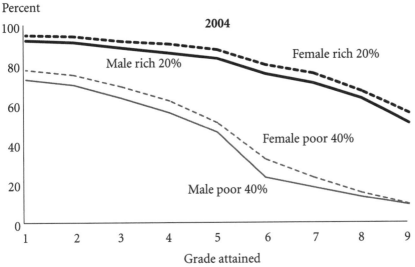

Note: Data are for children ages 15–19.
Source: Bangladesh Demographic and Health Survey 2004; Schuler 2006.

rural students may trail urban children in grade attainment or achievement, once mass education builds momentum location appears to make little difference, with both rural areas and girls catching up. Both Bangladesh and Tunisia targeted efforts to ensure that girls kept pace with boys, something that did not happen in the Republic of Korea.

Education and gender in heterogeneous countries

In heterogeneous settings participation in formal schooling by excluded groups continues to lag, even where girls' and boys' enrollment and completion levels converge. Where minority groups represent a significant proportion of the population, failure to educate children compromises countries' abilities to reach universal education. The cost of meeting the needs of children from linguistically distinct groups, nomadic tribes, or isolated ethnic clans far exceeds that of mainstream children, who are easier to reach and can be taught by existing teachers, books, and teaching materials. Minorities often need special attention, including outreach efforts and complementary programs, which can be expensive and administratively complex.

Ethnic groups that do not participate in the formal economy or reside in remote areas often remain reluctant to send their children to school due to distance, the opportunity cost of schooling, or the lack of apparent need for education. This is particularly the case for daughters, whom many parents are reluctant to let leave the house, particularly to attend school with boys (see chapter 2).

In some countries, minority girls have caught up with majority children and outperform minority boys. Brazil and South Africa (where blacks are the majority but are disproportionately disadvantaged) show such patterns (Guillebeau 1999). As education becomes universal and minority girls are given the opportunity, they overtake boys in achievement. Similar patterns emerge in developed countries among marginal groups. Girls take advantage of opportunity and leave boys behind, suggesting that lack of opportunity poses one of the greatest constraints to achievement among girls from ethnic and linguistic minority groups (see chapter 3).

Conclusions

Educating girls is desirable not only to reach universal coverage but also to help countries' meet their economic growth and social development objectives. There is strong support among both developing countries and donors for educating girls. The challenge is to ensure that shortcomings of current efforts are understood, that children who are not in school are given the opportunity to attend school, and that factors increasing retention are in place to promote completion.

Trends in education in general, and in girls' education in particular, are encouraging in much of the world. But some regions, such as the Middle East, South Asia, and Sub-Saharan Africa, are lagging, and pockets of nonparticipation exist in much of the world. Better understanding of the nature of exclusions in countries and subregions within countries is the first step in addressing barriers and devising effective policies and programs to overcome them.

Girls tend to be the most disadvantaged group in poorly performing environments and the most likely to be left behind in some well performing countries. Children from oppressed minority groups living in rural areas face multiple exclusions in gaining access to education. For girls, gender is an additional barrier.

Parity at the secondary level remains inadequate. Special efforts will be needed to ensure that girls can continue on to secondary school. Creative policies can help blunt the negative cultural effects that slow the process, but the narrowing of the gender gap cannot be accomplished overnight. The focus needs to be on secondary school, where the social and economic benefits help transform countries into equitable and prosperous societies.

2

Social exclusion and barriers to girls' schooling

Girls from ethnic communities face double exclusion—first as members of excluded minorities and second as excluded groups in developing countries that tend to disproportionately discriminate against females. Understanding the patterns of social exclusion across countries from multiple perspectives is crucial for identifying successful interventions. Multiple exclusion, based on both immutable and variable factors, is particularly relevant to education in developing countries, where children from excluded groups face many legal, household, social, and classroom impediments that affect their enrollment and achievement in school.

Multiple sources of social exclusion

Exclusion arises from multiple sources, some endogenous and some exogenous. Social exclusion from immutable factors—such as gender, ethnicity, or race—contributes to low educational participation for girls and sub-group members. Social exclusion from external factors—poverty, for example—not only contributes to low educational participation, but also to a cycle of exclusion based on poverty. Concatenating factors of exclusion lead to what is often called "multiple exclusion."

In developed countries, socially excluded populations are typically minorities. This is not the case in many developing countries, where the poor, the culturally and geographically isolated, and linguistic and ethnic minority groups can represent a majority of the population. Whether a majority or a minority, excluded groups suffer from lower educational participation, attainment, and achievement.

Long-term, self-imposed separation into self-contained clans, such as the Hmong in Southeast Asia, explains some exclusion. But exclusion in many parts of the world also stems from the lower status of excluded groups, leading to derogation and discrimination that denies opportunities and limits improved livelihoods. In some settings, a backlash by excluded groups has led to separation and rejection of dominant values, further distancing the possibility of assimilating into the mainstream culture. In others, communal violence erupts when excluded groups vent their anger at the dominant group.

Girls in excluded groups often suffer disproportionately from multiple sources of exclusion because gender is one of these sources. So girls living in impoverished families and in ethnic or linguistic "minority" communities that are remote from urban settings will require extra effort to bring them into the education mainstream.

What is exclusion?

Social exclusion sidelines certain groups, denying them social rights and protections that should be extended to all citizens (box 2.1). The term "social exclusion" emerged in Europe, following the perceived failures of the welfare system in the face of persistent poverty and slow economic growth in the early 1990s. It parallels concern in the United States in the late 1970s regarding the emergence of an underclass that appeared unable to climb out of poverty. Social exclusion aligns with Sen's (2006) characterization of group identity and the distance between the dominant group and others.

People who are socially excluded receive inadequate support from public institutions. Their opportunities are constrained because mechanisms and institutions exclude them. Although social exclusion is not synonymous with poverty, it is closely tied to the notion of poverty, bridging exclusion of certain groups and the concept of inequity (Loury 2000). Exclusion limits opportunities for marginalized groups through social isolation, limited access to education, and discrimination in schools and the labor market, all of which create an uneven playing field.

Social exclusion of an underclass emerges in heterogeneous, stratified societies that encompass a variety of ethnic groups, languages, and customs. Where subsistence agriculture predominates, geographic isolation effectively cordons off certain groups from mainstream society. Indigenous tribes in parts of the Amazon basin, for example, have only recently begun to interact with national governments and commercial interests, while environmental survey officials and gold miners encroach on their territory. But such geographical isolation is increasingly rare. More common is exclusion of specific groups that live within larger societies.

Box 2.1. What form does exclusion take?

Several factors can define excluded groups:

- Stigmatization by recent historical trauma at the hands of the majority population—a recent history of slavery (blacks in Brazil, Cuba, and the United States), indigenous groups dispossessed of their homeland (for example, native peoples in Canada), or outcasts who have been long time victims of economic and social discrimination (Roma in Europe, Dalits in India, blacks in South Africa prior to 1980).

- Ethnic differences, including groups differentiated by color, language, and religion as well as "tribes," "races," "nationalities," and "castes" (Horowitz 1985).

- Low status, because excluded groups are "ranked" in value below the majority population in the social hierarchy (for example, blacks were ranked lower than whites in South Africa during apartheid and in the southern United States before World War II; Roma, or Gypsies, are ranked lower than majority populations in Eastern Europe; "Dalits" are ranked lower than upper castes in India). In many cultures, women hold a lower social status than men.

- Involuntary minority status in the population.

Social exclusion sidelines certain population groups. It restricts excluded groups' economic mobility and prevents them from receiving the social rights and protections meant to be extended to all citizens. Discrimination by the dominant population effectively excludes these groups from mainstream activities, such as education and employment. In some cases, those who are socially excluded also face other exclusions that reduce their status and acceptance in society. Cultural differences, isolation, and even poverty can exacerbate discrimination and marginalization from the dominant population.

Source: Meerman 2005.

Ethnic populations or people whose mother tongue is not an official national language often remain outside the mainstream economy and society. Their identity comes from the ethnic group, not that of the larger society (Sen 2006). Laos, for example, has 50 ethnic groups, many speaking different languages. India's 573 tribal groups, which remain relatively isolated geographically, speak more than 270 languages. In Cameroon 280 languages are spoken, and in Central and South America, more than 350.

In many parts of the world, exclusion derives from colonization. The legacy of dominance over indigenous peoples created the excluded groups of Aborigines in Australia, First Peoples in Canada, Maori in New Zealand, and Native Americans in the United States. In much of Africa, borders were drawn arbitrarily by colonial powers, creating countries where the excluded group can be larger than the dominant group. The Hutus in Rwanda, for example, outnumber the Tutsis. Where significant ethnic and linguistic diversity has resulted from the cobbling together of nations, exclusion has occasionally erupted into civil conflict, as in Sri Lanka. In other cases, exclusion has led to genocide, as in Darfur and Rwanda.

Many "voluntary" immigrants share characteristics with excluded groups—stigmatization, membership in an ethnic minority, low status—following immigration, but their motivation to assimilate is different from that of other excluded groups. In part, because they perceive these characteristics as temporary, their tolerance for marginalization is greater. Immigrants or guest workers, such as Asians in Australia, Turks in Western Europe, or Caribbean blacks in the United States, for example, perceive both their low status and the discrimination they face as temporary costs of migration that can be overcome through hard work and education. Indeed, in the United States immigrants on average reach economic parity with the majority population within two to four generations; short-term discrimination is perceived as a small price to pay for economic opportunity (Ogbu 1991). However, some "temporary" immigrants or guest workers in Western Europe have become members of excluded groups largely because temporary immigration became permanent residency with limited integration.

In contrast, indigenous peoples and racial groups are involuntary minorities brought into society through slavery, conquest, or colonization. These groups compare themselves to the dominant group and attribute their lower status to being part of a disparaged minority group with limited if any opportunity for upward mobility. They view their situation as permanent and institutionalized and discrimination an inevitable part of their circumstances (Ogbu 1991).

Most of the children who are excluded from school in the developing world come from involuntary minorities. These are children whose parents differ from the dominant class, race, and ethnic group and who have historically been marginalized in their own societies. These children often adopt the expectations of their parents (Ogbu 1991).

Poverty both creates and is created by social exclusion. Loury (2000) points out that social exclusion focuses on the distributional aspects of poverty. Sen (1997) demonstrates how widespread unemployment, a major source of poverty, fuels inequality and social exclusion based on race or gender. Stewart (2001) points to the neglect of "horizontal inequalities" or the neglect of equality across groups, which reduces social welfare and inhibits individual welfare by placing restrictions on individuals within groups. She reviews the economic, social, and political disadvantages of certain groups in nine countries, including indigenous groups in Mexico, Afro-descents in Brazil; Fijians in New Zealand, and blacks in the United States, and shows their similarities in disadvantage and marginalization. Her horizontal inequity examples from the developing world highlight the plight of socially excluded groups.

Some countries have experienced a backlash from historically excluded groups, who aggressively reject mainstream values and substitute their own set of priorities—"minority values" that challenge majority behaviors. Excluded groups confront explicit and implicit discrimination as a way to build self-esteem, establish identity, and challenge the dominant expectations that together compromise learning, reduce social acceptance, and restrict upward mobility. But this may lead to self-defeating behaviors, particularly among the young. Sowell (1994) and Loury (2000) contend that group culture among American blacks (the refusal to "act white") devalues education and helps explain economic disparities between blacks and white. Similar behavioral responses of excluded groups, including rejection of education and other trappings of the majority group, have been observed among Jamaican immigrants in the United Kingdom (Modood 2005), the Roma in Eastern Europe, Aborigines in Australia, and, until recently, the Maori in New Zealand (Ringold, Orenstein, and Wilkens 2003; Ringold 2005). Some of these responses may reflect discriminated groups' efforts to forge a separate identity.

Alternatively, excluded groups may accept the dominant group's low esteem for them, lowering their own expectations for success and impairing their behavior in deference to the majority group (Ridgeway 1997a, 1997b). Steele and Aronson (1995) and Aronson and others (1999) argue that excluded groups may experience higher levels of anxiety in certain situations, arising from a fear of being discriminated against on the basis of stereotypes, and that this "stereotype threat" can lower their performance.

Whether members of an excluded group accept or reject the values of the dominant group, the consequences for their children's performance in school are severe. They are most severe when the children suffer from multiple sources of exclusion.

Measuring exclusion

Measuring exclusion allows comparisons and analysis to be made across and within groups. At the national level, ethnicity, language, location of residence, and other defining characteristics of particular communities can be identified and the degree of difference or heterogeneity measured. Such data provide a basis for defining and comparing conditions, opportunities, and achievements across groups.

From a policy perspective, such data are key. Rioting in France in 2005 and the plight of the Roma in Eastern Europe suggest inequities, but remedial measures are stymied because of lack of data with which to assess the problems, compare performance with majority populations, or track progress of excluded groups. In contrast, in the United States, disaggregated data permit tracking of educational enrollment, attainment, and achievement across ethnic and income groups. These data can be used to target policy initiatives and programs.

Some recent household surveys in developing countries capture ethnic distinctions. These data have been used to demonstrate the disadvantages facing indigenous groups in education (Hallman and Peracca forthcoming; King and van de Walle forthcoming; Hall and Patrinos 2006; van de Walle and Gunewardena 2001; Stash and Hannum 2001). They provide the basis for defining areas for public intervention.

Measurement offers the first step toward addressing social exclusion. Measuring exclusion at the national level is difficult, and differentiating countries by their degree of exclusion remains a challenge. In many countries, information on population groups does not exist or data are too old to be usable for policy analysis. Alesina and others (2003) have attempted to capture the degree of heterogeneity of countries by looking at ethnic and linguistic fractionalization. Ethnic fractionalization refers to racial and linguistic characteristics, taking into account physical attributes, social conventions, and accepted social definitions, including self-identification. Linguistic fractionalization is compiled separately from any racial or physical characteristics and reports the shares of languages spoken as "mother tongues" using census data. The data of Alesina and others cover 650 ethnic groups in 190 countries and 1,055 linguistic groups.

Both ethnic and linguistic heterogeneity, which tend to be highly correlated, are high in some of the poorest countries (table 2.1). Where both are high, as in Indonesia, Pakistan, and Uganda, the challenges of socializing children and building a nation-state with common objectives and goals are great. Although education offers an important tool for building trust across disparate groups, extending schooling to all groups in society can prove an economic and social challenge, particularly in socially and ethnically mixed populations. Indeed, 68 percent of all out-of-school children live in the highly linguistically fractionalized countries (UNESCO 2004). In contrast, where both ethnic and linguistic heterogeneity are low, as in Bangladesh, the Republic of Korea, and Tunisia, nation building can occur more smoothly.

Most developing countries are highly heterogeneous, outnumbering highly

Table 2.1. Ethnic and linguistic heterogeneity in developing countries and transition economies

Linguistic fractionalization	Ethnic fractionalization		
	Low[a]	Medium[b]	High[c]
Low[a]	Albania, Antigua and Barbuda, Argentina, Armenia, Azerbaijan, Bangladesh, Barbados, Burundi, Cambodia, Chile, China, Comoros, Costa Rica, Democratic People's Republic of Korea, Egypt, Honduras, Hungary, Kiribati, Lebanon, Lesotho, Marshall Islands, Poland, Republic of Korea, Russian Federation, Seychelles, Slovak Republic, Swaziland, Tunisia, Tuvalu, Uruguay, Vietnam, Western Samoa	Brazil, Croatia, Dominican Republic, Jamaica, Jordan, Mexico, Nicaragua, Romania, Saint Vincent and Grenadines, Syria, Turkey, Venezuela	Bolivia, Colombia, Ecuador, Guyana, Libya, Madagascar, Somalia, Trinidad and Tobago

Table 2.1. Ethnic and linguistic heterogeneity in developing countries and transition economies (continued)

Linguistic fractionalization	Ethnic fractionalization		
	Low[a]	Medium[b]	High[c]
Medium[b]	Papua New Guinea, Paraguay, Saint Lucia, Solomon Islands, Tonga, Vanuatu	Algeria, Belarus, Botswana, Bulgaria, Czech Republic, Estonia, Fiji, Georgia, Guatemala, Iraq, Latvia, Lithuania, Macedonia FYR, Mauritius, Moldova, Mongolia, Morocco, Myanmar, Oman, Palau, Panama, Sri Lanka, Tajikistan, Turkmenistan, Ukraine, Uzbekistan, Zimbabwe	Kyrgyz Republic, Mauritania, Peru, Suriname
High[c]	Philippines	India, Lao People's Democratic Republic, Nauru	Afghanistan, Angola, Belize, Benin, Bhutan, Bosnia and Herzegovina, Burkina Faso, Cameroon, Central African Republic, Chad, Congo, Côte d'Ivoire, Democratic Republic of Congo, Djibouti, Eritrea, Ethiopia, Gabon, Ghana, Guinea, Guinea-Bissau, Indonesia, Iran, Kazakhstan, Kenya, Liberia, Malawi, Mali, Micronesia, Mozambique, Namibia, Nepal, Niger, Nigeria, Pakistan, Senegal, Sierra Leone, South Africa, Sudan, Tanzania, Thailand, The Gambia, Togo, Uganda, Zambia

a. Fractionalization score of less than 0.3.

b. Fractionalization score between 0.3 and 0.6.

c. Fractionalization score of 0.6 or higher.

Source: Alesina and others 2003.

homogeneous ones by about three to two. Among homogeneous developing countries, about one-third are very small, with populations of less than 1 million (see table 2.1). Most children in developing countries will live in heterogeneous societies.

While hetereogeneity is often the consequence of former colonial status, it can also reflect voluntary migration and involuntary resettlement. Encounters with people from different ethnic or linguistic groups become more likely with economic development, social change, and urbanization. These encounters provide opportunities for a dominant group to judge a nondominant group against its own standards—and find it wanting. This leads to the emergence of socially excluded groups in many developing countries. Once confined to certain regions or self-contained communities, these groups now participate in a wider society dominated by unknown, mistrusted "others," who denigrate them for being different. Unless countered, this denigration leads to poverty, discrimination, and inequality in access to services.

Schools can play a special role in counteracting the negative effects of a heterogeneous society. Properly designed, schools can promote tolerance and build trust among ethnic and linguistic groups (Heyneman 2000). But building trust is a challenge, because distrust of others is a central feature of traditional societies (Putnam 1993; Inkeles and Smith 1974). Unfortunately, schools can also reinforce negative stereotypes and exacerbate differences.

Exclusion and the demand for schooling

Exclusion leads to lower parental demand for schooling and to inadequate and substandard public supply. Parents want to keep children home for many reasons, from general resistance to change, to a desire to retain a separate ethnic identity, to disinterest in what schools have to offer. Some parents identify discrimination and mistreatment by schools and teachers as a reason to keep their children out of school (Ringold, Orenstein, and Wilkens 2003; Narayan 2000). Direct and opportunity costs, lack of employment opportunities upon graduating, and low returns to those who have attended school also keep excluded children out of school.

Sending children to school entails a high opportunity cost without clear returns to the family, particularly in subsistence societies. Indeed, the need for child labor is the single most important reason for not sending rural children to school in developing countries, especially among the poorest families (Basu and Tzannatos 2003). Sending children to school means losing labor.

Recent research underscores the salience of safety factors in keeping girls out of school. Parents may want their daughters in school but worry about their safety away from home, traveling to and from school (Kim and Bailey 2003; Mbassa Mednick 2001; Mgalla, Boerma, and Schapink 1998; Ohsako 1997). Distance poses particular problems for girls in secondary school, when they become targets for rape and abduction, which is not only traumatic for the girls, but often compromises the social status of their households and their acceptance in the community. As demand for girls' education increases, reservations about safety could undermine the efforts of both households and governments in meeting that demand.

Reaching isolated groups in most societies tends to be costly, and as a lower public priority, the supply of schools and teachers tends to lag, which reinforces low demand. The direct costs of primary school—in the form of school fees, family contributions, and unofficial fees—can represent a high share of poor families' disposable income (Bray 1996; Kattan and Burnett 2004). These expenses can prevent families from enrolling their children in school (Kudo 2004; Narayan 2000). For the excluded, who typically have low incomes and limited demand, such charges can prove insurmountable. Other costs of education (school uniforms, textbooks, transportation) can also represent significant barriers. These costs may be particularly high for girls because of their lost household labor and the costs associated with safety en route to and at school (Birdsall, Levine, and Ibrahim 2005).

Families may have a preference for educating boys over girls, given better labor market opportunities for boys and the fact that girls in many societies are "married away," joining the husband's family and no longer providing for or living with their own families. The general preference for boys found among most excluded groups in developing countries adds to the disadvantage experienced by girls.

Most excluded groups are poor, in part because of lower economic returns to education. Excluded groups' educational attainment remains well below that of the majority population. Exclusion and gender discrimination lead to lower returns to almost all investments in comparison with similar investments aimed at the majority population, for several reasons. First, excluded groups tend to suffer multiple forms of discrimination. This lowers their economic and social status, which in turn shapes their attitudes toward education and reduces their motivation to learn. Second, expectations of limited economic returns to education among excluded groups reduce demand for education, particularly for girls, because women face greater labor market discrimination than do men. Third, the quality of public programs, including education, directed at marginalized groups tends to be inferior to those aimed at majority populations. Fourth, lack of role models and preschool preparation place excluded children at a distinct disadvantage when entering school, further reducing their motivation. Poor progress, high costs of schooling, and higher opportunity costs of sending children to school also make these children more likely to drop out. Thus even in countries where there are few structural barriers to girls' schooling, girls from excluded groups face clear disadvantages in enrollment and completion.

Public policies and funding favor the majority; limited voice and political representation reduce the attention afforded excluded groups. Indeed, with few exceptions, excluded groups have little say in the content, approach, or methods of teaching or in the selection or oversight of teachers. Because excluded groups by definition remain outside the mainstream, they do not participate in civic activities and have little if any knowledge about education. Public leaders marginalize their needs. Indeed, evidence for the United States shows that more ethnically fragmented communities are associated with less efficient provision of public goods, lower participation rates in social activities, and less trust within the community (Alesina and others 2003). All of these factors reduce access, participation, and performance.

The excluded suffer not only from inaccessible schools, but also from discriminatory treatment when they reach schools, which leads to dropout and to lower learning. A multi-country study estimates that the combined effects of gender, immigrant status (a proxy for exclusion), and isolated residence lowered mathematics scores a staggering 35 points, equivalent to one-third of the difference between the highest scoring country and the international average (Woessmann 2000). In a study of preschools in Kenya, Vermeersch and Kremer (2005) find that scores on both oral and written measures of learning were lower in classrooms in which ethnic heterogeneity was greatest.

Low returns to education exacerbate low demand. Using household surveys, Zoninsein (2001) estimates what the gains in GDP in Latin America would have been if excluded groups (indigenous peoples and black Afro-descendents) had had the same education, productivity, and earnings as whites. He concludes that the racial and ethnic exclusion have cost Bolivia 36.7 percent of GDP, Brazil 12.8 percent, Guatemala, 13.6 percent, and Peru 4.2 percent. The losses stem from differences in years of schooling and mean earnings between whites and excluded populations, controlling for age and gender.

At the household level the incomes of excluded groups consistently lag behind those of majority populations in most countries, except in Africa, where minority tribes can dominate, as in Rwanda and Malawi. Studies of Eastern Europe (Ringold, Orenstein, and Wilkens 2003), India (see India National Sample Survey at www.censusindia.net), Laos (King and van de Walle forthcoming), Latin America (Hall and Patrinos 2006), South Africa (Mwabu and Schultz 1998), and Vietnam (van de Walle and Gunewardena 2001) reveal significant gaps in average incomes between dominant and excluded groups.

In Latin America indigenous people and racial minorities earn less than white nonindigenous workers with the same educational attainment. Average incomes of indigenous men are 44–65 percent below those of nonindigenous men. The ability to climb out of poverty is hindered by restricted income-earning possibilities, which reduce the returns to education (Hall and Patrinos 2006).[1]

---

1. Hall and Patrinos (2006) find that disparities in educational attainment and location of residence best explain wage differentials across racial and ethnic groups. Average marginal returns across all groups for primary education are 7.8 percent, with the highest returns in Brazil, at 14.0 percent for primary education, 9.6 percent for secondary education, and 17.4 percent for tertiary education. Trends in the 1990s show a decline in the returns to secondary education and a rise in the returns to higher education. The increasing number of workers with secondary education could explain part of the decline, although Chile and Uruguay, both with relatively high-quality schooling and growing numbers of trained secondary school graduates, did not see returns fall. Duryea, Jaramillo, and Pages (2003) speculate that maintaining academic quality may have helped maintain rising wages for secondary school graduates.

In Peru nonindigenous white workers have higher average earnings than indigenous workers, after controlling for individual and household characteristics (Nopo, Saavedra, and Torero 2004). Being from a disadvantaged group raises the probability of being and staying poor; the combination of discrimination, lack of skills, and reliance on subsistence agriculture often pushes excluded groups deeper into rural poverty.

Earnings of excluded women trail those of excluded men and majority men and women. In Latin America the gender gap in earnings is closing, but indigenous females remain the most disadvantaged in every country in Latin America (Duryea, Jaramillo, and Pages 2003; Hall and Patrinos 2006). In countries with the largest indigenous or racial groups (Bolivia, Brazil, Guatemala, Guyana, and Peru), nonindigenous white men remain the best endowed with assets. The gender gap in income among indigenous peoples and people of African descent significantly exceeds the gender gap among nonindigenous white populations in Latin America (Hall and Patrinos 2006).

In 2001 Afro Brazilians earned half the average per capita income of white Brazilians. Although just 45 percent of Brazil's population is black, blacks represent 62 percent of poor households. Discrimination explains the 11 percent gap in white-black wages in the formal sector and the 24 percent gap among the self-employed. No social mobility appears to have taken place in Brazil, with income growth strongly correlating with initial income levels. White men remain the most privileged and black women the least so, a finding consistent with previous quantitative and qualitative evidence (Mario and Woolcock forthcoming; Narayan 2000).[2]

Excluded groups not only earn less, their ability to improve their (relative) economic circumstances is also more limited. For example, positive benefits from macroeconomic growth affect these populations less, due largely to their isolation, while the negative effects of economic decline tend to persist longer (Hall and Patrinos 2006).

Demand for education—or even the willingness to permit excluded children to attend school—is tied to expected returns. Parents who believe that education will yield long-term returns are more willing to send their children to school. The lack of returns can prove discouraging to households and communities, and it can lead to withdrawal from schooling. This is already occurring in some high-income OECD countries, as disadvantaged groups increasingly believe that discrimination undermines the value and returns to education. Policymakers and donors require a sound understanding of the returns to education in order to shape policies and interventions to rectify or compensate for impediments.

Gender, exclusion, and the supply of schooling

Low-quality inputs to schools and perceptions of the irrelevance of schooling further reduce the willingness of parents to send their children to school. In some cases parental

---

2. Mwabu and Schultz (1998) find mixed returns to education in South Africa.

participation in schooling in the past has not translated into an increased willingness to send children to school (for example, the Roma, Dalits, and some African Americans in the United States). Quality matters. Poor-quality schools, maltreatment in school, and low expectations of teachers lower demand among excluded groups. While incentives such as scholarships and other interventions may be able to break the cycle of resistance to school, low demand and inadequate supply reduce the opportunity for and interest in schooling for households and students.

A multitude of supply factors result in excluded girls never enrolling or dropping out of school early. Legal and administrative barriers typically affect the supply of schools and hence participation in schooling. Overt discrimination by a dominant group can affect the opportunity to learn, reducing both participation and performance.

Legal and administrative barriers

Legal and administrative barriers are usually overt, visible, and amenable to direct political and management action. While changing laws and regulations does not necessarily translate into behavioral change within households or schools, an appropriate regulatory framework is a necessary precondition for making changes at these levels. Experience from developed countries highlights the force of legislation and the application of existing laws in reducing barriers to equitable education (Hochschild and Scovronick 2003).

Legal barriers are not the main source of exclusion in education. Laws requiring discrimination, such as the apartheid laws in South Africa, have largely disappeared, and more than 90 percent of countries have legally binding rules requiring children's school attendance (UNESCO 2002; Benavot 2002). By 2002, 77 countries guaranteed free and compulsory education for all children, and another 29 had made strides in this direction (table 2.2).

Laws in some countries still limit access to education, however. Thirty-seven countries provide free and compulsory education only to citizens or legal residents, thereby excluding children of guest workers. Another 43 have no national or constitutional guarantees regarding education (Tomaschevski 2001). Others provide for education that is separate and possibly unequal for children of migrants or guest workers, on the assumption that their presence in the country is temporary and the children will be returning to their home country. Although laws can be, and are, disregarded, a legal framework that ensures education for all is important. The global consensus regarding basic education for all provides a strong impetus for eliminating remaining legal barriers in education.

Table 2.2. Prevalence of guaranteed free and compulsory education

Countries that guarantee free and compulsory education (77)	Countries with partial guarantees (29)
Albania, Algeria, Argentina, Australia, Austria, Azerbaijan, Barbados, Belgium, Belize, Bolivia, Bosnia and Herzegovina, Brazil, Bulgaria, Canada, Cape Verde, Chile, China, Colombia, Congo, Costa Rica, Croatia, Cuba, Denmark, Ecuador, Egypt, Estonia, Finland, France, Georgia, Germany, Ghana, Haiti, Honduras, Iceland, Ireland, Italy, Japan, Latvia, Liechtenstein, Lithuania, Macedonia FYR, Madagascar, Malta, Mauritius, Mexico, Moldova, Netherlands, Norway, Palau, Panama, Paraguay, Peru, Poland, Portugal, Republic of Korea, Romania, Russian Federation, Rwanda, Saudi Arabia, South Africa, Spain, Sri Lanka, Suriname, Sweden, Switzerland, Tajikistan, Thailand, The Gambia, Trinidad and Tobago, Tunisia, Ukraine, United Arab Emirates, United Kingdom, Uruguay, Venezuela, Yugoslavia	Bangladesh, Belarus, Benin, Bhutan, Cameroon, Comoros, Guinea, Guinea-Bissau, India, Iran, Iraq, Israel, Maldives, Micronesia, Monaco, Mongolia, Myanmar, Namibia, Nepal, Nigeria, Pakistan, Saint Kitts and Nevis, Sierra Leone, Sudan, Tanzania, Togo, Uganda, Uzbekistan, Zimbabwe

Countries in which guarantees are restricted to citizens or residents (37)	Countries with no national guarantees (43)
Armenia, Bahrain, Cambodia, Chad, Cyprus, Czech Republic, Democratic People's Republic of Korea, Dominican Republic, El Salvador, Equatorial Guinea, Greece, Grenada, Guatemala, Guyana, Hungary, Jordan, Kazakhstan, Kuwait, Kyrgyzstan, Libya, Luxembourg, Malawi, Mali, Morocco, New Zealand, Nicaragua, Philippines, Qatar, São Tomé and Principe, Seychelles, Slovak Republic, Slovenia, Syria, Turkey, Turkmenistan, Vietnam, Yemen	Angola, Antigua and Barbuda, The Bahamas, Botswana, Brunei Darussalam, Burkina Faso, Burundi, Central African Republic, Côte d'Ivoire, Djibouti, Dominica, Eritrea, Ethiopia, Fiji, Gabon, Indonesia, Jamaica, Kenya, Kiribati, Lao People's Democratic Republic, Lebanon, Lesotho, Liberia, Malaysia, Marshall Islands, Mauritania, Mozambique, Nauru, Niger, Oman, Papua New Guinea, Saint Lucia, Saint Vincent and Grenadines, Samoa, San Marino, Senegal, Singapore, Solomon Islands, Swaziland, Tonga, Tuvalu, United States of America, Vanuatu, Zambia

Source: Adapted from Tomaschevski 2001.

Gender barriers

Some administrative rules specifically affect girls. Within countries, educational administrative rules and practices can erect significant barriers to school participation.

Some of these rules appear to be gender or culture neutral, but a closer inspection shows that they are not. While national educational rules are often disregarded at the local level, their enforcement can block school participation, principally by affecting the supply of schools available for girls and members of sub-groups. Two important administrative rules affect girls' participation in school: specifying the number or "gender" of schools that communities must provide for primary students and expelling pregnant and married girls from school.

Single-sex schools. In many countries the requirement to provide single-sex schools, common in the Middle East and South Asia, often restricts the supply of schools for girls. Some communities disregard the rule prohibiting girls from attending boys' schools and allow very young girls to attend school with their brothers; young boys are also allowed to attend all-girls schools with their sisters. But girls in these communities are rarely allowed to continue schooling alongside boys beyond the first few grades. A survey of schools in 12 rural villages in Pakistan found that only 36 percent of girls enrolled at boys' schools were actually attending school, compared with 88 percent of girls enrolled at girls' schools (Sathar and others 2003). Without a girls' school in the community, girls are excluded from formal schooling. Differences across communities in willingness to educate girls alongside boys determines which regulations create the greatest barrier to girls.

Expulsion of pregnant girls. One of the main reasons why girls leave school in Africa is marriage or pregnancy. In many countries in Africa pregnant girls are routinely expelled from the formal education system. If they are allowed to rejoin the formal system after they give birth, they are required to return to a different school (Wilson 2004). Boys responsible for pregnancies are not dismissed from school. Although the Forum for African Women Educationalists has exposed this practice and the African Charter on the Rights and Welfare of the Child contains language recognizing pregnant girls' rights to education, countries vary widely in compliance. Although allowing girls to remain in or return to school does not deal with the underlying causes of teenage pregnancy, it could improve the lives of the affected girls.

Language barriers

In many countries the language of instruction in primary schools is a national or regional language, even though large shares of the population speak a different mother tongue. The cognitive demands on children who are required to learn multiple languages are substantial and contribute to barriers to schooling (Abadzi 2006).

Bilingual education programs are widely agreed to be the preferable approach for integrating nonnative speakers into the mainstream language (Hochchild and Scrovornick 2003). But even in developed countries few school systems have the resources to hire bilingual teachers. Hence children are often expected to "transition" to the dominant language without any pedagogical support.

Rules regarding the language of instruction often disproportionately affect girls, particularly in communities that seclude women. In these communities girls may lack the opportunities that their brothers have to learn the language of instruction before entering school (Benson 2005).

Even when teaching takes place in a local language, instructional materials may not be available in all mother tongues. The lack of relevant instructional materials puts some children at a considerable disadvantage. India, for example, with more than 1,000 languages and dialects, guarantees children the right to be educated in their mother tongue for the early primary grades, and most states publish textbooks in multiple languages (World Bank 1997). But according to the World Bank (1997),

> …textbooks in minority languages often arrive late or not at all. In most states, textbooks are first prepared and printed in a predominant regional language, and work on versions in minority languages often begins only after the majority language version has gone to press…. Yet states rarely purchase textbooks in a minority language from neighboring states in which that language holds majority status. For example, Andhra Pradesh struggles to produce a limited quantity of books for its Tamil-speaking children, even though neighboring Tamil Nadu produces the bulk of its books in Tamil. (p. 174)

In Morocco the official language is Arabic, but 30–50 percent of the population speaks one of three main Berber languages at home. Most instruction in Morocco is in Arabic at the primary level and in Arabic and French at the secondary and tertiary levels. Textbooks, however, are available only in Arabic and French (box 2.2).[3]

In Latin America significant shares of children in Bolivia, Guatemala, Mexico, and Peru speak indigenous languages. Many of these countries have begun to introduce mother tongue education in the early grades and to provide textbooks in indigenous languages. Performance of some indigenous children is improving (discussed in chapter 3).

Lack of schools in remote communities

Many of the world's poor people live in rural areas, where distance to school remains a highly constraining factor for school participation. In an extensive review of research, Lockheeed and Verspoor (1991) conclude that "the single most important determinant of primary school enrollment is the proximity of a school to primary-age children"

---

3. As of the 2005/06 academic year 317 primary schools started giving their first-year students lessons in the Berber language, fulfilling a promise made nearly 10 years ago by the late King Hassan to bring Berber into the classroom.

Box 2.2. Schools that fail Tashelhit-speaking Berbers in Morocco

In 2001 the Tashelhit-speaking Berber people in a remote rural village in Morocco worked hard to get a government school. Men toiled for weeks in the hot sun to create a flat platform on which a proper building could be constructed. Eventually, government workers arrived with cement and rebar. Up went the schoolhouse, with a toilet, glass windows, desks, blackboards, and a coat of shocking pink paint. The villagers were exuberant—even more so when the matriculating class received backpacks filled with school supplies. Finally, the government schoolteacher arrived. She was pious, wearing her scarf tight around her head at all times, and monolingual, an urban Arabic speaker who made no attempt to speak Tashelhit. The children could not understand anything she said. For the schoolteacher, Tashelhit was beneath consideration. She told people that Tashelhit was a language scarcely better than the babble of children. The school materials, designed for urban students, were entirely in Arabic and relied on pictures of things unfamiliar to rural children—crosswalks and refrigerators, streetlights and modern ovens. Enthusiasm for school quickly faded, and beatings were administered for lack of comprehension, absenteeism, and tardiness. The teacher became frustrated, extending her vacations, canceling school, and shortening the school day. Written school reports went home to parents who could not read them. The teacher asked for a transfer, and the students were released for the summer, having lost an entire school year.

Source: Crawford 2001.

(p. 146). Recent studies confirm this observation.

In a study of 22 countries, Filmer (2004) finds a strong negative correlation between the distance to a primary school and primary school participation of both boys and girls from the poorest 50 percent of households in about one-third of the countries.[4] King and van de Walle (forthcoming) find that distance to school is negatively related to school enrollment in Laos. The effect of having a school in the community is twice as large in rural areas than in urban ones, and the effect is much larger for girls than for boys. Lloyd, Mete, and Grant (forthcoming) report a strong positive effect of having a public school in a village in Pakistan on the probability of girls 10–14 being enrolled in school. Bilquees and Saquib (2004) find lower dropout rates for rural girls in Pakistan when the school is located less than 2 kilometers from the home.

Children are much more likely to attend schools located in their own village. For example, a school mapping study in Chad finds that enrollment increased sharply the closer the school was to the village, with gross enrollment rates of about 55 percent in villages that had schools compared with 35 percent in villages where schools were located up to 1 kilometer from the village and less than 10 percent in villages where schools were located more than 1 kilometer from the village (Mulkeen 2005). In Lesotho 69 percent of children who have never been to school live more than 30 minutes

---

4. Distance reduces girls' participation in Burkina Faso, Central African Republic, Chad, Haiti, Madagascar, Mali, Niger, and Zimbabwe. It reduces boys' participation in Benin, Burkina Faso, Central African Republic, Chad, Dominican Republic, Haiti, Madagascar, Mali, and Niger.

from a school (World Bank 2005a, cited by Mulkeen). Distance to school increases the opportunity cost for school attendance and the security risk to children walking to school.

Distance to a secondary school is also important in determining a child's educational attainment because it signals the opportunity for advancement. But many rural communities lack secondary schools. One study of rural schools in Mexico estimates that proximity to a secondary school increased attainment by more than one full year. The average number of years of schooling completed was 6.3 years for children living more than 3 kilometers from a secondary school, compared with 7.4 years for children living within 1 kilometer of a secondary school (Raymond and Sadoulet 2003).

Formal schooling is often associated with physical buildings in fixed locations. Yet children in remote communities, children of migrant workers, and children from nomadic communities, such as the Roma, may be underserved by schools in fixed locations. Distance education programs and traveling teachers have been tried as a means of reaching distant and migratory communities. Flexibility in providing access through distance programs and even mobile classrooms would open access to these children.

Selection examinations and tracking

Where the number of secondary school places is limited, examinations are often used to track and select the students who can enroll (Kellaghan and Greaney 1992; Binkley, Guthrie, and Wyatt 1991). In Algeria the number of students allowed to pass the primary school leaving examination in the mid-1990s was the same as the available number of places in lower secondary schools. In Tunisia in the mid-1990s a selection examination at the end of grade 6 combined with student grades determined which students were allowed to proceed to grade 7 (Lockheed and Mete forthcoming). In Jamaica efforts to equalize the share of male and female students at higher levels of education have led to reverse discrimination, whereby higher test scores are required for girls than for boys (Bailey 2004). In other countries opportunities for postcompulsory levels of education differ for boys and girls, and access is governed by examinations that allocate available places.

In recent years significant progress has been made in lowering examination-based administrative barriers in many countries by eliminating presecondary selection examinations. Selection examinations have the potential to exacerbate gender and ethnic differences in educational attainment, if test performance is lower for girls and other groups. Some research in the United States and India suggests that performance on tests is lower when "stereotype threats" are activated in the testing situation, as discussed below (Steele and Aronson 1995; Hoff and Pandey 2004, 2005).

Tracking students by ability often results in the separation of minority and majority children. While most segregation in the United States is attributable to residential segregation, a significant share of segregation in secondary school is related to ability grouping. A higher share of African Americans and children from homes in which English is not spoken are identified as "academically handicapped" and hence placed in separate schools or, more often, classes. A recent review of this literature observes that separating students by tracking leads to racial segregation (Conger 2005). In some states the practice has been challenged in court, and several school districts have been ordered to discontinue tracking. Tracking is common practice in developing countries. Roma children, for example, are often tracked into "special schools" for handicapped children.

Poor quality of schooling

Given the value of child labor in household production, sending children to school can be viewed as not worth the effort when the quality of the school is poor. There is little evidence on the quality of all-girl schools or schools attended by children of excluded groups. But there is considerable evidence on the quality of schools for poor people in developing countries: the schools are poor. Education services for the poor are weaker than education services for the more advantaged (World Bank 2004). The quality of the school affects learning, progress, and completion.

Good schools share many common features: a commitment to learning that is reflected in the knowledge and experience of the teachers and principals, the amount of time the school is open, the teaching methods, the richness of learning materials, and the safety and security of the school and its environs (Levin and Lockheed 1993; Scheerens 1999). Schools for poor people in developing countries often are of much lower quality than schools attended by the nonpoor. Teachers are less qualified and often less likely to come to work, fewer hours of instruction are offered, teaching methods emphasize rote learning more than investigation, textbooks and instructional materials are less likely to arrive on time (or to arrive at all), and the physical infrastructure of the school is more likely to lack electricity, water, sanitary facilities, and other basic features of a school.

Less knowledgeable teachers

Studies of teacher quality have focused on such proxies for quality as teacher salaries, formal qualifications, and experience. Such indicators are often weakly associated with student achievement, and they capture neither the quality of teaching nor the quality of teachers' knowledge (Behrman and Birdsall 1985; Hanushek 2003).

Empirical studies of the effects of teacher knowledge, as measured by tests, show more consistent effects on student performance than do teacher education, experience, or salary (table 2.3). In the United States among the 41 estimates for which teacher test scores were available 37 percent reported a statistically significant positive effect on student achievement. By comparison, statistically significant positive effects of teacher education were found in only 9 percent of the 170 estimates, and teacher salary was found to be positively associated with student performance in just 20 percent of 118 estimates (Hanushek 2003).

A recent multi-country study finds a strong positive relationship between the formal education of teachers and the math and science achievement of students, subjects for which teacher knowledge can be built in formal education (Woessmann 2000). Hill, Rowan, and Ball (2005) examine the effect of teachers' use of mathematical knowledge in largely minority classrooms in the United States. They find that for each standard deviation in teacher knowledge, children's scores on math tests rose by one-half to two-thirds of a grade-month. "Knowledgeable teachers can positively and substantially affect students' learning of mathematics, and the size of this effect…is in league with the effects of student background characteristics" (396). Students of teachers who know more and use this knowledge in the classroom perform better than other students.

Less evidence is available on developing countries, but a 1994 review reports that in all studies for which this factor was tested, teachers' measured knowledge was positively associated with student achievement (Fuller and Clark 1994). Test scores of teachers in Belize (Mullens, Murnane, and Willett 1996), Brazil (Harbison and Hanushek 1992), India (Kingdon 1998), Indonesia (Ross and Postlethwaite 1989), and the Philippines (Tan, Lane, and Coustier 1997) show that teacher knowledge contributes to student achievement, independent of other teacher and student effects.

Teachers in rural schools often lack a strong foundation in the subjects they teach. A study in rural India found that only half of the grade 4 teachers tested could correctly answer 80 percent of the questions on a grade 4 test of mathematics knowledge (Bashir 1994). In many developing countries people become teachers because they fail

Table 2.3. Effect of teacher quality on student performance in the United States

Variable	Number of estimates	Percentage statistically positive	Percentage statistically negative	Percentage statistically insignificant
Teacher education	170	9	5	86
Teacher experience	206	29	5	66
Teacher salary	118	20	7	73
Teacher test scores	41	37	10	53

Note: Figures based on 376 production function estimates for the United States.

Source: Hanushek 2003.

to obtain places in more competitive and desirable faculties, such as engineering or medicine. Teaching is viewed as a last resort. Because rural posts are viewed as highly undesirable, they are often filled by the least qualified new teachers.

The effectiveness of teachers in rural schools may also be compromised by their unfamiliarity with the language their students speak at home. Teachers who cannot communicate with their students cannot be effective. Students who speak a nonstandard mother tongue are at a disadvantage.

Less instructional time

Instructional time is often limited in urban areas as a consequence of multiple shifts and in rural areas as a consequence of teacher absenteeism. The effects on children are severe, as the amount of instructional time has consistently been found to correlate with student learning (Millot and Lane 2002; Woessmann 2000). In urban schools in Egypt multiple shifts resulted in loss of instructional time (Lloyd and others 2003). Crowded schools with split shifts in Africa provided 30 percent fewer instructional hours to students (Abadzi 2006, citing Kim 1999). Abadzi (2006) finds significant differences in Bangladesh, Honduras, and Mali between the number of hours in the official school year and the actual number of hours that schools were in operation. Amadio (1997) and Millot and Lane (2002) find substantial differences between actual and official instructional hours in Egypt, Lebanon, Morocco, Tunisia, and Yemen. In Bangladesh teachers assigned to rural schools typically arrive two hours late and teach for only two hours, effectively cutting learning time by 50 percent (Tietjen, Raman, and Spaulding 2003).

Teacher absenteeism is a major cause of reduced instructional time (Benavot 2004). A cross-country study of teacher absenteeism, observed through unannounced visits to about 100 randomly selected schools per country in seven countries, finds wide variation in teacher absenteeism, with an average of less than 20 percent of teachers absent in Ecuador and Peru compared with an average of 51 percent of teachers in India (Chaudhury and others 2005; figure 2.1). India's high rate of teacher absenteeism is an outlier—more than 13 percentage points higher than the next highest country. But high levels of teacher absenteeism are evident in other countries. In Kenya 57 percent of students surveyed in 39 schools reported a teacher absence the previous week (Lloyd, Mench, and Clark 2000). In 12 villages in the Northwest Frontier and Punjab of Pakistan, teacher absenteeism in public schools averaged 14 percent. The figure was much lower in boys' schools (11 percent) and private coeducational schools (9 percent) than average. These figures, while high, represent a significant decline in absenteeism in Pakistan, from an average of 20 percent in 1997 to 12 percent in 2004 across all schools (Sathar and others 2005).

Teacher absenteeism correlates with some school and community factors. Absenteeism is lower among female teachers, among teachers born in the district where the school is located, among teachers who work in schools with better infrastructure, and among teachers of children whose parents are more literate (Chaudhury and others 2005). In rural schools in Pakistan girls' enrollment and attendance are higher at schools in which the teacher lives in the community (and therefore is more likely to come to school) (Lloyd, Mete, and Grant forthcoming).

Absenteeism provides a window into the degree to which schools and teachers actually instruct children. In Zambia student learning suffers as a consequence of teacher absenteeism, due largely to illness and death in the family (Das and others 2005). In Indonesia higher teacher absenteeism is correlated with lower fourth-grade student performance on mathematics (but not dictation) among a representative sample of government schools in eight provinces, controlling for household characteristics, teacher quality, and school conditions (student-teacher ratios, presence of latrines).

While variations in instructional time are difficult to measure due to poor reporting, a few studies confirm the relationship between instructional time and girls' participation or achievement. In Egypt girls attending multiple-shift schools with fewer instructional hours were five to six times more likely to drop out before completing lower secondary (preparatory) school than were girls attending a single-shift school (Lloyd and others 2003). In rural India student achievement was higher in schools with more instructional

Figure 2.1. Teacher absenteeism is a serious problem in developing countries

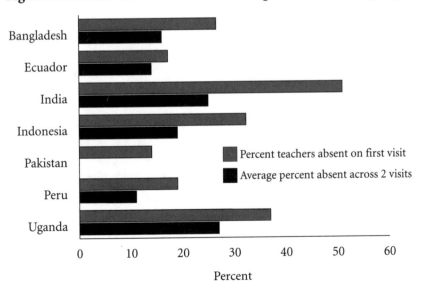

Percent teachers absent on first visit
Average percent absent across 2 visits

Note: Average for India is for three visits.
Source: Chaudhury and others (2005); Sathar and others (2005).

time. Schools with the highest achievement in one state reported more than 66 hours more instructional time per year than schools with the lowest achievement (World Bank 1997). Less instructional time translates into significantly fewer standard school years completed. The school year in Uruguay is only 455 hours, for example, less than half the standard year of 1,000 hours. Children completing six years of school in Uruguay thus complete the equivalent of only about three standard years of instruction (Motivans 2005).[5]

Fewer textbooks and instructional materials

Schools for poor people often lack basic instructional materials. Textbooks often reach remote schools well after the beginning of the school year—if they arrive at all (Tietjen, Raman, and Spaulding 2003). In Kenya, for example, less than half of seventh and eighth-grade students present in class had the required textbooks (Lloyd, Mench, and Clark 2000).

Availability of books in general poses a challenge to education in the poorest developing countries (figure 2.2). More than half of all sixth-grade students in eight countries participating in the Southern and Eastern Africa Consortium for Monitoring Educational Quality (SACMEQ) sample attended school without books. Providing books in second and third languages, especially those that are tailored to the language requirements of minority groups, is out of the question in settings where there is an overall lack of books.

Even when basic textbooks are available, schools in poor areas often lack other instructional materials. A study of poor districts in India found that while most schools in these districts have sufficient textbooks and learning materials for students, classrooms lack such supplementary materials as teacher guides, dictionaries, maps, globes, and instructional kits (World Bank 1997).

Textbooks and instructional materials are key to both participation and achievement. Increasing the quality of instructional materials boosted girls' participation in Laos (King and van de Walle forthcoming). A multi-country study finds that shortages of instructional materials significantly reduced math and science achievement (Woessmann 2000).

Poor facilities and physical inputs

The physical facilities of schools available to children of the poor are themselves poor. Many lack classrooms, electricity, blackboards, and basic sanitary facilities (Lockheed

---

5. Because Uruguay has not participated in any international survey of achievement, the effects of less instructional time cannot be estimated directly.

Figure 2.2 Millions of students in developing countries lack textbooks

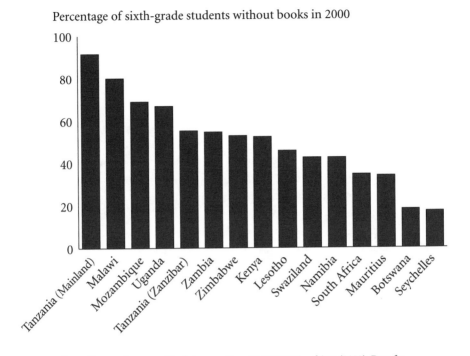

Percentage of sixth-grade students without books in 2000

Note: Data from all countries except Zimbabwe are from SACMEQ II archives (2000). Data for Zimbabwe are based on SACMEQ I archives (1995).
Source: UNESCO (2005), based on Ross and others (2004).

and Verspoor 1991). A study of school facilities in poor, low-literacy districts in eight states in India finds insufficient classroom space for enrolled students (less than 1 square foot per student, on average, against an international standard of about 10 square feet) and less than half of 31 other physical inputs, such as blackboards, safe drinking water, electricity, mats and furniture for students, and library books (World Bank 1997).

Lack of adequate facilities can affect other inputs, such as instructional time provided by teachers. A World Bank study finds that schools with better infrastructure have fewer teacher absences (Abadzi 2006). In Egypt girls are less likely to drop out when they attend schools with better physical facilities (Lloyd and others 2003). In rural Laos the physical quality of the school—with electricity, desks, nonleaking roofs—boosted enrollments of girls, particularly in rural areas (King and van de Walle forthcoming).

Inputs to school quality do not work in isolation. Adding ingredients one by one is not effective in improving student learning achievement. Simply providing textbooks to a randomly selected set of schools in rural Kenya did not increase the learning achievement of children in these schools (Glewwe, Kremer, and Moulin 2002). Good schools require a range of inputs that work together to boost learning. Ensuring that all these inputs reach schools in poor rural communities has proven difficult, because "leakage" in the flow of government funds to schools is greater for schools attended by poor children (Reinikka and Svensson 2001), and the supervision necessary to encourage "whole school" improvement is missing.

Discrimination and other barriers to the demand and supply of schooling

Unconscious discrimination, stereotypes, and expectations affect opportunities, motivation, and interpersonal behavior. These factors have particularly strong effects on student performance in heterogeneous schools and classrooms. Discrimination can reduce demand by leading families to keep their children out of what they perceive as predatory environments. It also leads to policies that favor households with higher incomes and political clout at the expense of marginalized groups, who are discriminated against both in the aggregate and as individuals.

Discrimination

Excluded children often face discrimination from teachers and classmates. Economists distinguish between discrimination based on preferences (tastes) and discrimination based on stereotyped information about skills and competencies (Arrow 1973; Becker 1971). Both types of discrimination are relevant to decisions made in schools. School administrators may selectively provide resources to schools that serve a particular community, and teachers may call on boys more frequently than girls to answer their questions.

Discrimination based on stereotypes about skills and abilities is widely practiced. Evidence comes from experiments that compare ratings of fictitious resumes and performances by musicians auditioning behind a screen to eliminate cues based on gender or race. Expert judges give higher ratings to musicians they believe are white or men (Ridgeway 1997a). Similarly, teachers subtly discriminate against children of excluded groups or girls based on longstanding stereotypes. In extreme cases this type of discrimination results in harsh treatment of children from excluded groups.

Discriminatory behavior can result in poorer schools for girls and marginalized children. It can also track girls or groups away from certain academic or vocational specializations (Lockheed 1993b). Perhaps most disturbing, discrimination by teachers in the classroom can affect children's opportunity to learn—by seating girls or minority students far from the teacher, by not giving textbooks to these students, by not calling on them in class. In Yemen researchers observed that primary school girls were typically seated at the rear of the classroom (World Bank 2004). Proximity to the teacher is important in learning; seating at a distance can lower achievement. It is possible that discrimination by the teacher led to the girls' lower performance on a standardized international test of mathematics, on which girls' scores were nearly one standard deviation below those of boys (Mullis and others 2003). In Jamaica children in disadvantaged schools spend instructional time sweeping the schoolyard instead of learning, ostensibly to prepare them for their future role in society (Lockheed and Harris 2005).

In India children from lower castes used to be excluded from classrooms—even their shadows were considered "polluting" (World Bank 1997). As Nambissan (1995) notes:

> ...the distinct message of social inferiority that is often quite clearly conveyed to [scheduled caste students] by teachers and peers. Personal narratives of [members of scheduled castes] educated just three decades ago offer glimpses of untouchability blatantly practiced in school—scheduled caste students being asked to sit separately from the classmates, refused drinking water or served in broken cups, made to dine separately. For instance, as many as 80 percent of the 1,030 students from Milind College, Aurangabad, who were surveyed in 1971–72 said that they were made to sit outside the classroom during primary schooling because of the practice of untouchability. (p. 20–21)

India has made great strides in rectifying past inequities. Caste remains salient, however (Hoff and Pandey 2005). In the mid-1990s tests of learning achievement in more than 1,200 primary schools in poorer districts found that primary students from scheduled castes and scheduled tribes performed significantly worse than their classmates on math tests in five of eight states and worse on reading tests in three of eight states, after controlling for multiple socioeconomic characteristics (World Bank 1997).

Whether discrimination is conscious and overt or subconscious and subtle, its impact is significant. Discrimination affects the availability of educational goods and resources at the school level as well as educational processes in the classroom. Discrimination can be observed in the amount of government resources that reach excluded groups. Government expenditures on education can be as much as four times higher for children from families in the top 20 percent of the income distribution than for children from the bottom 20 percent. In Guinea, Kosovo, FYR Macedonia, Madagascar, and Nepal more than 40 percent of government spending on education went to the richest quintile of the population, while less than 10 percent went to the poorest quintile (World Bank 2004).

Schools are social contexts; theories that explain differences in performance and interaction in social contexts are important. Two such theories relate to stereotype threats and performance expectations. While much research on both topics has been carried out in developed countries, recent research underscores their relevance to heterogeneous developing countries as well.

Stereotype threat in performance situations

Girls and minority students often perform poorly on tests of achievement, particularly in junior secondary school (see chapter 3). One explanation for this phenomenon focuses on the testing situation itself, where gender and ethnic stereotypes can be activated, to the detriment of those who feel threatened by the stereotype. This hypothesis has been the subject of dozens of laboratory experiments in the United States on black/white, white/Asian, gender, and social class differences in test performance (Steele and Aronson 1995; Spencer, Steele, and Quinn 1999). In all cases performance declined when stereotypes were activated. For example, the math performance of high-achieving white boys declined when they were told that Asian students usually outperformed whites (Aronson and others 1999). The test performance of high-achieving black students was poorer when they were told the test was a test of ability than when they were told it was a test about problem solving (Steele and Aronson 1995). Activation of the stereotype created higher levels of anxiety in the test takers, distracting them from the task and lowering their performance.

Stereotypes also affect performance in developing countries. One example comes from India, from an experiment carried out by Hoff and Pandey (2004). Low-caste junior high school boys performed as well as high-caste junior high school boys at a task when they were strangers and had no information about one another. When caste was announced, low-caste boys' performance dropped, while that of high-caste boys improved, and the difference became greater when the boys believed success in performance depended on subjective judgments made by the researchers. This suggests that the lower caste children inhibited their own performance in the presence of higher caste children.

Expectations and social interaction in the classroom

Expectations and social interaction also partly explain poor performance (Berger and Zelditch 1985). Research shows that discrimination based on stereotyped beliefs about abilities can be reduced by providing counter-stereotypical information (Aguero 2005). In contrast, discrimination based on more diffuse beliefs about social status is not sensitive to counteracting information (Ridgeway 1997a, 1997b). Excluded children, particularly girls, suffer from this sort of discrimination.

Expectations that create inequalities in social interaction have significant effects on underperformance in the classroom. Educators have long recognized that learning is enhanced through verbal interaction with classroom peers and teachers (Piaget 1926;

Rogoff 1990; Vygotzky 1962). But the heterogeneous classroom presents challenges for both teachers and students, as some children—often girls, students from nondominant ethnic groups, and the poor—remain comparatively silent (Cohen 1982, 1997). Children's participation in learning in the classroom can be constrained by status-based expectations regarding their own competencies relative to those of others in the class (Cohen 1984). Sociologists distinguish between such status-based beliefs, which influence social interaction, and simple discrimination or group identity effects "by the fact that those in the disadvantaged group overcome in-group bias and concede that the other group is more socially worthy" (Ridgeway and others 1998, p. 338).

Excluded groups have lower social status as well as other characteristics deemed undesirable by the dominant society. The generalized expectations about their competencies and abilities affect social interaction (Berger and others 1977; Webster and Hysom 1998; Ridgeway 1997). Teachers' performance expectations are often based on student social status. In a study of 48 primary schools in Minas Gerais, Brazil, for example, teacher expectations about the academic performance of fourth-grade children reflected their biases about gender, ethnicity, and household wealth (de Oliveira Barbosa 2004). Teachers' expectations were higher for girls and lower for black students and students from poorer households; after taking into account actual performance, only teacher expectations in favor of girls remained statistically significant. The authors note that higher expectations for girls may be a consequence of the fact that the teachers are women and that girls' behavior was better matched with the schooling context.

Cohen (1986) and her colleagues show that these expectations lead to differences in opportunities for interaction in school classrooms and hence affect children's opportunity to learn. In the United States "high-status" students talk more than "low-status" students in elementary and middle school classrooms (Cohen and Lotan 1995). Black children exercise less influence over group tasks than do white children (Cohen, Lockheed, and Lohman 1976). In Israel Jewish children from North African backgrounds exercise less influence over group tasks than do Jewish children from European backgrounds (Sharan and others1984). Research in the United States finds that gender is not a salient status characteristic at the primary school level, although it becomes salient among adults (Lockheed, Harris, and Nemceff 1983). Informal observations of schools in developing countries suggest that gender is salient even at the primary school level in some societies.

Other barriers

Many other factors present significant barriers to the multiply excluded. Cultural norms that require the seclusion of girls nearing adolescence or limit cross-sex interaction with nonfamily members contribute to female dropout. Norms that keep girls at home during menses reduce their time in school and lower performance.

In addition, schools catering to excluded groups are often at greater risk from corruption, conflict, and natural disasters. Corruption and mismanagement divert funds from intended uses. Remote rural schools suffer disproportionately. Studies in Ghana, Tanzania, Uganda, and Zambia tracking public expenditures show that an average of just 54 percent of nonwage budgets ever reached the intended schools. Zambia's school grants were an outlier, with a 10 percent leakage rate, particularly given the 76 percent loss documented for other public education transfer programs in Zambia (Reinikka and Svensson 2004). In India in the mid-1990s poor children were entitled to a variety of incentives to encourage school attendance, including shoes, books, and uniforms. One study found that few children actually received these incentives, and many parents did not know they were entitled to them (World Bank 1997).

One country that is trying to deal with the problem of leakage and corruption is Uganda. Expected funds are announced in newspapers and over the radio, and reports of funds received are tacked to school doors, allowing communities and parents to oversee public actions. The results of these efforts have been spectacular, with the percentage of funds received skyrocketing: from 22 percent in 1995 to 82 percent in 2001 (Reinikka and Smith 2004).

Conflict also affects the multiply excluded, with excluded girls often becoming the spoils and victims of war.[6] Horror stories from Darfur underscore the vulnerability of school-age girls to rape and murder during civil conflicts.

Natural disasters, such as earthquakes and floods, often have a disproportionate impact on remote excluded groups, resulting in lengthy school closings or total destruction of schools. The 2004 tsunami that hit Indonesia and Sri Lanka, which disproportionately affected fishing villages, and the 2005 earthquake in Kashmir, which destroyed hundreds of rural villages, are cases in point. The movements of communities away from disaster areas also results in reduced schooling for children.

---

6. One in three children out of school reside in countries that have experienced conflict in the past decade (International Save the Children Alliance 2006).

3

Multiple exclusions, educational attainment, and student performance

When it comes to schooling, being female is a disadvantage in developing countries, but, as chapter 1 demonstrates, it is rapidly becoming less of a disadvantage for most girls. But the girls that continue to be left behind are those who are doubly excluded—based on gender and social status. While most of the population shows a convergence in school enrollment, completion, and achievement, children from ethnically and socially separated groups, children in rural areas, and children from poor families have not benefited equally from the changes sweeping the globe.

This chapter addresses the impact of exclusion on the educational enrollment, attainment, and performance of excluded children, particularly girls. It draws on evidence from Organisation for Economic Co-operation and Development (OECD) countries, evidence on the determinants of educational attainment among disadvantaged children in developing countries, and new information on learning. The focus is on education determinants and performance.

Evidence from OECD countries

The history of education policies and interventions aimed at integrating excluded groups in high-income OECD countries suggests just how difficult such policies are to effectively design and implement—and how long the process can take. Achievements in Canada, New Zealand, and

75

Table 3.1. Educational outcomes of excluded groups have lagged behind those of majorities in Canada, New Zealand, and the United States

	Canada (2001)		New Zealand (2001)		United States (2000)		
	Non-indigenous	Aboriginal identity	Non-indigenous	Maori/Pacific Island	Non-indigenous	Black American	American Indian/Native American
Population	28,662,725	976,305	2,295,165	471,459	244,287,760	34,658,190	2,475,965
Percent of total population	96.7%	3.3%	83.0%	17.0%	86.8%	12.3%	0.9%
Male high school graduates, %[1]	69.0%	49.4%	54.9%	32.6%	81.2%	70.9%	70.0%
Female high school graduates, %[1]	69.3%	54.3%	52.6%	36.8%	81.7%	73.4%	71.7%

1. Canada: percent of population aged 15+; includes high school and equivalent, all trades certificates, and any post-secondary education; New Zealand: percent of population aged 15+, includes 6th form, HSC and other secondary qualifications, all vocational qualifications, and any post-secondary education; United States: percent of population aged 25+; includes high school and equivalent; vocational and community college, and any post-secondary education.

Source: Census of Canada 2001; Census of New Zealand 2001; United States Census 2000.

the United States have been modest, despite efforts to improve outcomes (table 3.1).

Seventeen percent of New Zealand's population and a little more than 3 percent of Canada's is indigenous. In the United States more than 12 percent of the population is black, and less than one 1 percent is Native American. (All of these estimates are based on self-reporting of ethnic identity from national census data.) In absolute numbers the United States has 37 million blacks and Native Americans, more than the combined populations of Canada and New Zealand.

In all three countries the percentage of the population graduating from high school is rising. Differences in gender are swamped by the stark variance in attainment across ethnic groups.[1] Male and female indigenous adults lag behind the majority by about 16–22 percentage points in New Zealand, 15–20 percentage points in Canada, and 8–11 percentage points in the United States (where Native Americans and blacks have similar attainment levels).

These figures highlight the difficulties even high-income countries face in providing indigenous or minority populations with education that can facilitate upward mobility and integration. Two caveats should be kept in mind in terms of the applicability of the findings to developing countries. First, gender is not a source of exclusion in education in industrial countries. Second, Canada, New Zealand, and the United States have already achieved basic educational attainment among the majority population, and all three countries are high-income countries with the flexibility and resources needed to effectively educate minority populations.

Canada

The evolution of schooling for indigenous children followed a path of boarding schools, public schools, and indigenous schools. In the 1870s religious orders began operating residential schools far from indigenous communities. Residential schools separated children from their families, and, as in the United States, incidence of physical and sexual abuse in these schools was high (CEA 2005).

By the 1950s the government began sending indigenous students to mainstream schools. Continued underperformance and the perception by the indigenous community that public schooling was part of the "process of destruction of identity" (Cummins 1997) led to a growing transition to schools operated by aboriginal tribes (Glenn and De Jong 1996). Greater community control of education was associated with increased participation of aboriginal children in secondary schools, which rose 60 percent between 1979 and 1989 (Cummins 1997).

---

1. These figures use comparable grade completion levels. Calculations of who actually graduates from secondary school can vary, and those in the table were selected because they are comparable across school systems (see Swanson 2004).

Table 3.2. Educational attainment by indigenous and nonindigenous peoples in Canada

Educational attainment (percent of population 15 years and over)	Non-aboriginal		Aboriginal	
	Male	Female	Male	Female
High school graduation and above	69.0	69.3	49.4	54.3
High school graduation certificate only	13.2	15.2	9.8	9.9
Some postsecondary education	10.6	10.9	11.3	13.7
Trades certificate or diploma	14.1	7.7	15.2	9.4
College/university diploma or degree	31.1	35.5	13.0	21.4

Source: Census of Canada 2001.

Despite this improvement, the academic attainment of Native peoples in Canada remains substantially lower than that of Euro-Canadians. Dropout rates are higher, and English proficiency is lower (Cummins 1997). Indigenous men have the least schooling of 13 ethnic groups: 9.5 years of schooling on average, 2–3 years less schooling than men of European descent (Sweetman and Dicks 1999). Even with the improvement in education that occurred between 1996 and 2001, the education gaps relative to the general population remain (Brunnen 2004).

Native peoples are less likely to graduate from high school, less likely to go to college, and slightly more likely to be in trades (table 3.2). Women achieve at a higher level, with 50 percent more women completing college than men. Euro-Canadian women are about 10 percent more likely to graduate from a university than are Euro-Canadian men.

New Zealand

Roughly 15 percent of New Zealand's population is Maori, making it a significant part of the population. During the second half of the eighteenth century Christian churches provided schools for Maoris in the Maori language. By the early 1840s more than half of the 90,000 Maori adults could read or write in their own language (Barrington 1991). Rising tensions between the Maoris and settlers, however, led to the Land Wars in 1860, the closure of missionary schools, and the elimination of government funding for Maori education. In 1867 the government introduced a national state system of Maori elementary schools (Barrington 1991). It required Maori communities to request a school, provide land, and share costs, and it banned the Maori language and culture from schools.

Maori educational opportunities improved in the 1930s with the election of a labor government that favored educational investments for Maoris (Barrington 1991). The Maori language continued to be excluded, but aspects of Maori culture were introduced into the curriculum. These "assimilation policies" failed to improve the educational attainment of the Maori.

Increased urbanization in the 1940s led to changes in the curriculum in Maori schools. In 1950 the government allowed them to integrate into mainstream school systems if favored by a majority of parents.

Today there is reemergence of Maori-based schools, including bilingual schools and classes; Maori boarding colleges, which have been important in providing secondary education; and informal community-based preschools. The preschools emerged as part of a strong grassroots movement by Maori communities—they now receive government funding (Ringold 2005).

As a group the Maori remain substantially disadvantaged. They have lower educational attainment, higher unemployment, lower incomes, lower rates of homeownership, and poorer health than do people of European descent or other groups in New Zealand (Gibbs 2005). Over the past decade females from both European and Maori descent have surged ahead of males in their ethnic group. The pace of improvement, however, has been more dramatic for people of European descent, with the Maori making significant progress in education only recently (figure 3.1).

The differences between urban and rural Maori has historically been significant, with those living in the countryside adopting non-Maori patterns more readily than their urban counterparts, despite the higher rate of acculturation in the cities. This trend may have to do with the fact that aspirations of rural Maori and non-Maori children are more similar than aspirations of Maori and non-Maori urban dwellers.

Family and community life influences the educational success of children, particularly among indigenous groups. Maoris value a sense of community, kinship, and derived status among their peers more than the qualities that form the foundation of the non-Maori educational system, such as punctuality and self-discipline (Ausubel 1960). The Maori worldview differs from the dominant value system, creating difficulties for Maori assimilation into the larger society.

Results from the OECD's Programme for International Student Assessment (PISA) offers insights into achievement differentials across ethnic and gender lines in New Zealand (table 3.3).

The United States

Two major groups are excluded in the United States: Native Americans and black Americans. The federal government began supporting schooling for Native American children when it faced the rising costs of subjugating Native Americans between 1865

Figure 3.1. Educational attainment of the Maori lags that of New Zealanders of European descent—but in both groups women outperform men, 2004

Population with at least sixth form education (%)

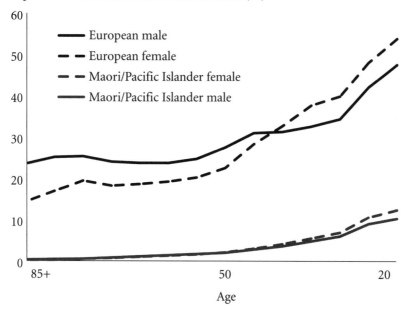

Source: New Zealand Ministry of Education 2004.

Table 3.3. Average PISA scores for 15-year-old students in New Zealand, by ethnic group, 2000

Test	White (Pakeha)	Maori	Asian
Reading Literacy	554 (3.0)	482 (4.3)	513 (7.9)
Mathematical Literacy	557 (3.3)	498 (9.4)	547 (7.5)
Scientific Literacy	553 (2.6)	483 (5.2)	517 (9.7)

Note: Standards errors are in parentheses. Average score for OECD countries is 500.

Source: Sturrock and May (2002).

and 1880. Both Congress and the Executive viewed reservations and education of In-dians in situ as more humane and less costly than military control (Hendrick 1976). In an effort to "civilize" the Native American population during the 1880s and 1890s the federal government created boarding schools, which focused on cultural adaptation and practical training relevant to coping in the "white man's world" (Hendrick 1976). The boarding schools proved ineffective and costly.

By the early 1900s the government turned to societal integration—providing public schools for Native Americans—with the goal of preparing them for citizenship. First federally funded and operated day schools were used, then state public schools, which increased attendance among Native American children substantially. In Califor-nia, for instance, the number of Native Americans attending school increased from 316 in 1915 to 2,199 in 1919, representing more than half the eligible children in the state (Hendrick 1976). Government efforts successfully raised enrollment, but the quality of these schools remained lower than that of schools for white children in the same vicinity. A major shift in the government's education policy occurred in 1932. Govern-ment assistance increased and sought to revitalize Native American culture, including by overturning earlier policies of English-only instruction (Hendrick 1976). Between 1930 and 1970 the share of Native American children attending public schools increased from 53 percent to 65 percent (Glenn and De Jong 1996). But increased enrollment was not matched by educational improvements. A 1960 report to the Special Subcommittee on Indian Education indicated that the government's policy had no positive effects on the education of Native American children (Glenn and De Jong 1996).

Federal policy shifts in 1991 encouraged self-determination among Native Amer-ican tribes, making them responsible for their children's education (Kramer 1991). Re-forms included a reversal of government policy suppressing Native American languag-es at schools run by the Bureau of Indian Affairs and other schools (Reyhner 1993), elimination of off-reservation boarding schools, development of culturally relevant curriculum and materials, and provision of community educational programs. Despite efforts by both federal and state governments, however, the educational performance of Native Americans remains among the lowest of any group in the United States, perhaps due to the alienation created by a failure to adopt rational policies earlier.

The history and evolution of the black population in the United States differs substantially from that of Native Americans. The single major turning point in im-proving educational opportunities and outcomes for blacks was the Supreme Court's *Brown v. Board of Education* (1954) ruling. It overturned the misguided policy of racial-ly segregated—"separate but equal"—schools, leading to more racially mixed schools, particularly in the South.

Mandatory desegregation plans in most southern districts by 1972 led to sig-nificant improvements in black-white enrollment balances (Armor and Rossell 2002) By 1980 the racial balance across schools was similar across the country. High school dropout rates among blacks declined in the 1970s by two to three percentage points, with desegregation explaining about half the decline (Guryan 2004). By the 1990s schools had become more segregated due to white flight to the suburbs and the concentration of low-income children in inner city schools (Armor and Rossell 2002). White flight offset about one-third of the initial reduction in segregation (Reber 2003).

What have these trends meant for schooling outcomes of black students? According to US Census data for 2000, roughly 70 percent of white females, just under 65 percent of white males, and about 60 percent of black males and females were enrolled in school at age 18–19 (figure 3.2). By age 20–24 both black and white women, and Hispanic women—the other large ethnic group in the United States—are more likely to be in school than their male counterparts. Girls, including advantaged girls, are on a par with boys through high school and outpace them afterward.

Has desegregation improved the achievement and performance of black students? On average, test scores show a persistent black-white gap. Although reading scores did not rise above late 1970s levels (Grissmer, Flanagan, and Williamson 1998), the racial gap fell markedly in the 1980s, leveling off in the 1990s (Hanushek 2001; Jencks and Phillips 1998). Desegregation in the South may have contributed to the narrowing of the gap, but because test scores also improved among black students in the Northeast, where segregation increased, the explanation is unsatisfactory (Grissmer, Flanagan, and Williamson 1998). Analyzing 2002 high school graduation data in southern states, Swanson (2005) finds higher graduation rates for both blacks and whites in less segregated schools. The role of desegregation remains unclear; other factors appear to have been more important.

Hanushek (2001) and Jencks and Phillips (1998) find no significant impact of funding on the black-white gap. Spending across segregated neighborhood schools is virtually identical, as are other quality measures, such as class size and teacher pay, education, and experience. These factors provide little explanation for persistent achievement and performance gaps across races.

The black American family has changed substantially since the 1960s. Parents tend to be better educated and families smaller (Hanushek 2001; Grissmer, Flanagan, and Williamson 1998). These gains have outweighed the negative impacts from the rise in single-parent households and young mothers in the 1990s. But the improvements have not been enough to offset the impact of resegregation by geographic residence, the negative peer pressure among black youth, and emerging anti-white biases that underlie the widening black-white gap (Hanushek 2001). Environment is increasingly being seen as crowding out the positive effects of family characteristics, resulting in deteriorating academic performance among black youth (Loury 2000).

Hanushek, Kain, and Rivkin (2002) find a negative association between achievement and share of student enrollment among blacks, particularly students of higher ability. The results suggest that blacks impose peer pressure on other blacks to underachieve, and teachers with a higher proportion of black students may reduce their

Figure 3.2. Net enrollment in the United States is fairly even, until age 16–17

Percentage of cohort

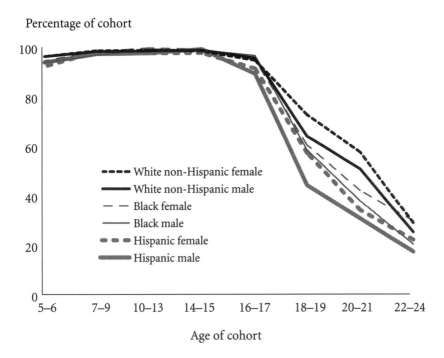

Age of cohort

Source: US Census 2000.

expectations for all blacks. Blacks have a cohesive group identity that leads to such behavior (Eberhardt and Fiske 1994). Peer pressure to underachieve in school is a form of resistance to the hegemonic social system, despite the adverse long-term effects that poor performance in school can incur, limiting future employment and educational prospects.

Girls from all ethnic groups are more likely than boys to take precalculus, an indicator of the seriousness of academic work and of likely future investments in education (figure 3.3). The largest gender gaps are observed among Native American and black adolescents, with boys the least likely to take precalculus. The smallest gender gaps are among whites and Hispanics. Asian girls are much more likely to take precalculus than are other students, including Asian boys. This suggests a higher willingness among girls to take on more challenges when given the opportunity and encouragement to do so. US schools have targeted girls to level the playing field. The fact that girls across ethnic groups are surging ahead may be the result.

The US National Assessment of Education Progress (NAEP) for eighth-graders revealed no meaningful gender differences in performance for mathematics in 2005

Figure 3.3. Across ethnic groups, girls are more likely than boys to enroll in precalculus in the US

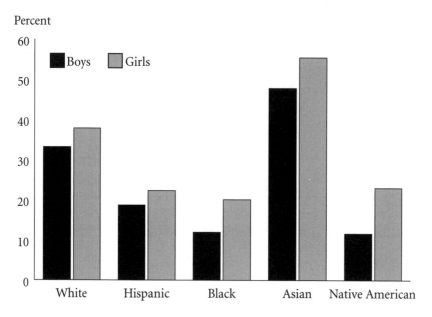

Source: Muller 2005, based on the US Adolescent Health and Academic Achievement Study 2001–02.

(figure 3.4). All three disadvantaged minority groups—blacks, Native Americans, and Hispanics—however, lag significantly behind whites and Asians in eighth-grade mathematics.

Despite government efforts, black, Hispanic, and Native American children have not caught up with non-Hispanic white children. School integration has enabled black and white students to interact more than they had under segregation, perhaps fostering greater tolerance, but policy levers have been only marginally successful in bringing black, Hispanic, and Native American children into the mainstream. Indeed, much of the black-white gap remains unexplained by the wide array of measures used. Despite a multitude of initiatives and careful evaluation aimed at informing policy, progress has been slow, suggesting the complexity facing countries with excluded, alienated minorities who encounter discrimination in education and the labor market.

Summary

No single approach emerges from the review of policies and programs in Canada, New Zealand, and the United States. But some strategies have paid off. Targeting

Figure 3.4. No meaningful gender difference in eighth-grade mathematics in the US

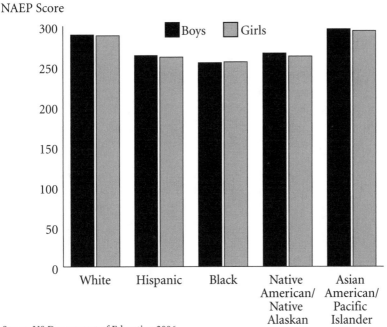

Source: US Department of Education 2006.

certain populations, adjusting education options to meet specific needs (providing bilingual education, adjusting the curriculum to reflect the concerns of minority groups), supporting faltering students, and encouraging integration into the mainstream—all have produced results, though inconsistently. Indeed, in some circumstances efforts to promote education and inclusion have led to a backlash and rejection of education.

Evidence from developing countries on gender, exclusion, and primary school enrollment and completion

The evidence on educational attainment and performance among indigenous and nonindigenous populations in some high-income OECD countries relies on a rich set of data largely unavailable for developing countries. It serves as a valuable background to research on the multiple determinants of girls' schooling in developing countries. Issues prominent in education in high-income OECD countries are just emerging in most developing countries.

This section examines the relationship between ethnicity and girls' primary school completion across countries. It reviews the country-level evidence of the factors associated with girls' primary school enrollment and completion, controlling for household, community, and school characteristics.

Cross-country evidence

Cross-country comparisons provide an aggregate look at the factors affecting girls' school enrollment, attendance, completion, and achievement. Such analysis is a crude tool—it offers comparators across countries yet masks factors that cannot be or are not measured. On the other hand, it provides a bird's eye view of the key policy concerns.

Development is a major determinant of girls' school participation, both across and within countries. In analyzing the sources of inequality in girls' net attendance within countries, Wils, Zhao, and Hartwell (2005) built an index of development, using girls' literacy and access to water, medical assistance, and media. The index compares 165 subregions of 9 countries (Bangladesh, Egypt, Ghana, Guatemala, Guinea, Malawi, Nicaragua, Uganda, and Zambia), finding substantial differences in development across subregions, often exceeding differences across countries or between rural and urban areas. Correlations between girls' net attendance rates and the level of development were high for eight of the nine countries, ranging from 0.60 in Guatemala to 0.90 in Egypt. Ensuring attendance in low-income countries is difficult, but regional differences may be important in explaining the inability of central authorities to ensure that children go to school.

The outlier was Bangladesh, where female attendance rates were unrelated to the degree of local development as measured by the index. Ethnicity and language disparities may explain the extreme differences in the results. Extending schooling to all children in a homogeneous setting is both easier and less expensive than in heterogeneous countries. Where the majority group, local authorities, and households all come from the same ethnic group, enforcement, trust, and shared values may facilitate both education in general and participation by girls in particular.

Cross-country correlations illustrate the significance of ethno-linguistic heterogeneity in female school completion (figures 3.5 and 3.6). The correlations between ethno-linguistic fractionalization and female primary school completion rates ($R^2 = -0.31$) and between ethno-linguistic fractionalization and gender differences in completion ($R^2 = -0.26$) are highly significant, suggesting the importance of a less fractionalized, or more homogeneous, society in fostering girls' education.

Lewis and Lockheed (forthcoming) further examine the importance of ethnic and linguistic heterogeneity across countries for the same two completion measures, with cross-country regressions that control for other socioeconomic factors. Their results suggest that linguistic and ethnic heterogeneity reduces the likelihood of primary school completion for girls and increases the gender gap in attainment. Average years

Figure 3.5. Higher ethno-linguistic fractionalization means lower girls' primary completion…

Female primary completion rate, as a percentage of relevant age group

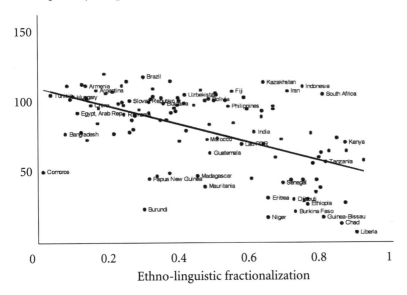

Ethno-linguistic fractionalization

Note: R² = 0.31; *N* = 118.
Source: Alesina and others 2003; World Bank 2005b.

of adult female education is an important predictor of primary school completion rates for girls. The degree of isolation (percent rural) and road density (a measure of accessibility) are contributing factors, but they are less important than heterogeneity in explaining completion rates. Countries with a socialist history have higher female primary school completion rates and smaller gender gaps, an expected finding due to their overall high level of school participation.

In explaining gender disparities, Lewis and Lockheed (forthcoming) find that the same factors play a role, although some evidence suggests that it is the countries with the highest fractionalization that are the most affected. Location has no effect on gender disparities, possibly because those most affected live in specific rural areas, not simply outside of urban centers.

Country-level evidence

Interest in gender, exclusion, and schooling is growing as the excluded are increasingly targeted in efforts to reach universal schooling. The few country studies conducted

Figure 3.6. ...and lower gender parity in primary completion

Difference in male and female primary completion rate

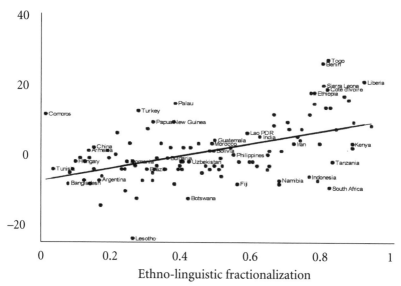

Note: $R^2 = 0.26$; $N = 118$.
Source: Alesina and others 2003; World Bank 2005b.

reveal the common thread of a distinct disadvantage of indigenous girls in terms of enrolling and staying in school, even when controlling for other family characteristics.[2]

Recent studies in Bangladesh (Schuler forthcoming); Bolivia (Jimenez 2004); China (Hannum 2002); Gansu province, China (Hannum and Adams forthcoming); Ecuador (Garcia Aracil and Winkler 2004); Guatemala (Hallman and Peracca forthcoming; Edwards and Winkler 2004); India (Wu and others forthcoming); Laos (King and van de Walle forthcoming); Mexico (de Janvry and Sadoulet 2006); Nepal (Stash and Hannum 2001); Pakistan (Lloyd, Mete, and Grant forthcoming); Tunisia (Lockheed and Mete forthcoming); and Vietnam (van de Walle and Gunewardena 2001) form the basis for the discussion in this section. Except for Guatemala, the results are not sourced and refer to the authors listed here for each country.

Virtually all studies find that indigenous boys and girls are less likely to enroll in school and more likely to repeat a grade than nonindigenous children. When controlling for ethnicity, location, and socioeconomic factors, indigenous girls are less likely to attend primary school or to enroll in secondary school (Hallman and Peracca forthcoming). In Bolivia, for example, indigenous girls are less likely to enroll in school than are Ladino (nonindigenous) girls or boys, and the first-grade repetition rate of indigenous

---

2. The section draws heavily on Lewis and Lockheed (forthcoming).

children is 43.4 percent—30 percentage points higher than those of nonindigenous children.

Indigenous girls drop out of school more often than do nonindigenous girls or boys. In many contexts, retention becomes a more important signal of participation levels than enrollment rates. Retaining children in school often poses more of a challenge than convincing parents to send their children to school. In Bolivia both Quechua-speaking and Aymara-speaking indigenous girls are more likely to discontinue their schooling prematurely than are Ladino girls or boys. Only 55 percent of indigenous children in Bolivia complete primary school—far lower than the 81 percent rate of nonindigenous children. Controlling for residence and socioeconomic status, in Guatemala the school completion rate for indigenous girls is about 40 percent that of Ladino girls and only a third that of all boys. At age 16, only 25 percent of indigenous girls in Guatemala are in school, while 45 percent of indigenous boys and more than half of all Ladino children are in school (Hallman and Peracca forthcoming). In Ecuador being indigenous raises the probability of rural dropout by close to 30 percent, and being female lowers the probability of rural school attendance by 35 percent.

Indigenous communities tend to be rural and geographically isolated. This affects the quality of schools or even whether a school exists in the community. In Vietnam restrictions on mobility and inequities in school provision lead to significantly fewer years of education among rural minorities than among the majority population. Absence of schools is also correlated with the absence of other essential infrastructure, such as roads, and with poor access to markets. In Laos so few indigenous families live in urban areas that the effects of isolation cannot be separated from indigeneity. However, the quality of schools is significantly higher in urban areas than in rural communities, where low- quality infrastructure (leaking roofs, no electricity) discourages enrollment.

Isolation appears to have a greater effect on girls than on boys. In Laos girls living in the highlands and other disadvantaged districts are less likely to enroll in school than are boys from the same communities. Location and schooling characteristics are key for minority girls but not for the majority Lao-Tai children.

The picture in China is mixed. In 1992 Han children were more likely than minority children to enroll in school due to differences in family backgrounds and county of residence. In rural counties where minorities accounted for roughly one-third of the population, minority participation rates were substantially lower than those of Han children. However, girls' participation was inconsistent across minority groups. Among 10 minority ethnic groups 5 were more likely to enroll girls in school while 4 were less likely to do so. In the Han group and in one minority group no gender differences in enrollment were observed.

In Guatemala enrollment rates are no lower in rural areas than in urban areas, but rural residence is associated with a higher age for primary school entry, lower grade for age, lower rate of primary completion, and lower secondary enrollment. In Ecuador the probability of primary school dropout is higher for girls in rural than in urban areas, and ethnicity is a factor explaining dropout from rural but not urban schools. Girls living in urban areas, whether indigenous or not, are 34 percent more likely than boys to stay in school, but girls living in rural areas are 35 percent less likely than boys to be in school. Indigenous girls living in rural areas particularly suffer low primary and secondary enrollment and depressed grade for age enrollment (Hallman and Peracca forthcoming).

Lack of nearby schools in rural areas is often responsible for lower school participation. In Bolivia, Ecuador, and Peru school attendance disparities between urban and rural communities largely disappear when the availability of a local school is taken into account (Hall and Patrinos 2006). In a few countries, such as Indonesia, significant efforts have been made to provide schools in rural areas—and have led to universal primary school participation. In Chile efforts to improve the quality of the poorest performing schools have had spillover effects on rural schools attended by indigenous children (McEwan 2004).

Cultural factors work to remove rural and indigenous girls from school in many countries, particularly after primary school. When controlling for a variety of socioeconomic factors, majority Hausa-speaking girls in Nigeria are shown to be 35 percent less likely to attend school than are minority Igbo- or Yoruba-speaking boys (UIS 2005). In China variations across ethnic minority groups in girls' school participation could reflect cultural differences. In Pakistan single-sex education has been the norm, based on religious and cultural norms that require separation of the sexes. It has raised the cost of education, limiting the quality and availability of girls' schools and slowing the process of universal education. Evidence in Guatemala suggests that parental concern over allowing adolescent girls to mix with boys and the lack of separate latrines are the most important reasons for keeping girls at home (Hallman and Peracca forthcoming).

Dropouts often attribute their departure to disaffection or boredom with school, as in China, or to lack of interest, as in Guatemala (Hallman and Peracca forthcoming). Parental concern for their children's dissatisfaction with school has also been voiced in Mexico (Sadoulet 2006 personal communication) and in Vietnam, possibly helping to explain the difficulties of encouraging minority households to send their children, especially their daughters, to school.

Cultural factors would be expected to play a role in reducing schooling for girls in Bangladesh, but unlike the other South Asian countries (except Sri Lanka), girls no longer trail boys in education. This dramatic shift over the past two decades can be attributed to such factors as strong government policies aimed at increasing female education and nongovernmental organization (NGO) efforts to complement and partner with government. Its effects have altered cultural practices. Coeducational schools made universal education affordable in Bangladesh. This outcome is in sharp contrast to that in Pakistan, where separate schools for boys and girls have imposed extra costs and curtailed opportunities, particularly for girls.

An important cultural shift stemming from more education is that educated Bangladeshi girls have become more desirable marriage partners. They also face less abuse from mothers-in-law and husbands than do illiterate wives. Education has become a substitute for dowries because, with income earning capacity, educated women become the dowry. Cultural shifts can and do occur, but they take time, with efforts on multiple fronts.

Caste—associated with ethnicity, occupation, and residence—is important in India and particularly Nepal, where it overwhelms all other factors in explaining school enrollment and completion. Its effect is only slightly mitigated by household characteristics. In India children from scheduled castes are less likely than children from higher castes to attend school. According to one study (UIS 2005), the probability of a girl from a scheduled caste attending school is 9.4 percent lower than that of a boy from a nonscheduled caste. The size of the difference between low caste girls and high caste boys was about the same as the difference in the probability of attending school between the most highly literate state, Kerala, compared with all other states.

Poverty compounds the effects of social exclusion and isolation in lowering girls' school participation. The UIS (2005) study reports that in half of the 68 countries examined, children in households from the lowest income quintile are less likely than children from higher income quintiles to attend school. And poor minority families are more likely than other households to invest in the education of sons rather than daughters. In Laos household income has a strong effect on whether minority but not Lao-Tai girls go to school. The greatest gender disparities in enrollment exist among the Chinese ethnic groups who face the highest rates of poverty. Forty-five percent of minority households and 30 percent of Han households cite poverty as a reason for not sending boys to school. For girls, the figures are 53 percent of minority households and 45 percent of Han households. Poverty thus seems to have a disproportionate effect on girls in minority households in China.

In Pakistan income prevents many households from sending rural girls and boys to school. Girls' school attendance rates are 45 percentage points below those of boys in the lowest income group but only 15 percentage points below boys in the highest income group. Rural households in the upper third of income earners are by far the most likely to send girls to primary school, suggesting that income is much more important than location in explaining school participation in Pakistan. Higher income communities are more likely to have public single-sex schools and private coeducational schools, with private schools providing the largest increase to school supply over 1997–2004.

In Guatemala poor Mayan girls have the lowest school participation and are least likely to remain in school. By age 16, only 4 percent of extremely poor indigenous girls attend school, compared with 20 percent of poor indigenous girls and 45 percent of nonpoor indigenous girls. Indeed, poverty is the most persistent and significant variable in explaining why children do not enroll in or complete primary or secondary school. In one multivariate analysis, an interaction term for indigenous girls and poverty was significantly correlated with girls' school attendance, suggesting that the gender-poverty effects were greater than simply the sum of the two characteristics considered independently (Hallman and Peracca forthcoming).

Girls suffer more than boys from economic shocks. In rural Pakistan unanticipated economic shocks such as crop losses reduce the likelihood that girls, but not boys, attend school. In Uganda negative income shocks (as proxied by variations in rainfall) are associated with sharp declines in girls' school enrollment and girls' performance on the primary leaving exam; the impact on boys is much smaller and only marginally significant (Bjorkman 2005).

Girls have benefited, at least initially, from public programs that offset the direct costs of schooling. Under Mexico's *Progresa/Oportunidades* program, girls benefited more from conditional cash transfers in the first year, when the program attracted female dropouts back to school.[3] However, indigenous boys living in a community without a secondary school disproportionately gained from the expansion of secondary education. In a similar conditional cash transfer program in Ecuador enrollment rose 3.7 percentage points and dropouts declined, but the program did not differentially affect girls or minority students (Schady and Araujo 2006).[4]

Gender gaps in schooling are exacerbated by ethnicity and poverty, leading to large differentials in enrollment and completion. In Guatemala being female and indigenous decreases the probability of enrollment, both individually and together. Income raises the likelihood of enrollment, but the probability of enrollment varies considerably across indigenous groups. Speaking Spanish is an important factor in raising the probability of indigenous boys enrolling in school, but it did not increase enrollment for girls in two of five indigenous groups (Edwards and Winkler 2004).

Education of parents or household head affects enrollment in most settings. In 93 percent of the countries analyzed in the UIS (2005) study mothers' education was a significant correlate of school attendance. Children of mothers with any formal schooling were much more likely to attend schools than are children of mothers who had never attended school.

In Guatemala both mothers' and fathers' educational attainment has a sizable and significant impact on enrollment, especially if they have completed primary school (Hallman and Peracca forthcoming). Education of the head of household has a larger and more significant effect on enrollment in urban than in rural areas in Laos, but mothers' education has a significant impact only in rural areas. In rural Pakistan if a

---

3. *Progresa* allows families to enroll separately in the different components of the program. The uptake for cash transfers was 95 percent; the uptake for the education transfer was only 76 percent. Households could enroll in the income transfer program and enroll all, some, or none of their children in the education component. Not enrolling in the education transfer program cost families roughly $200 per child a year in foregone income.

4. The fact that indigenous groups make up only 6 percent of the Ecuadorian population led to a small sample of indigenous families, which may have contributed to the limited measured impact of the program.

mother has ever been to school it significantly increases the probability that her daughter is enrolled, but it has no effect on boys. In Nepal children of mothers with some formal education are 2.5 times more likely than children of mothers with no formal education to attend school. In rural China, where school participation at the primary level is almost universal, mothers' educational attainment is associated with higher school enrollment.

Demographics also affect enrollment. In Laos children from households with a larger number of children under 6 years old are less likely to go to school—and the effect is even more important for girls. In Guatemala age is associated with school completion for boys but not girls, who are more likely to drop out early (Hallman and Peracca forthcoming). More than 50 percent of all children and 75 percent of indigenous boys and girls are overage for their grade, reflecting a combination of late entry, repetition, and dropout and returns. Among girls in Guatemala enrollment is negatively associated with family size and positively associated with a recent birth (Edwards and Winkler 2004). In India and Nigeria children from families with more children under the age of five are significantly less likely than children with fewer young siblings to attend school (UIS 2005).

These results show considerable divergence across and within countries. The determinants of enrollment often vary across subgroups within countries. Poverty and isolation play a role, as do parental characteristics, but the importance of ethnicity and community characteristics of indigenous groups persists in all countries. In Nepal socioeconomic factors and location have no impact because caste overwhelmingly determines girls' enrollment, suggesting the difficulty in reaching certain populations and the need to experiment with alternative ways of engaging and including girls who are outside the mainstream.

The evidence base is thin, as are the data available with which to analyze the effect of exclusion, particularly among marginalized populations. More and better data, broader experimentation to engage hard to reach groups, and more in-depth research will be required to develop an adequate evidence base to guide policy.

Evidence from developing countries on gender, exclusion, and learning

Participation in schooling is important, particularly for girls. But learning is also important, as it translates into benefits at the individual level (by increasing skills and self-esteem) and the country level (by increasing economic growth). From the perspective of excluded groups, it also provides a basis for employment and upward mobility. Without learning, productivity and earnings stall.

A major challenge is ensuring that excluded groups not only go to school but finish basic education and continue to secondary or higher education at the same rate as the majority group. While parental education is associated with an increase in the demand for children's schooling in most contexts, this does not appear to be the case for excluded children. Having an educated mother does not ensure that black children in the United States finish high school or that Roma children in Europe even enroll in school. As OECD policymakers have learned, targeted programs to promote schooling are needed to bring excluded children into the school system and keep them there. Focusing on learning is critical if the cycle of poverty and exclusion is to be broken.

This section focuses directly on the learning outcomes of schooling and on the differences in achievement of multiply excluded children in developing countries after they enroll in school. Evidence from international studies of reading, mathematics, and science achievement shows consistently lower performance for students in schools attended largely by minorities or indigenous groups and by students living in rural areas or attending schools in which most of the students are poor. Given selection effects, it is difficult to establish whether these performance differences reflect the effects of the school or of student characteristics.

Cross-country evidence on ethnicity and learning

Heterogeneity affects learning outcomes, through mechanisms discussed in the next section. The cross-country correlation between heterogeneity and learning achievement is negative (Lewis and Lockheed forthcoming). The measure of learning comes from a recent study by Crouch and Fasih (2004), who developed an "imputed learning score" for each country based on its actual performance on various international tests and equated to a common measure. This score is negatively correlated with ethno-linguistic fractionalization in developing countries—the greater the fractionalization, the lower the learning (figure 3.7).

Using these data in cross-country multivariate analysis of 55 developing countries, Lewis and Lockheed (forthcoming) find a negative effect of heterogeneity on achievement after controlling for a country's socialist history, the female labor force participation rate, road density, and the percentage of rural population. To control for national variations in school participation, they introduce the female primary school completion rate, which is positively associated with overall learning achievement. The percentage of the population that is rural is negatively associated with learning, while road density (a measure of the ease of reaching the whole population) positively affects learning. In short, ethnicity, female school participation, location, road density, a socialist history, and female labor force participation explain a good deal of the disparity in national learning scores.

Table 3.4. International assessments of primary and lower secondary school learning achievement

Assessment	Sponsor	Measures	Frequency and student population	Countries in most recent assessment
Progress in International Reading Literacy Study (PIRLS)	International Association for the Evaluation of Achievement (IEA)	Reading competencies	Administered on four-year cycle to students completing four years of primary school (2001, 2005)	35 mainly OECD and Eastern European countries
Programme for International Student Assessment (PISA)	OECD	Reading, mathematics, scientific literacy, problem solving	Administered on three-year cycle to 15-year-old students (2000, 2003, 2006 in progress)	30 OECD and 26 other mostly middle-income countries
Trends in International Mathematics and Science Study (TIMSS)	International Association for the Evaluation of Achievement (IEA)	Mathematics and science curricular domains	Administered on four-year cycle to students in grades 4 and 8 (1995, 1999, 2003, 2007 in progress)	46 countries, including 26 low and middle-income countries
Southern and Eastern African Consortium for Monitoring Educational Quality (SACMEQ)	International Institute for Educational Planning	Mathematics and reading competencies	Administered in mid-1990s and 2000 to students in grade 6	15 countries in Africa
Laboratorio Latinoamericano de Evaluación de la Calidad de la Educación (LLECE)	UNESCO	Language and mathematics	Administered in grades 3 and 4	Seven countries in Latin America

Source: International Association for the Evaluation of Achievement website; Organisation for Economic Co-operation and Development website; United Nations Educational, Scientific and Cultural Organization website; and Southern and Eastern African Consortium for Monitoring Educational Quality website.

Learning, development, and economic growth

Learning boosts economic growth. In a cross-country analysis of 80 countries Hanushek and Kimko (2000) find a positive association between average achievement (as measured by standardized tests) and economic growth. They estimate that increasing average mathematics and science test scores by one standard deviation would boost average

Figure 3.7. The higher the level of ethno-linguistic fractionalization, the lower the level of learning

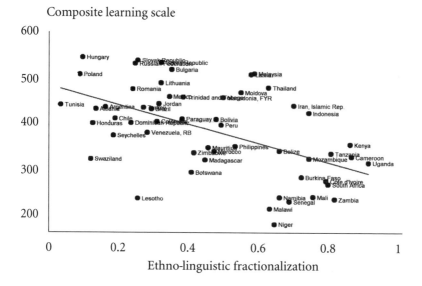

Note: $R^2 = 0.28$; Number of cases = 55.
Source: Crouch and Fasih 2004; Alesina and others 2003.

annual real growth by more than 1 percent.[5] They also test for the impact of growth on achievement, and find no effects, underscoring the direction of the causality.

Developing countries lag developed countries in learning achievement, to the detriment of their economic growth. Since the early 1970s international studies have demonstrated consistently that students in higher income countries score higher than students in lower income countries on internationally comparable tests of achievement (table 3.4).[6] Average differences are quite large, with 2003 TIMSS eighth-grade mathematics scores in developing countries ranging from one-half to more than two standard deviations below the standardized international mean score. Scores in seven countries (Egypt, Indonesia, Iran, Jordan, Lebanon, FYR Macedonia, and Tunisia) were half a standard deviation below the standardized mean. Scores in six (Botswana, Chile, Morocco, the Palestinian Authority, the Philippines, and Saudi Arabia) were one full standard deviation below the standardized mean. And scores in two (Ghana and South Africa) were two standard deviations below the mean. Only one non-European middle-income country, Malaysia, achieved a score at or above the standardized mean.

The differences are also meaningful in terms of what share of students reach rea-

---

5. Hanushek and Kimko (2000) note that this estimate seems implausibly large.
6. International sample-based tests are typically administered to samples of about 5,000 students in about 200 schools per country. The results are thus representative of achievement at the country level.

sonable performance standards. On the 2003 TIMSS assessment in 45 countries, for example, fewer than 20 percent of students in 12 countries, all developing—Bahrain, Botswana, Chile, Ghana, Iran, Morocco, the Palestinian Authority, Philippines, Saudi Arabia, South Africa, and Tunisia—reached the "intermediate international benchmark" on eighth-grade mathematics ("students can apply basic mathematical knowledge in straightforward situations") (Mullis 2004:62). By comparison, more than 65 percent of students in 14 countries reached this level of achievement. Of these, six were the East Asian "tigers"—Chinese Taipai; Hong Kong, China; Japan; Malaysia; Republic of Korea; and Singapore—and nine were Eastern European or OECD countries—Australia, Belgium, Estonia, Hungary, Latvia, Netherlands, Russia, and Slovak Republic (see Martin and others 2000, 2004 for science benchmarks; Mullis and others 2000 for earlier mathematics benchmarks).

Comparing developing countries with OECD countries across five international studies of learning achievement, 1984–2001, Pritchett (2004) notes that with the exception of the East Asian "tigers" and countries in Eastern Europe, students in developing countries and transition economies have lagged far behind in achievement for nearly two decades. These differences in achievement could translate into annual real economic growth rates of 1–3 percent below what would have been achieved had these countries had higher learning outcomes.

Even when school participation rates are high, high achievement does not necessarily follow. Raising a county's level of achievement requires improving the quality of education offered to all students, with particular attention paid to those whose achievement lags behind.

Gender and learning

At the primary level the performance of girls does not account for the lower average performance of developing countries. All major international surveys that include tests of achievement find limited gender differences at the primary level. Where such differences are found, the studies find that girls outperform boys on reading. On tests of fourth-grade reading girls outperformed boys in all 35 countries participating in the PIRLS 2001 assessment, including the developing countries of Argentina, Belize, Colombia, Iran, Morocco, and Turkey (Mullis and others 2003) (figure 3.8).[7] Across all countries, 55 percent of girls scored in the top half of reading achievement in their country, compared with 45 percent of boys, for a 10 percent advantage. On international tests of reading in Latin America among third- and fourth-graders girls outperformed boys in six of seven countries participating in the *Laboratorio Latinoamericano de Evaluación de la Calidad de la Educación* (LLECE) (Carnoy and Marshall 2005).

---

7. These differences favoring girls were found for both literary reading and reading for informational purposes.

Figure 3.8. Fourth-grade girls outperform boys in reading in many countries

PIRLS test scores, 2001

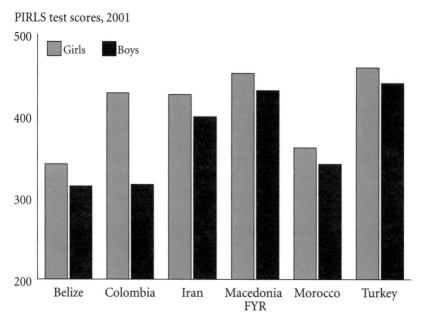

Source: Mullis and others 2003.

On tests of fourth-grade mathematics and science girls' achievement was equal to that of boys in nearly two-thirds of countries. Where gender differences were observed the countries were equally split between those in which boys outperformed girls and girls outperformed boys (Martin and others 2000, 2004; Mullis and others 2000, 2004). No gender differences on the 2003 TIMSS fourth-grade mathematics tests were found in Iran, Morocco, or Tunisia, while in Armenia, Moldova, and the Philippines girls achieved significantly higher mathematics scores (figure 3.9). The same pattern was observed in science, except that girls outperformed boys in science in Iran. In Latin America, however, third- and fourth-grade girls fell behind boys in mathematics in five of the seven LLECE countries (Carnoy and Marshall 2005).

On tests of reading literacy, girls continue to outperform boys throughout middle school, with most countries showing statistically significant differences favoring girls (table 3.5). In Africa in sixth grade, girls outperformed boys in reading in 6 of 14 countries participating in the SACMEQ assessments (Botswana, Lesotho, Mauritius, the Seychelles,

Figure 3.9. Fourth-grade girls in many developing countries perform at least as well as boys in mathematics and science

TIMSS Math Scale Scores, 2003

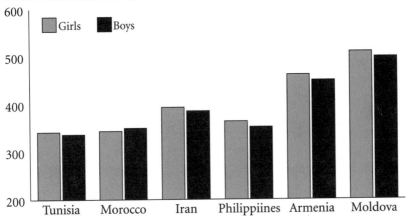

TIMSS Science Scale Scores, 2003

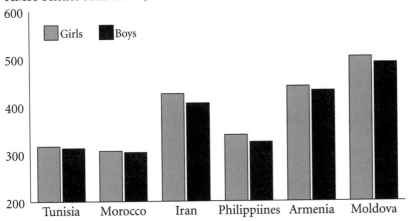

Note: Based on results of 2003 TIMSS mathematics and science assessments.
Source: Martin and others 2004; Mullis and others 2004.

South Africa, and Swaziland). Boys outperformed girls in three countries (Malawi, Tanzania, and Zimbabwe). No gender differences were found in the rest.[8] Among OECD countries, 15-year-old girls outperformed 15-year-old boys in reading literacy in all 40

---

8. For this study, a substantial difference is defined as one greater than two standard errors; the SACMEQ Web site does not report the level of statistical significance of gender differences. Data for Tanzania (Mainland) and Tanzania (Zanzibar) are presented separately.

countries participating in the 2003 PISA assessment. In Brazil girls outperformed boys on national assessments in Portuguese in eighth and eleventh grades (Rosenberg 2004).

In mathematics and science, however, girls' achievement begins to fall behind the achievement of boys in middle school, and the share of countries that report gender differences favoring boys increases. Three recent international studies of mathematics and science achievement, covering 45 developing and more than 25 developed countries between 2000 and 2004, provide a consistent picture of the global emergence of gender differences in mathematics and science achievement after primary school (table 3.5).[9]

On international tests of sixth-grade mathematics achievement in 13 African countries, boys substantially outperformed girls in 5 countries (Kenya, Malawi, Mozambique, Tanzania/Zanzibar, and Zambia), girls outperformed boys in just 2 countries (Botswana and the Seychelles), and no gender differences were observed in 6 countries (SACMEC data from Web site). On the 2003 PISA mathematics assessment in 40 countries, boys outperformed girls in 27 countries, whereas girls outperformed boys in only one country (Iceland); no gender differences were observed in 12 countries. By comparison, in the 2003 TIMSS mathematics assessment, no gender differences were observed in 27 of 45 countries. An equal number of countries (nine) reported differences favoring girls (including the developing countries of Jordan and FYR Macedonia) and differences favoring boys (including the developing countries of Chile, Ghana, and Lebanon).

On the 2003 TIMSS science tests, eighth-grade boys outperformed girls in 27 of 45 countries (including the developing countries of Botswana, Indonesia, and Malaysia), whereas girls outperformed boys in only 7 countries (including the developing countries of Jordan and FYR Macedonia), and no differences in achievement were found in 11 countries (Martin and others 2004). Among 15-year-olds tested in science achievement on the 2003 PISA assessment, boys outperformed girls in 13 of 40 countries, whereas girls outperformed boys in only 3 countries; no gender differences were observed in 24 mainly OECD countries (OECD 2004).

The emergence of gender differences can be traced in three of the six developing countries participating in the 2003 TIMSS that reported scores for both fourth and eighth grades. In Iran, where girls outperformed boys in fourth-grade science, the gender gap disappeared by eighth grade. In Tunisia and Morocco, where gender differences in fourth-grade mathematics were not statistically significant, boys outperformed girls by eighth grade. In the other three countries (Armenia, Moldova, and the Philippines) differences favoring girls remained for both subjects.

The decline in girls' performance also emerges from two smaller studies in Brazil. McEwan (2004) finds that girls' advantage in reading in third grade disappears by sixth

---

9. A similar pattern was observed in developed countries in the 1980s, but it has since disappeared due to targeted efforts in the 1980s and 1990s to boost girls' mathematics and science achievement (Klein 1985).

Table 3.5. Gender differences in learning in middle school in selected countries, 2000–03 (percent of countries showing statistically significant differences)

Assessment	Number of countries	Girls outperform boys	Boys outperform girls	No gender difference in performance
Reading				
Grade 6 (2000)	15	40	20	40
15-year-olds (2004)	40	98	0	2
Mathematics				
Grade 6 (2000)	14	14	43	43
Grade 8 (2003)	45	20	20	60
15-year-olds (2004)	40	2	68	30
Science				
Grade 8 (2003)	45	12	62	26
15-year-olds (2004)	40	8	32	60

Source: Author computations based on data from SACMEQ (various years circa 2000); TIMSS (2003); PISA (2003).

grade and that girls, who performed as well as boys in mathematics in third grade, were underperforming boys by sixth grade. Rosenberg (2004) shows that girls' mathematics scores were equivalent to those of boys in fourth grade but fell behind in eighth and eleventh grades.

These results indicate that the pattern of faltering performance by girls in middle and secondary school holds for mathematics and particularly science, but generally not for language. One reason for these emerging gender differences is that in many countries different courses are offered to girls and boys during middle school. Girls may attend home economics classes while boys attend shop classes, which provide additional support in learning science. In some countries middle schools may not be coeducational, and the quality of science teachers and facilities may be lower in all-girls schools. Expectations about women's roles in society may become more pronounced in middle school, particularly in countries with larger shares of traditional subgroups, as in Africa. These speculations are no more than that, however, as research in these areas has not been conducted in developing countries in recent years (see Lee and Lockheed 1990 for earlier reviews). What is clear is that the initial gender equality in primary school achievement erodes to gender inequality in achievement in some countries by middle school.

Excluded groups and learning

Once children from excluded groups enroll in school, their performance may be handicapped by the discrimination of peers and teachers—and by their own attitudes, values, and expectations. The evidence regarding the relationship between exclusion and academic achievement is confounded by the declining rates of participation of children from excluded groups—those who remain in school tend to be higher performers than those who drop out. Nevertheless, the evidence is clear that students attending rural schools, students who do not regularly use the language of instruction at home, and students from some groups that are discriminated against underperform compared to other groups on international tests of learning achievement, such as the TIMSS, PIRLS, PISA, and SACMEQ, as well as on nationally administered tests for which scores are reported for children from different ethnicities and home languages (see table 3.4). This section reviews the available evidence regarding exclusion factors related to differences in learning achievement.

Students attending rural schools scored significantly lower than students attending urban schools on the 1999 TIMSS tests given to eighth-grade students in Indonesia, the Republic of Korea, Japan, Malaysia, the Philippines, and Thailand (Nabeshima 2003). Urban-rural differences were highest in the countries with the greatest ethnic diversity (Indonesia, with a 72-point difference on an 800-point scale, and the Philippines, with a 73-point difference) and lowest in the countries with the lowest ethnic diversity (Japan, with a nonsignificant 6-point difference, and the Republic of Korea, with a 15-point difference). Urban-rural differences in achievement in Malaysia and Thailand were 31 points.

Country studies in Latin America echo these results. In Peru students in urban schools significantly outperformed students in rural schools on tests of fourth-grade reading and fifth-grade reading and mathematics, a difference that held after controlling for household assets (Cueto and Secada 2004). In Ecuador the scores of students in urban schools were half again as high as those of students in rural schools in language and twice as high in mathematics (Garcia Aracil and Winkler 2004). In Bolivia urban-rural differences in performance on tests of third-grade Spanish and mathematics were small, after controlling for school and household effects (McEwan 2004).

In Africa children attending schools in small towns outperformed students in remote rural schools in all countries reporting data (figure 3.10). Reading and mathematics scores of children attending urban schools were significantly higher than those of children in either remote rural schools or schools in small towns.

Average test scores in schools with high shares of indigenous children are lower than scores in schools with few indigenous children. In Mexico, two studies find that the average fourth- and sixth-grade Spanish scores of students in indigenous schools were significantly lower than scores of students in nonindigenous public schools. They were also significantly lower than scores of students in other rural or urban schools (Paqueo

Figure 3.10. Sixth-grade mathematics scores are higher in small towns than in rural areas in Africa, 2000

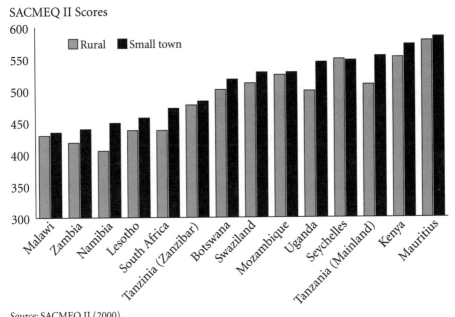

Source: SACMEQ II (2000).

and Lopez-Acevedo 2003; Lopez-Acevedo 1999). When Lopez-Acevedo (1999) ranked Mexican schools according to their average test scores, she found that only 6 percent of students in indigenous schools were enrolled in the highest quintile of schools, compared with 21 percent of students in public urban schools.

In six Latin American countries, the indigenous "effect size" exceeded one-third of a standard deviation for both Spanish and mathematics, but the Spanish test score gaps exceeded those for mathematics in all countries. This reflects the language barriers indigenous children face in schools teaching in the majority language (McEwan and Trowbridge 2005) (table 3.6).

Another study found that test scores in Mexico were significantly lower for indigenous students in all years and grades in 1999–2002 (figure 3.11 reports data for sixth-grade students in 2002) (Shapiro and Trevin 2004).

In Bolivia being indigenous has a strong negative effect on performance. Indigenous students scored significantly lower than nonindigenous students on third-grade tests of Spanish and mathematics and sixth-grade tests of Spanish, controlling for parental education and household assets. In Chile indigenous students scored significantly lower on fourth-grade and eighth-grade tests of Spanish and mathematics (McEwan 2004). McEwan and Trowbridge's (2005) analysis of Guatemalan students' performance on third- and sixth-grade mathematics and Spanish in a national sample

Table 3.6. Gaps between indigenous and nonindigenous student achievement in Latin America (effect size units)

Country/grade	Gap in Spanish	Gap in mathematics
Bolivia		
Grade 3	−0.33	−0.27
Grade 6	−0.48	−0.35
Chile		
Grade 4	−0.39	−0.37
Grade 8	−0.47	−0.40
Ecuador		
Grade 5	−0.43	−0.20
Guatemala		
Grades 3 and 4	−1.06	−0.85
Mexico		
Grade 5	n.a.	−0.69
Peru		
Grades 3 and 4	−0.77	−0.69

n.a. is not available.

Note: Figures show the mean difference between indigenous and nonindigenous students' test scores, divided by the standard deviation in the pooled sample.

Source: McEwan and Trowbridge 2005, based on multiple studies of achievement in Latin America.

of 236 indigenous and 432 nonindigenous schools shows consistently lower performance by indigenous children, when controlling for gender, parental education, and home assets (third grade only). Decomposition analyses indicate that the largest part of these differences are attributable to between-school effects rather than differences in family background, but the analyses provide no information about which factors are operating at the school level.

In Ecuador fifth-grade students speaking an indigenous language score significantly lower than Spanish-speaking students on tests of language and mathematics, but Spanish-speaking Afro-Ecuadorian score well below indigenous children, suggesting that ethnicity can have an even more powerful negative effect on student performance than language (Garcia Aracil and Winkler 2004). In Brazil black and mixed race students consistently underperform whites on national assessments in grades 4, 8, and 11, with the differences largely reflecting differences in socioeconomic status and schooling quality (Rosenberg 2004).

Figure 3.11. Sixth-grade indigenous students underperform nonindigenous students by a wide margin in Spanish and mathematics in Mexico, 2002

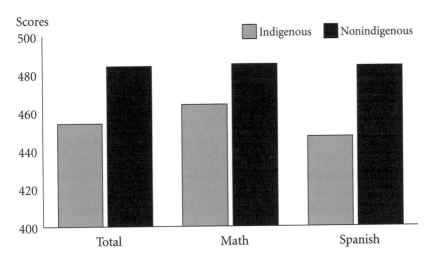

Source: Shapiro and Trevin 2004.

In India caste and tribal status are important determinants of learning outcomes. After adjusting for household welfare, a World Bank study of approximately 24,000 students in 1,800 schools in low-literacy districts of eight Indian states found that fourth- and fifth-grade students from scheduled castes and tribes in five of the states scored significantly lower than other students in mathematics, with differences up to 20 percent of a standard deviation. In reading, students from scheduled castes and tribes scored lower than other students in three of the states (World Bank 1996). Another study found that fourth-grade students from scheduled tribes scored lower on achievement tests than other students in 12 of 15 major states for which data were available (World Bank 1997).

Evidence from Serbia and Montenegro for Roma and non-Roma children shows significant differences in performance. On a national test administered at the end of third grade, average grades for Serbian language were 4.01 (out of 5.00) for non-Roma and 2.79 for Roma. In mathematics the average scores were 3.75 for non-Roma and 2.4 for Roma. Eighty percent of Roma pupils performed below the national average (Mihajlovic 2004).

Children who speak a language at home that is different from that used in school (or on tests of achievement) often encounter both discrimination and learning challenges. Children in Argentina, Colombia, FYR Macedonia, and Turkey who never or only sometimes spoke the language of the test at home scored significantly lower on a test of reading literacy at fourth grade (Woessmann 2005). The differences amount to as much as half the difference between the international average and scores in the highest scoring country (figure 3.12).

Moreover, lack of opportunities to learn the language of instruction before entering school may disproportionately disadvantage girls in countries where they are secluded and not allowed outside the home, giving them little exposure to the language of instruction before entering school (Benson 2005). In Morocco Berber boys are allowed to travel outside the home with their fathers and thus encounter Arabic before going to school. But girls are not allowed outside the home. In Guatemala isolation exacerbates problems for girls in Mayan communities, where they do not leave their communities like boys do and have little exposure to Spanish before entering school (Hallman and Peracca forthcoming).

In Peru the ability to understand the teacher (a measure of the extent of potential language difficulty) emerges as an independent, positive, and statistically significant factor explaining performance on fourth- and fifth-grade mathematics and language comprehension tests, suggesting a lingering effect of mother tongue on student performance. Speaking Aymara at home, but not Quechua, led to lower scores in language comprehension (Cueto and Secada 2004).

Figure 3.12. Reading scores of fourth-graders who never or only sometimes speak the test language at home are lower than those of fourth-graders who speak it regularly, 2001

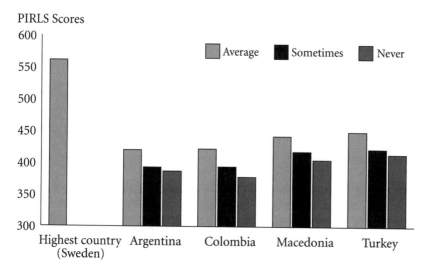

Note: Based on results of grade 4 PIRLS 2001 assessment.
Source: Woessmann 2005.

Gender, exclusion, and learning

One might expect that girls from rural, indigenous, minority, language minority, or poor communities would be doubly disadvantaged in learning. But the evidence suggests the contrary: once in school, girls from excluded groups often perform as well as or even better than boys at the primary level. This may be due to selection effects. If fewer excluded girls go to schools, they may be more likely to be higher achievers. Moreover, although certain school policies and practices can exacerbate gender or ethnic gaps in achievement, others can mitigate them. Studies in developed countries provide evidence that gender, racial, and ethnic gaps in achievement can be mitigated by improved school quality.

Evidence from developing countries is limited, coming mainly from international assessments of reading, mathematics, and science, in which most participating countries are members of the OECD. Only rarely are learning achievement data disaggregated by students' gender within other categories of exclusion. One exception is data disaggregated by gender within home language, which in some countries can serve as a proxy for ethnicity. Another exception is data disaggregated by gender within indigenous groups in Latin America and the Caribbean, where research is increasingly taking ethnicity into account.

Language is a key indicator of exclusion, with excluded groups often speaking a language at home that is different from the dominant language. Thus Native American indigenous languages, the Maori language, countless tribal languages in much of Africa and India, and many others often signal ethnic differences and may signal exclusion, along with other signals such as skin tone. Using language as a proxy for ethnicity it is possible to examine the combined effects of gender and ethnicity on performance, drawing on data from selected international tests of achievement (principally the TIMSS and PISA). Differences in language are indicated by students' reports of the frequency with which they use the language of the test at home.

In South Africa the 2003 TIMSS tests were given in both English and Afrikaans, corresponding to the school's language (medium) of instruction. Only about 30 percent of test takers reported always or almost always speaking the language of the test at home, suggesting that the majority of test takers spoke an indigenous African language at home. Those who always or almost always spoke the language of the test at home significantly outperformed those who did not, with students in Afrikaans-medium schools systematically outperforming students in English-medium schools (figure 3.13). However, in English-medium schools, gender differences in performance were insignificant among those who spoke English rarely (only sometimes or never), whereas in Afrikaans-medium schools, gender differences were substantial and favored boys for those who spoke Afrikaans rarely. Thus disadvantage was doubled in Afrikaans-medium schools, whereas it was not in English-medium schools.

In FYR Macedonia, ethnic Albanians, who have been historically discriminated

Figure 3.13. In South Africa, eighth-grade mathematics scores are lower for children who rarely speak the language of instruction at home

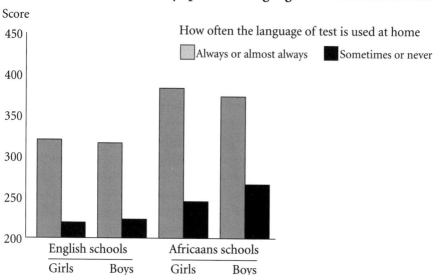

Note: Data are unweighted averages. Authors' analysis of data from 2003 TIMSS mathematics assessment.
Source: 2003 TIMSS data downloaded from the Web.

against, represent about 25 percent of the population. The education system includes schools taught in Macedonian and Albanian, and the 2003 TIMSS was administered in both languages, corresponding to the school's medium of instruction. Students in Albanian-medium schools underperformed students in Macedonian-medium schools, and students who spoke the language of instruction less often at home underperformed those who spoke it more frequently at home. In both kinds of schools, however, girls slightly outperformed boys, suggesting that girls can take advantage of schooling opportunities, a pattern observed in OECD countries.

Two smaller studies from Ecuador (Garcia Aracil and Winkler 2004) and Peru (Cueto and Secada 2004) provide inconsistent evidence regarding the double disadvantage of gender plus ethnicity or remoteness of community. In Ecuador tests administered at the end of fifth grade to children in 42 schools produced Spanish and mathematics scores that do not show a consistent double disadvantage for indigenous girls or girls attending rural schools (Garcia Aracil and Winkler 2004). Indigenous girls scored lowest in Spanish—lower than nonindigenous students of either sex and lower than indigenous boys. In mathematics, however, indigenous girls' performance was second only to that of nonindigenous boys (table 3.8).[10] The urban-rural discrepancy

---

10. In Ecuador, indigenous groups are not homogeneous; performance varied across ethnic groups. Quechua speakers outperformed other indigenous groups, but Afro-Ecuadorian students achieved much lower scores, 5.00 for Spanish and 0.98 for mathematics, well below indigenous groups. See table 3.8.

Table 3.7. Fifth-grade Spanish and mathematics scores in Ecuador, by gender, ethnicity, and location, 2000

	Spanish	Mathematics
Nonindigenous		
Boys	7.58	6.35
Girls	7.90	6.07
Indigenous		
Boys	6.21	4.02
Girls	6.00	6.18
Urban		
Boys	9.61	9.25
Girls	9.08	9.35
Rural		
Boys	6.27	4.34
Girls	6.79	4.76

Source: Garcia Aracil and Winkler 2004.

in performance was most pronounced, with rural students of both sexes significantly underperforming urban students of both sexes. Rural girls, however, performed slightly better than did rural boys on these tests. The picture is mixed.

A study in Peru of 29 schools from predominantly Spanish-, Aymara-, and Quechua-speaking communities examines differences in fifth-grade mathematics and reading comprehension (Cueto and Secada 2004).[11] Rural Aymara girls are doubly disadvantaged in both mathematics and reading achievement, scoring lower than urban girls and rural Aymara boys. In addition, urban girls outperform rural girls, and urban boys outperform rural Quechua boys but not rural Aymara boys (table 3.8). There were no significant gender differences among urban students or rural Quechua students.

Multivariate analyses of the Peruvian sample controlling for family, schooling, and classroom effects suggest that being male raises mathematics scores but being a rural Quechua does not. In contrast, gender does not explain language comprehension performance, but being rural Quechua does make a difference (Cueto and Secada 2004).

The association between heterogeneity and achievement found in Lewis and Lockheed's (forthcoming) cross-country regressions strongly suggests that gender differences in achievement may result from heterogeneity. And data from Africa provide some support for this conclusion (figure 3.14). In Malawi, a highly heterogeneous country, reading and mathematics scores favored boys, whereas in South Africa and Botswana—the first benefiting from affirmative action programs and the second comparatively homogeneous—girls outperform boys.

11. This sample was meant to be representative of schools across the three languages.

Table 3.8. Fifth-grade reading and mathematics scores in Peru, by gender, ethnicity, and location, 2000

	Reading	Mathematics
Urban		
Boys	25.9	13.8
Girls	27.3	14.2
Rural Aymara		
Boys	25.6[a]	12.9[a]
Girls	21.2[a, b]	10.9[a, b]
Rural Quechua		
Boys	17.7[b]	9.8[b]
Girls	18.4[b]	10.4[b]

a. Differences between girls and boys are statistically significant ($p < 0.05$).

b. Differences between urban and rural are statistically significant ($p < 0.05$).

Source: Cueto and Secada 2004.

Figure 3.14. Gender differences in achievement may result from heterogeneity, 2000

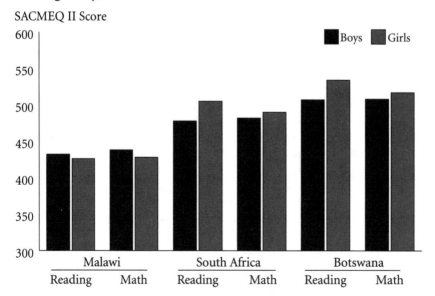

Source: SACMEQ II (2000).

Conclusion

When girls are given the same opportunity as boys to attend school, their performance is comparable—and in many cases superior—to that of boys. And this applies to both developed and developing countries. In countries where women have held significant positions of authority, such as in the Philippines, or past socialist regimes, and where equal opportunities for women have been provided, girls' test scores exceed those of boys not only at the primary school level but also at the lower secondary or middle school level. In some countries, however, girls fall behind boys in mathematics and particularly science, which are "stereotypically male" subjects. In other countries, particularly those in Sub-Saharan Africa, the status of women in the larger society appears to affect girls' performance in school during middle school. In these countries, girls fall behind boys in mathematics and science after primary school. Heterogeneity matters, and girls excel in more ethnically homogeneous countries.

4

Strategies for addressing the multiple sources of exclusion faced by girls

Reaching universal education means ensuring that all children complete school. Progress in recent years has been impressive in improving access, especially for girls. Achieving universal education is within the grasp of international efforts. But significant barriers facing excluded groups need to be addressed. Policy guidance from several sources provides a basis for action by donors and policymakers alike. The need for documented evidence suggests a significant role for public and private players in helping excluded girls catch up with the rest of their cohort.

Different and more intensive efforts are needed to get girls who face multiple exclusions—based on ethnicity, language, social stigmas—into school and keep them there. Experience in developed and developing countries reveals how difficult it is to reach these girls and to ensure that they enroll in, complete, and perform in school. The environment these children live in can counter incentives that in other circumstances have brought children, particularly girls, into the school system. Policy options need to build on accepted interventions (see Herz and Sperling 2003), focus on the exceptional circumstance of the target group, and effectively change behavior by ensuring that excluded girls receive the support they need to obtain an education.

Policies to spark progress with the remaining out-of-school populations will require actions on various fronts:
- Altering education policies and addressing discrimination by changing laws and administrative rules.

113

- Expanding options for schooling out-of-school children, especially girls.
- Improving the quality and relevance of schools and classrooms by ensuring that excluded girls receive basic educational inputs and providing professional development to help teachers become agents of change.
- Supporting compensatory preschool and in-school programs that engage and retain excluded children, particularly girls.
- Providing incentives for households to help overcome both their reluctance to send girls to school and the costs of doing so.

Efforts to target disadvantaged groups with effective programs are handicapped by the lack of solid evidence on what works in reaching and teaching them. The evidence on what is effective for girls is particularly sparse. But even in the high-income Organisation for Economic Co-operation and Development (OECD) countries the evidence base is thin. The exception is the United States, where there is an extensive body of evidence on social integration, educational enrollment, and educational achievement differentials across population subgroups. Finland has made concerted efforts to reach the Lapp population, but no literature exists on the effectiveness of its efforts. Virtually no evaluations have been conducted of Spain's extensive efforts to integrate Roma children. And little has been done to assess the effectiveness of New Zealand's investments in Maori development. Moreover, where evaluations exist, they rarely look at gender differences in program effects.

Some evaluations have been conducted in developing countries, but the quality is uneven and certainly incomplete. We hope that the studies reviewed in this book will provide an impetus for greater investment in evaluation, so that research can help guide policy and program development.

Two other issues are important in the context of how to do more and do better in reaching excluded girls in developing countries. First, the countries furthest behind and those with the most challenging problems are often among the poorest, with the fewest resources and most limited capacity to implement programs or systemic reforms. Long-term affordability needs to be taken into account in designing and implementing targeted programs. Interventions must align with national budget realities and entail straightforward designs that are technically and economically feasible given county circumstances. Even so, sustained donor support may be needed.

Second, governance is weak and corruption deep and widespread in most target countries. Under-the-table payments, politicization of teacher hiring, and lack of accountability, among other abuses, undermine efforts to improve the supply of education (Lewis 2005). Corruption often diverts funds from programs aimed at excluded groups. Experience suggests that the quality and effectiveness of such programs often fall short of average government performance (Alesina and others 2003; World Bank 2003). Part of the problem is the lack of the target populations' voice in government policy. Combined with uneven public sector management, this may cause public service performance to suffer. These problems need to be kept in mind in designing interventions.

Strategies need to grant excluded groups a level playing field in the labor market and raise the quality of their schools so that parents can justify sending their children to school. Once members of excluded groups leave school, low skill levels and discrimination work against them, hurting their prospects in life (Birdsall and Sabot 1996). Girls and women are particularly hurt by discrimination in the labor market, where the economic returns to education are measured. In Latin America, for example, the returns to primary and tertiary education exceed those for secondary school (Behrman, Duryea, and Szekely 1999). Only secondary school students who go on to tertiary education earn returns on their investment in secondary school, so dropping out or not enrolling at all makes economic sense to most poor households. In some countries returns to education among excluded groups are compromised by explicit and implicit discrimination in the labor market and society at large, which bars access to better paying jobs and upward mobility (Mario and Woolcock forthcoming; Narayan 2000). Addressing education for excluded groups must include attention to problems such as labor market discrimination.

Recent evidence suggests the importance of economic growth in expanding employment and creating political space for investments in minority populations (Friedman 2005; Meerman 2005). In their analysis of 18 Latin American and Caribbean countries Behrman, Duryea, and Szekely (1999) show that weak macroeconomic conditions in the 1980s were the most important factor explaining the weak gains in schooling across the region. Current expansion of education in the region effectively targets excluded groups, because primary education is near universal for the majority populations. While economic growth may be necessary, Latin America's recent investments in education cannot be construed as sufficient.

If universal education is not on developing countries' agendas, the likelihood that excluded groups will be considered in setting policies and budgets is small. Donors can spark new ideas and demonstrate the value of paying attention to neglected areas—as the Bangladesh Rural Advancement Committee (BRAC) has done—but government commitment is key, given the need for a legal framework and long-term investment. It is rare for disadvantaged groups to receive basic services such as education at the expense of the power elite. Commitment to broad educational coverage is critical to any efforts aimed at reaching excluded children, but it alone will not be not enough to make a difference.

Altering education policies and addressing discrimination

Policy setting determines the environment in which excluded groups must maneuver, and it affects the credibility of government in efforts to reach children who are out of school. Although policies alone ensure little, having clear mandates against discrimination, a legal system that enforces both entitlements and rights of all citizens, administrative rules that foster enrollment of all children, and an articulated policy regarding excluded groups in education all reinforce the credibility of government and offer a foundation for both taking action and coalescing target populations. Good legal systems, rules, and policies also provide a context for engaging donors in advocacy for marginalized groups and in reaching underserved regions with education programs.

Anti-discrimination legislation

Anti-discrimination laws undergird both legal and policy efforts in fighting exclusion. Clear legal protection offers a beginning in reversing implicit and explicit discrimination. It has proved critical in Canada, New Zealand, and the United States. Racial discrimination was widespread in South Africa during Apartheid and in Cuba before Castro took power, and data on discrepancies in academic performance, employment, and earnings by race in Brazil suggest that discrimination is prevalent there as well (Meerman 2005; Skidmore 2003).

These countries have legally barred discrimination. Brazil's anti-discrimination legal action is the most recent (Htun 2004). India passed anti-discrimination laws banning discrimination against Dalits (widely known as "untouchables") in the 1950s, soon after independence, in tandem with affirmative action and preferential policies. Much of Latin America has adopted some form of legal prohibition against discrimination, although enforcement of statutes remains weak. Malaysia has adopted affirmative action toward the indigenous Malay population, but at the expense of ethnic Chinese and Tamil, in order to promote Malay prospects and foster greater equity and political harmony across ethnic groups (Lee 2005).

Japan has avoided legislating against discrimination. This policy has left the minority Burakumin clan—which despite being ethnically Japanese has existed on the margins of society for centuries—without legal protection against abuse by government, employers, and the public. The Japanese believe that nondiscrimination should evolve from within rather than be legislated. Efforts to educate the population about fair treatment for the Burakumin have been only partially successful, however (Meerman 2005).

In the past few decades European countries and the European Union have introduced legal protection against all forms of discrimination. The Roma throughout Europe now have protection under human rights laws and European Union legal agreements on ethnic minority rights, which explicitly address treatment of minorities. Despite these advances, the transition to democracy in Eastern Europe has been accompanied by a rise in discrimination and violence toward the Roma and the emergence of local restrictions regarding their access to public places. Legal protection has led to recent efforts to seek redress for egregious injustice, but discrimination against and marginalization of the Roma persist (Ringold, Orenstein, and Wilkens 2003). Private donors have been pivotal in promoting the rights of the Roma in Eastern Europe and improving their access to mainstream schools.

In most high-income OECD countries anti-discrimination laws spawned multiple initiatives to integrate minorities, particularly with respect to school enrollment. Some success has been recorded, but despite legal protection and increasingly flexible policies aimed at bolstering the prospects and achievements of excluded groups, minorities continue to lag behind the majority population in education, employment, and earnings.

Anti-discrimination efforts must extend beyond schools. Unless discrimination is aggressively addressed in the labor market, returns to education and the demand for schooling will be suppressed. Discrimination disproportionately hurts girls, as discussed in chapter 2. While discrimination is a broader issue, it is essential to raise it in this context, because the economic consequences of barring trained workers from jobs on the basis of ethnicity, language, or cultural differences has direct links with education.

While not a panacea, the legal framework provides protection and a source of arbitration for excluded groups. Its effectiveness is a function of enforcement and internalization by the majority population.

Affirmative action and preferential policies in education

Affirmative action attempts to establish equal opportunity, compensate for a history of discrimination, provide advantages to certain groups to hasten upward mobility, and break the intergenerational transmission of low human capital and poverty. Affirmative action is an outgrowth of antidiscrimination efforts, turning discrimination into a positive force to assist the victims of negative discrimination. It has implications for government, the private sector, and households.

Critics of affirmative action argue that it undermines merit as the basis for schooling or employment, skews benefits to a few better off minorities, reduces incentives for self-improvement, and creates divisions within society, which in countries like India and Sri Lanka have led to violence or civil war. Wariness of the credentials and competency of target populations often undermines the effectiveness of affirmative action (Sowell 2004). Ascertaining the impact of affirmative action has proved elusive, though there are some indications that it can have positive effects. But do the benefits outweigh the costs to both the target group and society as a whole?

Affirmative action can take the form of quotas. It can also be less intrusive, by tipping marginal decisions in favor of candidates from disadvantaged groups. The 2003 Supreme Court decision in the United States (Grutter v. Bollinger) ruled that ethnicity can be one of many criteria for selection to university, but it cannot serve as a filter on its own.

Loury (2000) proposes an alternative "preferential" affirmative action, which emphasizes bolstering the performance of disadvantaged students while maintaining common standards. Summer math programs or after-school enrichment programs can strengthen skills and make disadvantaged children competitive. This approach is based on the assumption that minority groups suffer from deficits that can be remediated through tutoring, behavioral guidance, or other compensatory interventions. The approach avoids the distortions introduced by traditional quota arrangements but projects "a direct concern about group inequality and involves allocating benefits on the basis of group identity" (p. 248). Some of the school-based compensatory programs discussed below describe these kinds of interventions.

Despite reservations and only modest results, affirmative action has been embraced by countries as varied as Brazil, India, Malaysia, South Africa, and the United States, all of which have heterogeneous, highly stratified societies based on class, ethnicity, and skin color. This subsection discusses the policies of various countries in attempting to reach out to excluded groups in education.

Brazil. Brazil considers itself a positive example of multiculturalism, but it has an intricate social stratification system based on shades of real and perceived skin color. The "color caste" system is based on both cultural perceptions and structural differences; one can be considered lighter or darker depending on one's socioeconomic status (Guillebeau 1999; Htun 2004). This creates difficulties for policymakers attempting to define disadvantaged minorities.

In acknowledging the prevalence of racial inequality, the Brazilian government implemented a quota system in government, higher education, and the private sector. Imposing quotas for nonwhite students undermines the merit-based university entry culture (based on examinations), but it compensates for the higher quality of private secondary schools available to the more advantaged (Lockheed and Bruns 1990). Critics note, however, that affirmative action strikes at the very heart of Brazilian identity as a harmonious multiracial society (Skidmore 2003).

India. Affirmative action policies in India are referred to as "compensatory discrimination." These polices are intended to counteract centuries of past injustices against and repression of the Dalit. Affirmative action in India began in the nineteenth century, when the British established quotas for Indians from certain disadvantaged groups. It is enshrined in the Constitution and takes the form of quotas in education, government jobs, and elected officials. In the 1950s under the leadership of Jawaharlal Nehru the Constituent Assembly devised the category of "socially and educationally backward classes," an amalgamation of more than 4,000 castes. This category includes non-Hindu tribal groups, known as scheduled tribes; low castes on the government schedule for preference, known as scheduled castes; and "other backward castes" (Deshpande 2005; de Zwart 2000). The three groups are similar in socioeconomic status and conditions and account for a significant share of the total population—about 16 percent of the population belongs to scheduled castes, about 8 percent to scheduled tribes (Census of India 2001). In 1980 it was estimated that other backward castes constituted 52 percent of the population, but this caste-based classification is made on a state by state basis and no recent national estimates are available (Kumar 2005).

The quota "reservation" system in educational institutions reserves 15 percent of places for scheduled castes and 7.5 percent for scheduled tribes (Boston and Nair-Reichert 2003). The results of such policies have fallen short of the intended outcomes. For example, in 2000 at the University of Delhi only 8.6 percent of students were from scheduled castes and 2 percent from scheduled tribes (Deshpande 2005). The quotas have nevertheless improved the status of Dalits relative to higher castes (Galanter 1991).

Malaysia. Affirmative action in Malaysia was established in 1971 under Article 153 of the Constitution. Its historical roots are in stipulations by the British colonizers in 1948 that gave preferential treatment to ethnic Malays (bumiputeras) for their elite administrative service. This constitutionally sanctioned policy entitles Malays to preferential treatment that is nonnegotiable and intended to "safeguard [the] 'special position' of the Malay community" (Lee 2005:212). The success of these preferential policies has lead to a significant and visible Malay professional class in both the public and private sectors. It has also led to increased Malay migration to cities—historically, ethnic Chinese and Indian immigrants dominated business in urban areas, and the Malay majority was engaged primarily in agriculture.

The practice of ethnic segregation in Malaysia under affirmative action has created "ethnic enclaves" and distortions in access to equal opportunity. For example, although 25 percent of the population is Chinese and 7 percent Indian, just 2.1 percent of Malaysia's public primary school students are Chinese and just 4.3 percent are Indian (Lee 2005). As the Malay middle class grows, so do opportunities for children born into these families to take advantage of preferential policies. Although the original aim of Article 153 was to create equality across the major ethnic groups, the policies have greatly favored ethnic Malays more than other indigenous groups (Lee 2005). Despite these problems, Malaysia has seen robust growth over the past 20 years and a rise in equity. Whether affirmative action played any role is arguable, but it is clear that affirmative action at the very least has not forced a compromise between peace and prosperity.

South Africa. In South Africa blacks have been the beneficiaries of educational and employment opportunities since the end of apartheid. These efforts have been directed at black men, leaving women with limited access to education and higher paying jobs. This is largely due to the continued inherent sexism among the nation's leaders and the presence of institutional discrimination against women (Guillebeau 1999).

Despite its endorsement by the African National Congress, affirmative action has been "passionately resented, even among blacks" (Adam 1997). Affirmative action in South Africa is problematic for two reasons. First, it has been accused of being apartheid in reverse. Second, it has benefited only a small segment of the black population. Sowell (2004) makes the same arguments in criticizing affirmative action efforts in India, Malaysia, Nigeria, Sri Lanka, and the United States. In contrast to the United States, the private sector in South Africa has voluntarily embraced affirmative action because it has widened the pool of available talent and brought in black managers who can help capture the expanding market of black consumers (Adam 1997). The end of apartheid has made discrimination against the majority a poor business decision, which may help explain the response of South African business.

United States. In the United States affirmative action takes the form of legal rulings and executive orders. Much of the initiative entails "goals and timetables" for hiring minorities and women in a largely voluntary program. Preferences in university admissions meant to compensate for past discrimination have been successfully contested. Legally, universities can only use preferences for underrepresented minorities as one of many criteria for assessing applicants for admission. Thus, in many respects, affirmative action is a relatively weak instrument in the United States. Nonetheless, laws tend to be systematically enforced (Deshpande 2005).

Administrative rules

Ministry of Education administrative rules often serve as barriers to girls and children from excluded groups. These consequences are often unintended. Analysis of the negative impact of administrative rules on gender was highly effective in bringing about change in the United States. Some analysis of administrative rules has been undertaken in developing countries. The Forum for African Women Educationalists has shown how administrative rules in Africa on expulsion of pregnant girls prevents them from continuing their education (Wilson 2004). Researchers in Pakistan have examined the impact of administrative rules that require communities to provide single-sex schools (Lloyd, Mete, and Grant forthcoming). As community resources may be limited, boys' schools tend to be built first while schools for girls are often neglected. Administrative rules regarding use of a national language of instruction often serve as barriers to school participation by children from families who do not speak the national language at home, with particularly negative effects on girls (Benson 2005). Many countries have made strides in providing mother-tongue instruction in the earlier grades. Schools in India offer mother-tongue instruction at the primary level. In Sri Lanka public schools offer instruction in Tamil and Sinhalese.

Administrative rules that require tracking children by ability in the early grades exclude many children from more demanding programs, limiting their future opportunities. Multi-country studies of student tracking have found that grouping students by "ability" has long-lasting negative consequences for subsequent performance, particularly when students are tracked into different types of schools (Hanushek and Woessmann 2006; Gamoran 2001; Nonoyama 2005). The results of the Primer Estudio International Comparativo in Latin America reveal that schools that did not group students by ability had higher achievement (Willms and Somers 2001). While early tracking of children through competitive examinations has largely been discontinued in developing countries, informal tracking continues.

Implications for donors and policymakers

Donors can expedite integration by fostering alternative forms of positive discrimination and expanding opportunities for girls who otherwise would have no options. The Open Society Institute provided extensive assistance to local nongovernmental organizations (NGOs) and governments in their efforts to initiate laws and regulations that protect the Roma and make schools safe havens for Roma children. Similar initiatives could be funded in other settings. Donors could also support the analysis of the unintended consequences of administrative rules in education, to raise awareness of these issues.

Expanding options for schooling

Many of the changes that complement overall expansion of educational opportunities entail efforts that facilitate access by tailoring schooling to the needs of specific populations and addressing concerns of households and communities. For girls this may prove critical, because mainstream schools are not an option for many excluded girls, due to the barriers identified in chapter 2. One of the lessons from the high-income OECD countries is that targeted, tailored programs are essential to complement overall schooling investments if excluded populations are to be reached and excluded children are to stay in school.

Increasing school supply

A first step in improving access is making schools or school substitutes available to excluded groups. While expanding access generally occurs under programs for "education for all," without targeting or tailoring to excluded groups, increasing the number of school places often results in greater access for the historically excluded. In Indonesia a massive school construction program added 64,000 schools over five years (Duflo

2000). A recent analysis shows that this program halved the gender gap in educational attainment, from about 1.4 years to about 0.7 years of schooling, while reducing the urban-rural gap in educational attainment (Jayasundera 2005). Indonesia saw nearly 100 percent of children in school after the investment.

In India a centrally sponsored scheme for districts in which female literacy rates were below average, the District Primary Education Programme (DPEP), added 15,000 new schools and expanded existing schools by 14,000 new classrooms. Enrollment in target districts grew slightly more rapidly (about 1.3 percentage points more) than enrollment in matched nonprogram districts, reaching children who were not in school and having a greater impact for older girls (Jalan and Glinskaya 2003). The program also had a positive net impact on primary school completion. No studies are available that compare student achievement in DPEP and non–DPEP schools.

Establishing community schools

Community schools are educational initiatives grounded in the decisionmaking of communities and designed to shape schooling to meet the needs and ensure the involvement of community members. Community schools are the ultimate means of giving parents voice in the running of local schools. They are formal schools that teach the normal curriculum, adapted to local conditions. They are particularly valuable in reaching girls by offering flexibility in timing, venue, and curriculum, which accommodate the domestic demands, safety concerns, and relevancy requirements of parents.

South Asia pioneered the community school approach with its *Shiksha Karmi* (SSK) Project in Rajasthan, India, in 1987. The project used paraprofessional teachers, allowed the community to select and supervise teachers, and hired part-time workers to escort girls to school. Targeting students from scheduled castes and scheduled tribes, the project increased enrollments in SSK schools to 202,000 girls by 2001. A comparison of public and SSK schools in West Bengal shows higher attendance, lower teacher absenteeism, and greater parent satisfaction with SSK schools. In Rajasthan SSK students had higher enrollment, attendance, and test scores at all grade levels compared to their public school counterparts (World Bank 1999). These programs led to better performance and greater satisfaction of parents and students.

In 1997 Madya Pradesh, with support from the DPEP, launched its Education Guarantee Scheme and Alternate Schools programs, which adopted approaches similar to the SSK but with midday meals added to meet the needs of remote communities (Sipahimalani-Rao and Clarke 2003). By 2000 more than 26,500 schools had been built and 1.2 million children, or about 20 percent of the cohort in government schools, enrolled. Girls' attendance rose 47 percent, and their dropout rate fell 35 percent. Nine other states followed suit with support from the DPEP, establishing 32,000 alternative schools enrolling 1 million students. The Education Guarantee Scheme and the Alternate Schools program targeted girls and remote communities, but their effects on these groups are difficult to determine because of data gaps (Gomes 2004).

Community schools represent an important share of all schools in several Sub-Saharan African countries. Gershberg and Winkler (2003) report that 20 percent of primary schools in Togo, 32 percent in Mali, and most primary schools in Ghana are managed by the community, with the curriculum and in some cases textbooks provided by the central government. According to studies reviewed by Miller-Grandvaux and Yoder (2002), community-based schools in Ghana, Guinea, Mali, and South Sudan increased girls' participation in primary education and in many cases reached greater gender equity in enrollment than government schools. A rigorous analysis in Malawi finds that learning was higher in community schools than in comparable government-run schools (Dowd 2001).

The experiences of these Sub-Saharan African countries is substantially different from those of South Asia. Community schools in Africa have generally emerged as a response to crisis—neglect during the colonial period, an ineffective centralized model in the 1960s and 1970s, and economic and political upheavals in the 1970s and 1980s—rather than a strategy for improvement (Watt 2001). Recently, governments and donors have turned to communities to accommodate the rapid expansion of enrollment associated with the abolition of primary school fees (Riddell 2003). Community involvement in education in Africa remains largely limited to cash and in-kind contributions generally associated with school and classroom construction and maintenance (Watt 2001). The majority of community schools in Sub-Saharan Africa are funded and managed by NGOs. This is in contrast to South Asia, where governments have been active partners in many of the major community school programs.

Because of the dominance of NGOs in Sub-Saharan Africa, data limitations are greater than for other regions. As Gershberg and Winkler (2003: 27) note, "The studies that provide evidence [on the impacts of community-based school management on educational outcomes] must be interpreted with caution, since many are self-studies commissioned by the programs being evaluated, and few have the necessary baseline data and experimental controls to provide statistically reliable results."

Creating alternatives to formal schooling

Two major alternatives to formal schooling are nonformal schools and distance education. Nonformal schools address gaps or compensate for limitations of formal schools. In some cases they provide basic literacy training, in others they prepare students for mainstream schools. Nonformal schools can be very important in preparing disadvantaged children academically and in developing appropriate social skills and self-discipline. The major drawback of the many nonformal alternatives is their lack of evaluation, which prevents their adoption on a large scale (Gomes 2004). The BRAC program is an exception.

BRAC is an NGO that established a nonformal primary education program in Bangladesh in 1979 to provide schooling for unenrolled children and dropouts from poor families in rural areas. The program focused on girls, who were least likely to be able to attend school. BRAC schools offer a two- to three-year program that enables 8- to 16-year-olds to transfer to formal schools (Rugh and Bossert 1998). Seventy percent of its students are girls—far higher than the 46 percent female enrollment in government schools. Classes are run out of one-room schoolhouses and taught by paraprofessional teachers (local woman with at least nine years of schooling). Student-teacher ratios are low, pedagogical practices (including cultural activities) child-based, and schedules flexible to allow students to perform agricultural activities and household chores.

Spin-offs of BRAC operate in other countries, including India and Morocco (Jain 2003). Community involvement in BRAC schools exceeds that in traditional government schools. Parents participate with BRAC staff in selecting a local teacher; establishing a school calendar; committing to sending their children, especially their daughters, to BRAC schools regularly; and agreeing to attend monthly meetings. In addition, along with the school management committees, parents manage and maintain the schools and ensure regular student and teacher attendance, playing an important monitoring role (Rugh and Bossert 1998).

The BRAC nonformal education program, which currently serves about 8 percent of primary school children in Bangladesh, has significantly increased the availability of schooling, especially among low-income households and girls. Between 1985 and 1999, 1.5 million students graduated from nonformal schools.

BRAC has had a significant impact on attainment and performance. Dropout rates among BRAC school children are one-quarter those of children at government schools, and, according to an assessment of 720 randomly selected children across rural Bangladesh, BRAC graduates are about 2.6 times more likely to have achieved basic education skills (as measured by test scores in life skills, reading, writing, and numeracy) than graduates from the formal system (Nath, Sylva, and Grimes 1999). Given its adaptability, strong focus on implementation, and emphasis on girls, the BRAC approach offers a viable and adaptable approach to other countries for enrolling and retaining excluded girls.

Informal classes, often provided in conjunction with income-generating activities for women, typically provide short-term literacy training. Other informal classes for excluded children offer instruction in the language used in school, teach social skills, and supplement formal school activities with culturally relevant activities. Because they typically are NGO driven, informal classes reflect the community in design and rely on the community for implementation. Programs are shaped around cultural themes and respect the local calendar for times and days for teaching. Involving parents and investing in topics of interest to them has prodded change (Gomes 2004).

At the primary level distance education rarely provides a suitable alternative on its own because it usually relies on the ability of learners to manage their own learning. Where distance education has been effective with young children, as in the Australian outback in the 1950s, parents provided the supervisory structure for its success (Conway 1989). But there are many substitutes for educated parents. Even in remote areas radios are usually available. Primary education programs that combine radio delivery of a high-quality curriculum with local monitoring of children's progress have been rigorously evaluated and found to boost learning.

The most widely evaluated program is interactive radio instruction, which has broadcast professionally developed curricula to children in remote regions of Belize, Bolivia, Cape Verde, Costa Rica, the Dominican Republic, El Salvador, Guatemala, Honduras, Lesotho, Papua New Guinea, South Africa, Thailand, and Venezuela (Bosch 1997). Lessons teach core instructional material, each curriculum is designed according to proven instructional design principles, and each 30-minute lesson incorporates sound pedagogical principles, including the active participation of students. Randomized control evaluations have found that the programs increase learning by as much as 2.1 standard deviations for rural children, compared with an increase of 2.8 standard deviations from a year of traditional schooling, with 70 percent greater cost-effectiveness (Bosch 1997). Despite its proven effectiveness and cost-effectiveness, because interactive radio instruction has been largely donor driven it has not been widely adopted after donor support ended.

Establishing girls' schools

Girls' schools have proven effective in attracting, retaining, and teaching girls, particularly in countries where girls and women are secluded or isolated. In developed countries single-sex education is typically confounded with private education, and many of the early positive findings regarding the effect of single-sex education on girls' learning achievement may be attributed to different selectivity and schooling arrangements (Lee and Lockheed 1990). In New Zealand Maori girls in single-sex schools outperformed other 15-year-olds on the Programme for International Student Assessment, but their higher performance has been attributed to the higher socioeconomic status of private school students (New Zealand Ministry of Education 2004).

In some developing countries, such as Pakistan, the requirement that primary education be segregated by gender combined with poor performance in the construction and staffing of girls' schools has led parents to send their girls to nonpublic coeducational primary schools (Lloyd, Mete, and Grant forthcoming). In contrast, Bangladesh has made dramatic inroads with coeducational primary schools combined with targeted efforts to bring girls into both primary and secondary school (forthcoming 2006).

A few studies from developing countries suggest that the absence of boys in the school creates a more positive learning environment for girls, resulting in higher performance, particularly at the secondary level. In Nigeria and Thailand in the 1980s girls in single-sex secondary schools outperformed girls in coeducational schools on math tests, but the results may have reflected the schools' greater selectivity (Jimenez and Lockheed 1989; Lee and Lockheed 1990). In Kenya girls' probability of dropping out of coeducational secondary schools was affected by their in-class experience: preferential treatment by teachers given to boys and harassment of girls by male classmates increased girls' dropout rate. In contrast teachers who considered that difficult subjects were important for girls reduced girls' dropout rate (Lloyd, Mensch, and Clark 2000). In rural northeast Brazil math performance by primary school girls was substantially lower than that of boys in classes taught by male teachers, while there were no gender differences in classes taught by female teachers, suggesting some discriminatory practices (Harbison and Hanushek 1991). In some cases the quality of inputs to girls' schools is lower than the quality of inputs to boys' schools. In Egypt the major difference in quality between all-girl and all-boy schools is the level of discipline, which is stricter for boys (Lloyd and others 2003). The benefits from single-sex schools are thus likely to be situation specific.

Creative approaches to secondary school: teaching an international language

Creative alternatives may help reach girls. Munshi and Rosenzweig's (forthcoming) study of English-language and Marathi-language schools and labor force participation in Bombay, India, suggests that certain types of education can overcome caste-based discrimination. They find that both boys and girls educated in English-language schools had higher achievement and enjoyed higher rates of return to education than did students educated in Marathi-language schools. This finding is not surprising, as competence in English is a major means of upward mobility in India, eclipsing traditional routes. Because of social networks built around traditional male working class occupations, boys are more likely to be sent to the Marathi-language schools than are girls. As a consequence, girls are able to take advantage of the returns to English education in both labor and marriage markets, with better employment options, higher relative wages, and the opening up of the marriage market outside of their caste. Indeed, 31.6 percent of the older siblings of students in English-language schools married outside their caste, compared with 9.7 percent of the older siblings of students in the Marathi-language schools (Munshi and Rosenzweig forthcoming). Targeting disadvantaged girls with programs teaching an international language may offer a low-cost alternative that provides high returns in marriage and income.

Separate schools for the excluded: not a good idea

Building separate schools for children from ethnic, cultural, and linguistic minorities has not succeeded as a policy. Canada, New Zealand, and the United States sought to educate their indigenous populations through separate day schools, special schools on reservations, and boarding schools away from reservations. Similar programs have been implemented for educating children from scheduled tribes in India. Because these programs often removed very young children from their families and were often designed to socialize the children for their subordinate place in society, they failed to bridge gaps in educational attainment. Moreover, separate schools are inherently unequal and suffer from poor quality.

Implications for donors and policymakers

A trust fund for multilateral programs targeting excluded girls could provide the financial basis for expanding successful efforts of donors and governments. Lack of funding often prevents experimentation with innovative means of expanding schooling to difficult-to-reach groups or adapting effective programs to new contexts.

First, donors can play a catalytic role in devising and financing alternative schooling options. NGOs and donors have already demonstrated success in increasing school enrollment and completion through such programs as BRAC in Bangladesh and the *Shiksha Karmi* projects in India. Both launched innovative approaches and financed them for extended periods, demonstrating the feasibility of alternative schools in raising educational levels for girls. Donors could expand these kinds of approaches to other settings.

For older children, innovative programs, such as immersion classes in an international language such as English or computer training as an alternative to secondary school, could be effective. These programs could provide girls with marketable skills in a global marketplace.

Second, a girls' education evaluation fund to finance rigorous evaluations of new and ongoing programs aimed at reaching girls would help fill a major gap and offer guidance to both policymakers and donors eager to use their resources to promote girls' education. A particularly glaring omission is knowledge regarding exclusion, gender, and schooling in Africa. Too little is known about a continent that is home to more than 30 percent of the world's out-of-school girls and an estimated 40 percent of excluded girls.

Third, alternative schooling offers an ideal opportunity for donors to complement public efforts and meet the needs of an out-of-school population that is underserved and relatively expensive to reach. Governments in low-income countries struggle to provide basic education; the alternatives proposed here go beyond what these countries can afford. Donor financing is thus critical to finance complementary investments that help bring children up to a basic level and permit them to join the educational mainstream.

Improving the quality and relevance of schools and classrooms

Keeping girls in school is as important as getting them into schools. It is particularly important for excluded groups. Improving the quality of the schools these children attend is essential, given past histories of neglect.

Providing basic inputs

Children from excluded groups often attend schools that lack the basic inputs needed for learning.[1] Failure to provide basic inputs drives even the poorest people away and lowers achievement of those who remain. In Pakistan there are fewer schools for girls, and those that do exist lack essential inputs. As a consequence, parents withdraw their daughters, preferring to send them to private coeducational schools. The surge in girls' enrollment in private coeducational schools reflects the poor quality and lack of public schools (Lloyd, Mete, and Grant forthcoming; Andrabi, Das, and Khwaja 2006).

While there is some debate about the importance of basic inputs in boosting achievement (see, for example, Hanushek and Luque 2002), provision of basic inputs to the poorest schools has yielded positive results. In Brazil, for example, measures of school quality—education of teachers, quality of physical facilities, private ownership of schools—were associated with significantly higher test scores (Albernaz, Ferreira, and Franco 2002). In northeast Brazil a program designed to deliver basic inputs—physical facilities, writing materials, and textbooks—to schools resulted in significant gains in achievement, with no gender differences (Harbison and Hanushek 1992). In Egypt lower quality schools—those with multiple shifts and temporary teachers—increased the likelihood that girls left school, whereas schools with adequate facilities and in-service teacher training decreased their likelihood of dropping out (Lloyd and others 2003).

Schools targeting indigenous children in four of Mexico's poorest states (Chiapas, Guerrero, Hidalgo, and Oaxaca) were provided with supplementary funding to ensure the necessary quantity and quality of books, didactic materials, teachers, school infrastructure, distance education technologies, and institutional strengthening to bolster local management and budget functions. Spanish tests scores rose 42.3 percent in the program group compared with 16.5 percent in the control group. The impacts were greatest for the poor, but the program had less impact on the poorest, the excluded population in

---

1 Basic inputs include knowledgeable teachers, sufficient learning time, good curriculum and instructional material, and an adequate physical environment (Lockheed and Verspoor 1991).

Box 4.1. How Chile reduced the achievement gap between indigenous and nonindigenous students

About 5 percent of Chile's population identifies itself as indigenous, 90 percent of them Mapuche. In 1997 Spanish test scores for indigenous eighth-grade students were nearly half a standard deviation below scores of nonindigenous students, and math test scores were nearly as low. Three years later, these gaps had dropped 30 percent for Spanish and 25 percent for math. Two-thirds of the Spanish test score convergence and all of the math score convergence occurred within rather than across schools, among students with similar family characteristics, largely due to school reform.

Three education reforms were implemented in Chile in the 1990s: the 900 schools program, or P-900; the Equity and Quality Improvement in Education (MECE) program; and the Full School Day reform. Beginning in 1990 the P-900 program provided the lowest performing 10 percent of schools, as identified from test scores, with a package of school inputs, including textbooks, in-service teacher training, and tutoring for low-achieving children. In 1992 all publicly funded schools received a wide range of instructional materials from the MECE. The program also funded school improvement projects intended to boost student learning achievement and provided special assistance in multigrade learning to small, publicly funded primary schools. The third reform, initiated in 1997, subsidized an extended school day in publicly funded schools, initially in schools that were not operating on a split-shift system, such as rural schools.

None of the three reforms targeted indigenous schools, and neither mother tongue nor ethnicity was a criterion for participation. Because indigenous students' performance is lower than that of nonindigenous students and they more frequently attend small rural schools, however, the effect of the reforms was greater in indigenous schools. By 2000, 45 percent of indigenous students and just 23 percent of nonindigenous students were participating in the P-900 program, and 26 percent of indigenous and 8 percent of nonindigenous students were participating in the Full School Day program. Thus without specifically targeting ethnicity or language differences, Chile was able to significantly improve the learning of indigenous children.

Source: McEwan (2006).

---

rural Mexico. The gender differential of impact was not addressed (Paqueo and Lopez-Acevedo 2003). In Chile 10 years of programs providing additional support to the worst performing schools have significantly reduced gaps in achievement between indigenous and nonindigenous students (McEwan 2006) (box 4.1).

Targeting school resources to the poorest performing schools and improving management help retain excluded children, particularly girls, in school. It also boosts these students' learning achievement.

Offering mother tongue–based teaching and bilingual education

The issue of language in OECD countries has proved central to progress in indigenous education. For example, in New Zealand an emphasis on bilingualism has raised the importance and relevance of the Maori language and improved secondary school retention and completion by Maoris. The 2001 census showed improvement in educational attainment for Maori and non-Maori alike, a shift from the stagnation among the Maori between 1986 and 1996 (Census of New Zealand 2001).

A mismatch between the home language and the language of the school has several negative consequences for children (Benson 2005). It may reduce their likelihood of enrolling in school because parents may not understand communications from the school regarding enrollment procedures. It may increase their likelihood of dropping out, as not all of these children acquire sufficient proficiency in the target language to remain in school. And failure and fear of failure may lower these children's aspirations for further education. Girls suffer disproportionately, as they have less access to the world outside their communities and therefore less familiarity with the national language than do their male counterparts.

Corson (1993) notes that "unjust" language policies are particularly detrimental to poor girls who do not speak the language of instruction. Effective bilingual education programs start by developing the child's reading, writing, and thinking skills in the home language, which requires that the teacher be fluent in that language. At the same time, the target language is taught as a subject. The United Nations Education, Scientific, and Cultural Organization (UNESCO) (Benson 2005) describes some bilingual education programs but notes that they are often poorly implemented, as understanding of the theory on which they are based is often lacking, leading to poor design. However, research (Klaus 2003, King and Benson 2003, Hovens 2002, and Benson 2002, all cited in Benson 2005) finds that mother tongue–based bilingual education can help break down barriers faced by girls:

- More girls enroll in school when they can learn in a familiar language.
- Use of the home language in school increases parent participation and influence.
- Teachers from the same linguistic and cultural communities as their students are less likely to exploit girls.
- Girls in bilingual classes stay in school longer.
- Girls learn better and can demonstrate their learning in their mother tongue.
- Bilingual teachers treat girls more fairly than do teachers who do not speak their language.
- Bilingual women are more likely to become teachers and role models for excluded girls.

Parker, Rubalcava, and Teruel (2005) find that access to a bilingual school mitigates the negative effects of a monolingual indigenous mother on enrollment in Mexico. In Guatemala students in bilingual primary schools have higher attendance and promotion rates, lower repetition and dropout rates, and higher achievement scores in all subjects, including Spanish (Hall and Patrinos 2006). Despite the higher cost of bilingual teachers and supplementary curriculum materials, bilingual education pro-duced cost savings of $5 million in 1996—equivalent to the cost of primary school education for 100,000 children in Guatemala—due to lower repetition rates. In Mali bilingual programs led to sharp declines in dropout and repetition, with rural children in bilingual schools outscoring urban children (World Bank 2005c).

Bilingual programs provide access to excluded groups and may be a necessary means of making public schools acceptable to families, particularly for girls. The down-side of bilingual education is that if the program is not well implemented children do not master the majority language, limiting their opportunities for upward mobility.

Strengthening curricula and classrooms and making them more open to diversity

Schools need to reflect the diversity of children in them. Early efforts focused on text-books and included such actions as ensuring that girls and women were represented by nonsteroetyped images, that pictures of people from excluded groups appeared in textbooks, and that textbooks did not refer to urban or international experiences that would be foreign to rural children. These changes were intended to improve student motivation and their perceptions that schools were relevant to them. The effect of these interventions on learning achievement were not evaluated, but the changes are believed to have other benefits, such as those given above (Lockheed and Verspoor 1991).

Pedagogical processes in the classroom need to be changed to increase inclusion. Status expectations that shape interpersonal behavior in classrooms can be addressed by restructuring the learning environment to celebrate differences. Approaches such as cooperative learning or complex instruction require that students work together on complex tasks—teachers are trained to point out the positive contributions of each student in the group's completion of the task (Cohen and Lotan 1997). Evaluations of complex instruction find significant treatment effects. Students in treatment classrooms or groups gained more than those in control classrooms or groups, and the gains were larger for low-status children (Bower 1997; Sharan and Shachar 1988). Cooperative learning and complex instruction approaches can be taught to teachers and become sustained in schools with appropriate levels of supervisory support (Cohen 1997). In a review of major Latin American school interventions to boost learning, Anderson (2005) finds that in-service training for teachers that focused on better pedagogy in the classroom is highly effective in boosting the language achievement of children from poor areas, raising scores 0.8 standard deviations.

Implications for donors and policymakers

Donors can help children transition into mainstream schools by underwriting bilingual schooling to complement public education programs. Donors could, for example, finance informal or community schools for preprimary-age children in difficult-to-reach areas, providing local teachers, materials, and books in local languages. The need for bilingual entry for all children, but especially girls, is crucial for both enrollment and retention of students who come from homes where the national or regional language is not spoken.

Teachers can be agents of change and tolerance, a characteristic of particular importance in ethnically mixed classrooms. Bilingual teachers in particular are often torn between their cultural roots and integration into the national culture. They have the opportunity to change perceptions and behaviors by majority and minority populations (Kudo 2004). Sensitizing teachers and providing them with tools to cope with and address inevitable ethnic and gender tensions in the classroom can contribute to both learning and the integration of cultures.

Donors can support classroom improvements in poorly performing or underfinanced schools by providing school improvement grants. By complementing or supplementing public investments, such grants could support activities designed jointly with recipient communities and teachers to respond to local conditions, build in local monitoring and oversight capacity, and ensure an impact on learning. School improvements benefit both boys and girls, but families consider dilapidated environments less suitable for girls. Combined with concerns over safety, inadequate facilities may tip the balance away from enrollment of girls. Such investments therefore have a strong gender component.

Supporting compensatory preschool and in-school programs

As the OECD experience suggests, simply providing adequate schools will not ensure that excluded children are educated. Additional initiatives are needed.

"Book flooding" to overcome language problems

Millions of children are required to learn, to read, and to write in languages they do not speak at home. One way of helping these children master the language used in school is to "flood" their classrooms with books in the target language and to train teachers in using these books effectively. Variations on the "book flood" strategy have been evaluated in Fiji, New Zealand, Singapore, South Africa, and Sri Lanka (Elley and others 1996). In all of these settings students whose teachers used the approach made rapid and sustained gains in learning the target language.

In a Sri Lanka evaluation involving 16,000 students in 20 book flood schools and 10 control schools, pretest to posttest progress for students in the intervention schools was nearly three times that of students in the control schools (test scores rose about 11 percent for the test group and less than 4 percent for the control group). In a review of interventions in Latin America, Anderson (2005) finds that having a classroom library boosted language achievement by 0.8 of a standard deviation, but it was not effective for the subsample of students from poor areas.

Compensatory preschool programs

Compensatory programs have had mixed results in OECD countries. Programs that remove children from their classes for compensatory instruction have not been successful, while extending the school day or adding programs shows promise.

Evaluations show that the most effective and long-lasting compensatory education programs occur during preschool (Myers 1995). Evidence from the United States and a number of developing countries suggests the vital importance of preschool for children whose parents did not go to school. In developing countries preschool programs need to encourage parental involvement, so that parents are aware of what goes on in classrooms, and to ensure that children are prepared to stay in school once they enter primary.

One of the earliest programs aimed at excluded children whose parents had little if any education was the Head Start program in the United States. Head Start focused on cognitive development, school readiness, and social and emotional development of disadvantaged children between the ages of three and five. Financed by the federal government in the 1960s, Head Start now covers 17 percent of preschool enrollment and has been supplemented by state and municipal programs that provide additional services to low-income parents. Head Start focuses on child development and socialization of children and parents, and it requires the participation of parents. Head Start and programs like it offer outreach services and counseling to parents to help them bridge the gap between home culture and preschool for their children. Recent evaluations find positive impacts (Garces, Thomas, and Currie 2002; Love and others 2005). Similar approaches have been adopted in various forms by many countries and programs.

A study of early childhood programs in Brazil finds that the number of years of preschool has a positive and statistically significant impact on the schooling ultimately attained. It also has a positive and significant impact on the probability that children will reach a given grade at a specific age. An additional year of preschool also reduces repetition by 3–5 percentage points (Pães de Barros and Mendoça 1999).

In 1982 researchers at Boğaziçi University in Istanbul, Turkey, conducted a randomized evaluation of a program to see whether educating poor mothers of three- and five-year-olds improved their children's learning outcomes and whether the effects lasted longer than those of programs that only educated children. The program was evaluated at the end of the project and again seven years later. A series of assessments, tests, and interviews were used to establish a baseline. Mothers were divided into three groups: those with children in an educational preschool, those with children in a custodial daycare center, and those with children at home. Both treatment and control groups were established by random assignment. The intervention involved early childhood enrichment and mother training in low-income areas of Istanbul. All mothers in the project had similar socioeconomic and demographic characteristics—young, rural residence, low levels of education and income. After seven years 86 percent of the children whose mothers had received training were still in school compared with 67 percent of the children whose mothers had not been trained. Scores on primary school math tests were significantly higher for the mother-trained group. Verbal cognitive performance was also higher (Kagitçibasi 1996; Kagitçibasi, Suna, and Bekma 1993).

In Bolivia a large-scale, home-based early childhood development and nutrition program, *Proyecto Integral de Desarrollo Infantil*, provides daycare, nutrition, and educational services to children who live in poor, predominantly urban areas. Children between the ages of six months and six years are cared for in groups of 15 in homes in their own neighborhoods. The community selects local women to become home daycare mothers. These nonformal, home-based daycare centers, with two to three caregivers, provide integrated child development services (play, nutrition, growth screening, and health referrals). The women receive child development training before becoming educators, but they are usually not highly trained and come from the same socioeconomic backgrounds as the parents. Scores of children 37–54 months old participating in the program improved about 5 percent on tests of bulk motor skills, fine motor skills, language skills, and psychosocial skills (Behrman, Cheng, and Todd 2000).

In 1982 an early childhood education project was launched in six states in India, with four more states joining in subsequent years (Bihar, Goa, Karnataka, Madhya Pradesh, Maharashtra, Nagaland, Orissa, Rajasthan, Tamil Nadu, and Uttar Pradesh). The project established 65 early childhood education centers in underprivileged, underdeveloped regions of each state, all attached to primary schools. The centers offered a development-oriented curriculum and encouraged parent participation. Dropout rates were lower among children with early childhood education experience than among children without early childhood education. Retention in primary grades was greater for girls than for boys, especially through grade 4 (Kaul, Ramachandran, and Upadhyaya 1993).

Compensatory primary in-school programs

Compensatory programs may be critical to keeping children from excluded group in school and compensating for the absence of educational reinforcements at home. They may also be necessary to keep students on track and able to keep up with their peers.

The preferential policies that Loury (2000) identifies fall into this category: extra investments for students to ensure that they can raise their skill and capacity levels to effectively compete.

In the United States "accelerated schools" offer programs for ethnic and social minorities to compensate for deficits at home (Hopfenberg and Levin 1993). After-school programs for the disadvantaged have also shown positive effects. In the state of Minas Gerais, Brazil, an extensive after-school program focuses on socialization, tutoring, and curriculum enrichment. Schools with the program enjoyed higher enrollments, lower repetition and dropout rates, and rising tests scores (Pães de Barros, Mendoça, and Soares 1998).

An education program launched in 20 Indian cities by a Mumbai-based NGO provides remedial education to groups of 15–20 children who are lagging behind. Using young female high school graduates from the same slum communities in which the schools are located, the *Balsakhi* program teaches core competencies (basic numeracy and literacy) to second and third-graders. Teachers follow a core curriculum, but there is considerable flexibility in tailoring it to the needs of the children. Teachers are paid \$10–\$15 a month, and turnover is high, suggesting that the program is built on a workable concept rather than the charisma of a leader or the commitment of a few teachers.

A randomized evaluation of the *Balsakhi* program in two Indian cities reveals significant academic progress. Participation in the program increased learning by 0.15 standard deviations in the first year and 0.25 in the second year, with the largest gains recorded for the most economically disadvantaged students. In Vadodara, one of the two cities, test scores of children in the program rose 40 percent more than those of children outside the program. Comparisons between children in the public schools without remedial education and those in the *Balsakhi* program show that remedial education is more than 10 times more cost-effective, suggesting that it may be more efficient than expanding the public teaching force to compensate for repeaters (Banerjee and others 2003).

Spain's School Monitoring Program in Madrid has developed partnerships with Roma-focused NGOs to help integrate Roma children into the public school system. Part of the effort entails tracking the attendance and progress of students. The program promotes preprimary education, completion of compulsory education, and improvement in education habits and socialization skills. The program works with Roma families, social workers, and teachers on education topics, using their input to adjust the curriculum and extracurricular activities to engage Roma children. As of 2000, 16 schools in 3 districts had launched School Monitoring Programs. Student absenteeism is down, participation and engagement in extracurricular activities is high, and contact between Roma and non-Roma students is growing (Martin 2000).

Some Roma parents in these districts still keep their children at home, which points to the difficulty of reaching parents from excluded groups and finding the right mix of enticements and comfort levels that will allow countries to reach the last 1–5 percent of children. These families require affirmative action or preferential policies to convince them that they and their children will not be worse off if their children go to school.

Supplementary assistance appears to pay off for minorities and other excluded groups. Two separate effects appear to be at work: parental education and the achievement levels in the community that reinforce demand for education. Policies that can overcome lack of parental education may need to be supplemented with additional support when "neighborhood" effects must also be overcome.

Parental involvement and support for education

Excluded children typically come from illiterate, disadvantaged families who live in marginalized communities. Parents often lack the time and the capacity to provide educational support to their children.

Research has repeatedly shown parent involvement as a strong predictor of student achievement (for example, Postlethwaite and Ross 1992). Parent involvement includes engaging parents and communities in the governance of schools as well as encouraging parents to provide a supportive home environment in which children can learn. Involving parents also helps assure them that their girls are safe at school.

Children of parents who have not been to school, are illiterate, or simply do not have books at home are at a disadvantage. Books in the home signal a commitment to education—their absence suggests not only a low regard for education but also restricted access to books and reference material that enrich and support education, explicitly and implicitly. Numerous studies have identified the impact of parental support of education on achievement. The International Association for the Evaluation of Achievment's (IEA) 1991 international assessment of reading literacy across 26 countries finds that such proxies for parental support of education as the number of books in the home were positively correlated (corr. = 0.20 or higher), with achievement in 19 of the countries studied (Postlethwaite and Ross 1992). IEA's 1995 international assessment of mathematics achievement finds that students from homes with large numbers of books, a range of educational study aids, or parents with university-level education had higher mathematics achievement (Martin and others 2000; Beaton and others 1996). A repeat of the study in 1999 (TIMSS) involving 41 countries created an index of home educational resources that included books in the home, study aids (a computer, a study desk or table for the student's use, and a dictionary), and at least one parent with a university education (Mullis and others 2000). Across all countries, students with a high level of home educational resources scored 128 points (about 1.25 standard deviations) higher than students with a low level of home resources—about the same difference as between the highest scoring country (Singapore) and the international average.

IEA's 2001 international assessment of reading achievement at the primary level in 35 countries (PIRLS) finds that children of parents who engaged in early home literacy activities (such as reading a book, playing with alphabet toys, or reading aloud signs or labels) scored 40 points higher (about half a standard deviation) than did children whose parents did not engage in such activities—about two-thirds of the difference between the highest scoring country (Sweden) and the international average (Mullis and others 2003).

Evidence from OECD countries suggests the importance of local activism and control over schools (Lindert 2004). In Colombia, Iran, and Thailand local decision-making about supplies and the hiring of teachers led to higher test results in both mathematics and science (Woessmann 2000). In the Republic of Korea the establishment of parent-teacher associations under the US occupation following World War II increased parental involvement in and contributions to primary schooling, which drove the surge in enrollment and completion in the 1960s (Lewis 2005).

Reaching parents as part of efforts to attract excluded children, particularly girls, is fundamental to success in developing countries as well. Town meetings, one-on-one canvassing, and other means of reaching parents to explain the purpose and the plan for education programs are critical. For example, in Himachal Pradesh, India, regular meetings of parents and local officials have led to effective community oversight of teacher attendance and performance and a shared burden in overseeing student attendance and the safety of schools for girls (De and Drèze 1999).

Busing

Sometimes reaching a better school rather than upgrading an existing one represents the best or most affordable option, especially where geographic divisions are effectively segregating schools. Integrating schools through busing proved both highly controversial but highly effective in the United States (Weatherford 1980). Integrated schools provide the ultimate socialization for excluded children.

In Vidin, Bulgaria, the Open Society Institute and a local NGO experimented with busing Roma children to mainstream schools as a way of improving the quality of education. The program encompassed intensive efforts with school administrators, teachers, and Roma parents. School monitors ensured that Roma children were not mistreated, a common complaint of Roma parents. Roma children were also provided with free lunches and shoes. The results were 100 percent enrollment, a doubling in the initial number of children in school to 920, and parity in test scores with non-Roma children, a major achievement (Ringold, Orenstein, and Wilkens 2003). It is not clear whether parents responded to the free lunches or shoes, the monitors, or the schooling option. What is evident is that the package of interventions made a significant difference in altering behavior of a large group of out-of-school children.

Implications for donors and policymakers

Financing the compensatory costs associated with reaching excluded children can pro-vide parents with a major incentive for keeping children in school. After-school super-vision and academic support, remedial programs for those behind on entry, special summer enrichment initiatives, and the like have been shown to be effective in OECD countries. They deserve attention and investment in low-income settings.

Children who do not receive reinforcement at home need school-based support to succeed. But like other extras, such programs are not generally affordable in develop-ing countries. Simple after-school activities can build social capital among children or ensure that students have a place to complete homework. Both kinds of efforts deserve donor attention. Ensuring that girls in particular have a place to do their homework is critical because they are more likely to to be expected to perform domestic chores, which reduce the time available to complete homework.

Financing transportation for excluded children, possibly separately for girls, could respond to the safety concerns of parents whose daughters must travel to other villages for secondary school. In less accessible locations older women could be paid to accompany girls to schools outside their villages. A logical extension of the transporta-tion issue is construction of basic infrastructure, not only roads but communications as well. Roads make it easier for teachers and textbooks to reach schools and students; communication and electrical infrastructure broaden the schooling options beyond teachers and textbooks. Traditional school buildings, materials, and latrines tend to be underfinanced, especially in the poorest areas.

"Flooding" rural schools and those serving disadvantaged groups with books and libraries—and training teachers to encourage students to use them—can only help fos-ter reading. A major impediment to demand for literacy among adults is the limited need for literacy skills. Most schools in developing countries lack libraries. What better way to reinforce classroom learning than by making books available on loan?

Parents from socially excluded groups need to be involved if new programs are to be successful. Programs that engage parents in parent-teacher associations or other venues that get them involved help parents who have never been to school understand the process and objectives of schooling and bring them into the decisionmaking pro-cess. Not including them can prove disastrous if they see little value in the innovations offered to their children, and the greater sensitivity regarding daughters means that involving parents is particularly important for girls.

Middle-income countries, such as Brazil, Chile, and Mexico, have pioneered means of reaching the excluded, but many countries cannot afford the extra efforts. It falls to donors to pick up the cost of these necessary but costly initiatives.

Creating incentives for households to send girls to school

Cultural taboos, the opportunity cost of labor, low demand for education, and reluctance to allow children, especially girls, to enter mainstream schools contribute to low enrollment, completion, and achievement rates among excluded groups. Several efforts to overcome some of these concerns—or simply to make it financially worthwhile for families to change their views regarding schooling for girls—have shown promise. With few exceptions, efforts have not yet focused on excluded groups, who may require more than income supplements to send their girls to school. In targeting the poor, however, they are more likely to capture marginalized girls.

Conditional cash transfer programs implicitly embrace Pritchett's (2004) contention that getting children into school pays off whether or not learning occurs, because girls who attend school will send their daughters to school, initiating a virtuous cycle. There is strong evidence that paying parents to send their children to school increases attendance. But simply going to school may not be enough with excluded groups, as the behavior of blacks in the inner cities of the United States, the Japanese Burakumin, and the Roma, among others, demonstrate. Conditional cash transfers alone may not yield the payoffs achieved in homogeneous populations because of the discrimination and pain excluded groups suffer at heterogeneous schools. But this hypothesis has yet to be tested.

Scholarship programs for girls have also demonstrated their effectiveness in encouraging parents to send girls to school and in helping girls complete school. Whether underwriting education costs will be sufficient to attract and keep excluded girls in school remains to be seen.

Conditional cash transfers

Conditional cash transfers provide resources to households that engage in desirable behaviors, such as enrolling and keeping their children in school. Although challenging to administer in many settings, conditional cash transfers offer incentives to families to invest in education (at least in terms of the opportunity costs of their children's labor) and put the onus on the family to make sure that children go to school—something that school officials often find impossible to do. Seven major conditional cash transfer programs have been evaluated (table 4.1).

Brazil's *Bolsa Escola* was the first such program. It remains the largest, currently enrolling more than 5 million families. *Bolsa Escola* has proven to be one of the most successful anti-poverty programs in Brazil, and school attendance has risen nationwide, reflecting expanded school attendance by low-income children. The program has recently undergone a radical restructuring that combines multiple social programs under a single federal agency with a new name, *Bolsa Familia*.

Table 4.1. Impacts of selected conditional cash transfer programs

Program (country and date)	Design	Coverage
Bolsa Escola (Brazil 1995)	Federal program administered by local government for dedicated credit card–based transfers to mothers in poor households, conditional on children 6–15 maintaining 85 percent attendance. Participants must attend after-school activities and cannot work.	5 million families, 8.6 million children in 98 percent of municipalities in Brazil.
Bono de Desarollo Humano (Ecuador 2003)	National program targeting poorest families. Program links school attendance to cash transfer to women of $15 a month.	1,391 households, 3,072 school-age children, representing 40 percent of poorest households.
Food for Education (Bangladesh 1993)	Centrally designed and administered monthly food transfer program to poor households conditional on 85 percent attendance by primary school-age children (ages 6–10).	2.1 million students (12 percent of all primary students) in 1,247 municipalities covering all 64 districts.
Programa de Asignación Familiar (Honduras 2000)	Centrally designed and implemented program for cash transfers to mothers. Phase I: Education voucher provided to mothers of up to three children in grades 1–3. Phase II: Education voucher for primary school–age children conditional on attendance; program included nutrition and health voucher component.	70,000 households in 50 municipalities of 7 departments.
Progresa/ Oportunidades (Mexico 1997)	Federally designed and administered program for cash transfers to mothers in poor households, conditional on school-age children maintaining 85 percent attendance. Grants increase with grade, higher for girls in secondary school. Noncompliance leads to temporary or permanent loss of benefit.	2.6 million families in 2,000 municipalities and 31 states (40 percent of all rural households).

Targeting mechanism	Impact[a]
Municipal eligibility determined by poverty indices, child eligibility determined by local committee. Child is ineligible if per capita monthly income of family is more than $36 (half the minimum wage).	*Enrollment:* No formal estimates of impact. Earlier school entry age. *Attendance:* Rose 79 percent on average. *Dropout:* 0.40 percent (5.6 percent for nonbeneficiaries). *Performance:* 80 percent promotion rate (72 percent for nonbeneficiaries), no difference in learning outcomes between beneficiaries and nonbeneficiaries.
Obscure eligibility criteria led to poor targeting. Current targeting uses a poverty index (Selben) based on household characteristics.	*Attendance:* Rose 10 percentage points, with largest increases in secondary school, where all new enrollments occurred. *Dropout:* Declined 3.1–3.6 percentage points.
Backward areas identified by the government. Households chosen by local committees of parents, teachers, local representatives, education specialists, and school donors.	*Enrollment:* Rose 44 percent for girls, 28 percent for boys. *Attendance:* Rose 70 percent (58 percent in nonparticipating schools). *Dropout:* 6 percent (15 percent for nonbeneficiaries).
Municipality-level targeting based on height-for-age data for first graders. All households in municipalities with children in relevant age group are eligible.	*Enrollment:* No measurable change in primary school enrollment. *Dropout:* Some reduction.
Localities identified by "marginality index" of poverty and illiteracy, with verification by local officials. Eligible households informed of responsibilities at local general assembly.	*Enrollment:* Increased 0.7–1.1 percent for boys and 1.0–1.5 for girls in primary school, 7.2–9.3 for boys and 3.5–5.8 for girls in secondary school. Earlier school entry age. *Attendance:* No impact. *Dropout:* Lower dropout rates and higher school re-entry rates among dropouts. *Completion:* Increase in transition to secondary school (6th to 7th grade): 20 percent for girls, 10 percent for boys. *Performance:* Better grade progression. No change in achievement test scores.

(Continues on next page)

Table 4.1. Impacts of selected conditional cash transfer programs (continued)

Program	Design	Coverage
Red de Protección Social (Nicaragua 2000)	Centrally designed and administered cash transfer program providing education subsidies to households with children 7–13 enrolled in grades 1–4, conditional on 85 percent attendance. Health subsidy conditional on scheduled health visits and information lectures.	10,000 households in 6 municipalities in 2 of poorest states.
Subsidio Unitario Familiar (Chile 1981)	Local government–administered program that provides mothers in eligible families (income < $2,400) a family subsidy if pregnant, caring for invalids, or with school-age children in school. Covers children up to age 18. Eligibility reassessed every two years.	5.6 million people (36.5 percent of population).

a. Impact reported only for some countries and for some characteristics.

Source: Morley and Coady 2003; Schady and Araujo 2006.

While Nicaragua's *Red de Protección Social* increased primary enrollment 18 percentage points, other conditional cash transfer programs in Central America have met with mixed success (Morley and Coady 2003). For example, Honduras's *Programa de Asignación Familiar* showed no impact on primary enrollment, though it did lead to a modest decline in dropout rates, due in part to enhanced administrative and oversight capacity (Caldes, Coady, and Maluccio 2004; Coady 2004).

Mexico's *Progresa* program is three separate transfer programs—for social assistance, health, and education—each with its own eligibility criteria. In education mothers receive bimonthly stipends contingent on sending their children to school at least 80 percent of the time. Results show a 3.4 percent increase in enrollment for grades 1–6. This achievement is less than it appears at first sight, as primary education was already close to universal (Schultz 2004). Lower secondary school enrollment was 64 percent before the program was introduced and 76 percent afterward. Enrollment by girls rose almost 15 percentage points (figure 4.1). Although the program targeted the poorest states in southern Mexico, it did not explicitly address ethnicity; the degree to which indigenous groups participate is not known.

De Janvry and Sadoulet (2004) suggest that the efficiency of the *Progresa* program could be enhanced by adjusting eligibility criteria, particularly at the lower secondary school level. Their proposal would directly affect excluded groups in remote areas, as these are the least served and the most difficult to reach. Sixty-four percent of those receiving transfers would have gone to secondary school without the transfer, and 24 percent of eligible children do not attend school, meaning that their parents choose to

Targeting mechanism	Impact
Poor municipalities targeted on basis of education and health access and organizational capacity. Submunicipal units and houses were then targeted on basis of poverty and marginality index; 21 treatment units, 21 control units.	*Enrollment:* 22 percent increase in new enrollment, 29 percent increase in continued enrollment. *Dropout:* 41 percent decline. *Performance:* Grade progression increased 8.2 percent for progression from first to second grade, 7.3 percent from second to third, and 6.2 percent from third to fourth. Additional improvement for beneficiary cohort that progressed beyond grade 4.
Proxy means test based on household data. Responses scored according to a weighting scheme; 90 percent of benefits go to poorest 40 percent of population.	

forgo the roughly $200 a year stipend. De Janvry and Sadoulet argue that focusing on cases where the conditionality will alter behavior would improve efficiency. Targeting difficult-to-reach children, those with an indigenous parent, or girls living in communities without a secondary school would help bring the most excluded into the schooling system and would disproportionately affect girls. Attracting and retaining girls in lower secondary is the needed next step.

Ecuador's *Bono de Desarollo Humano* program showed much more impressive results than Mexico's program, with primary school enrollment rising 10 percentage points. The difference probably reflects initial variations in national enrollment levels. Ecuador's primary enrollment averages 90 percent, but the figure is lower in rural, indigenous, and low-income areas. Average years of schooling are 6.5, with the rate for indigenous groups half that. The largest program effects occurred among poorer households and older children who continued on to secondary school. Contact with parents regarding the need to send children to school in order to receive the transfer fueled the growth in enrollment, particularly at the secondary level. Despite the lack of enforcement, enrollment increases have not been reversed, possibly because households may not want to risk losing the transfer (Schady and Araujo 2006).

In Bangladesh, where in-kind rather than cash transfers are provided, impact assessments consistently show improved attendance, declines in child labor, and increased completion. The transfers had the same effect on school attendance as cash transfers, but child labor declined only slightly, in contrast to other settings (Ravallion and Wodon 2000).

The Community Support Program in Balochistan, Pakistan, provides a variant

Figure 4.1. Mexico has had some success in education under its *Progresa/Oportunidades* program, 1998

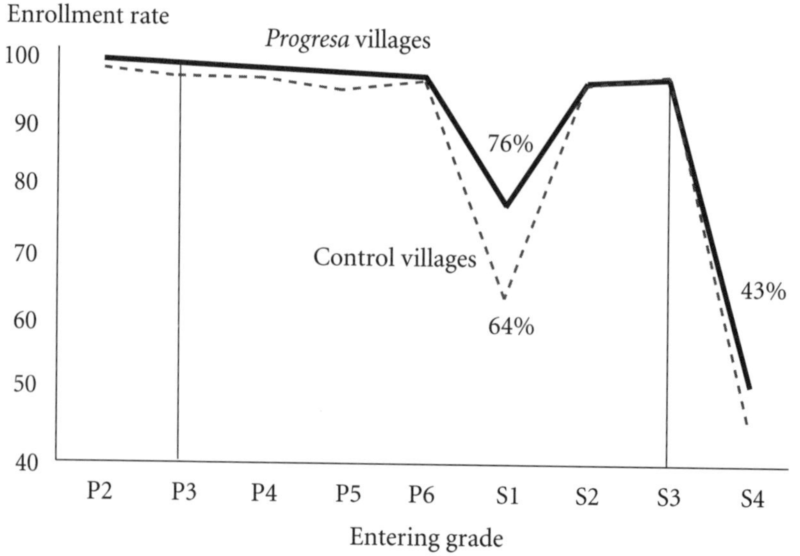

Note: *Progresa* intervention starts in the third year of primary and ends after the third year of secondary. P = primary, S = secondary.
Source: De Janvry and Sadoulet 2004.

on the conditional cash transfer by targeting communities without schools and communities with low schooling attendance among girls. The successful program included roles for the community and parents as well as transfers to households. Because it is the only conditional cash transfer–type effort with a parental involvement component and there were no controls, no conclusions are possible, but it suggests the importance of linking conditional cash transfer with other initiatives when attempting to reach the hardcore holdouts to primary schooling (Kim, Alderman, and Orazem 1998; Khalid and Mukhtar 2002).

Other incentives and subsidies for households have shown promise in bringing girls into school. Using a randomized evaluation Kremer, Moulin, and Namunyu (2002) show that in-kind provision of textbooks and uniforms (as well as classroom construction) to seven schools in rural Kenya led to a 15 percent increase in schooling after five years—two years sooner than in schools that did not receive the intervention.

In Japan Burakumin children attend secondary school at about two-thirds the rate of the majority population. National programs to provide free textbooks for Burakumin students in the 1970s, as a way to induce school attendance, initiated the practice of government-financed textbooks in Japan. In addition, some jurisdictions provide stipends to encourage parents to send their adolescents to school (Meerman 2005).

Significant administrative capacity is needed to ensure that transfers reach target families and that the link between school attendance and stipends is maintained. In countries with limited capacity, operating a conditional cash transfer may not be feasible if done through government channels.

Scholarships for girls

Scholarships for girls offer both financing for and encouragement to stay in secondary school (Herz and Sperling 2004). Scholarships compensate families for the direct and indirect costs of education. For them to attract new students into the system, households must view cost as an impediment. Scholarships for excluded girls may need to be accompanied by other forms of compensatory support to help them succeed. In the United States offers of college tuition payments have led to mixed results among minorities, partly because children did not have the academic fundamentals needed to excel and partly due to peer effects of the community.

The best known and most effect scholarship program for girls is in Bangladesh. It produced remarkable results in a short time. Introduced in a quarter of Bangladesh's administrative districts, the program increased girls' enrollment to 44 percent—roughly twice the national average—after five years (Khandker, Pitt, and Fuwa 2003). The program was then expanded nationwide. Girls recently overtook boys in school completion in Bangladesh, which may partly reflect the expansion of the program. Given its homogeneous population, Bangladesh may not provide the best example for reaching excluded groups, but it does demonstrate that conservative parents in developing countries will respond to financial incentives and that their reluctance to educating their daughters can be overcome.

Stipend programs compensate parents in much the same way that scholarships and conditional cash transfer programs do, though they are at least notionally tied to school inputs such as uniforms, books, materials, and transportation. These efforts can be linked to specific purchases or provided as transfers to households that allow them to allocate the funds as they see fit. The programs offer flexibility and avoid the bureaucratic management of funds for books and school supplies. For this reason, stipends may be particularly relevant in some settings, especially those with weak administrative capacity.

Stipend programs have led to significant increases in enrollments, often in alternate schools. In Kenya learning and performance rose among girls who received scholarships. Test scores of nonscholarship boys and girls attending schools in which some girls received scholarships also rose, teacher and student attendance increased, and study habits improved—all positive externalities of the program (Kremer, Miguel, and Thornton 2004). Because the stipends were meant to cover fees and school costs, teachers and schools benefited from reliable, if not increased, revenues.

School feeding programs

School feeding programs appear to be tied to higher attendance and enrollment. In some cases they have also been associated with reduced dropout rates and higher student achievement.

Many of the relevant evaluations have been plagued by statistical problems. For example, studies based on unrepresentative samples, biased selections of schools or unreliable data result in ambiguous findings. Often socioeconomic status cannot be captured, as studies tend to be school-based, so the equity implications cannot be drawn.

Some studies have overcome these obstacles. Based on evaluations in eight countries, Levinger (1986) concludes that school feeding programs are most effective in meeting school attendance objectives. Success is enhanced where attendance is relatively low at the outset and children come from low socioeconomic households.[2] Attendance declines, however, sometimes dramatically, when food programs are suspended (Levinger 1986; Del Rosso 1999). Evidence from India suggests that school feeding has contributed to increases in school enrollment (Drèze and Kingdon 1999).

Despite the uncertain long-term effects of feeding programs, they offer a means of drawing families into the school system. Parent committees often manage the food or prepare the meals, increasing their concern and involvement in school issues (Levinger 1986; Janke 1996; World Food Program 2004). Low-income communities outside Buenos Aires operate community gardens to grow food for the lunches that local women prepare for underprivileged school children. Parental engagement is a valuable byproduct of school feeding programs (Lewis 2005).

In Kenya, one of the world's most heterogeneous countries, a randomized evaluation shows that school meals in 25 schools raised attendance 30 percent relative to 25 schools without the free lunch. Test scores rose 0.4 standard deviations in contrast to the control schools that showed no change in scores (Vermeersch and Kremer 2004). But the program appeared to benefit boys more than girls. The program boosted the weight of boys but not girls, and it boosted girls' written test scores, but not their oral performance, a pattern often associated with negative expectations of teachers. While small, this carefully conducted study suggests the potential value of providing food for children. Obviously, the long-term implications are not clear. But the Vermeersch and Kremer (2004) study reinforces the findings of less rigorous studies, and the food program serves to attract otherwise out-of-school children into the educational system.

Implications for donors and policymakers

Governments and multilateral donors have forged partnerships for conditional cash

---

2. Programs in Colombia, Jamaica, and the Philippines had minimal impact, because enrollment and attendance were already close to universal (Levinger 1986; World Food Program 2004).

transfers in much of Latin America. Expanding these initiatives to additional countries and to harder to reach groups could increase enrollment of excluded girls. Providing conditional cash transfers to families of excluded girls and initiating rigorous evaluations would help determine whether these initiatives work. Testing such programs in Africa is a priority, given the dearth of evidence and the lack of experimentation and evaluation across the continent. Donors could finance and manage conditional cash transfers for low-income countries that lack the managerial capacity and resources to conduct such programs.

Scholarships for girls have demonstrated such promise that donor initiatives to expand such programs to lower secondary, higher secondary, and tertiary education would do much to increase the stock of educated women in low-income countries. These women, who are not from the elite, offer both potential leadership and role models for girls. Stipend programs also hold promise. Donors could provide the funding needed to ensure that girls enroll and stay in school.

Financing school meals can attract children to school. Feeding programs also provide employment for and involve parents, reinforcing the school as a focus of community life. Meals offer a potentially important draw for excluded families in poverty. The ability of such programs to attract excluded girls remains untested. Donors could fund feeding programs targeting excluded girls to determine whether such programs are effective. Such programs offer an entry point to help upgrade schools, and provide the potential for additional help to children from excluded groups whose attendance or performance are faltering.

Conclusions and recommendations

The evidence suggests a menu of possible interventions for increasing enrollment and achievement by girls, particularly girls from excluded groups. All options will not be appropriate in every setting. Some options to consider include:

- Eliminating legal and administrative barriers to girls' education.
- Expanding opportunity through a trust fund for multilateral programs targeting excluded girls. The fund could support alternative schooling options, innovative programs for adolescent girls, transportation for excluded girls, and some targeted construction of basic infrastructure.
- Improving the quality of schools serving excluded girls by underwriting primary schools, financing the provision of books and textbooks, training teachers to promote tolerance and inclusion, and providing school improvement grants.
- Establishing safe havens for girls in school by creating an inviting environment that gives parents confidence that their daughters will not be harmed or abused. Gender diversity training for teachers, which can be provided inexpensively, could help.

- Promoting positive discrimination through compensatory interventions that help excluded children overcome past inequities.
- Creating demand by financing compensatory costs associated with reaching excluded children, promoting outreach programs for parents, building partnerships for conditional cash transfers, providing scholarships for girls, and providing school meals.
- Supporting heterogeneous countries to participate in international assessments and to measure learning outcomes generally and across subgroups.
- Expanding the knowledge base about what works to improve the school participation and achievement of excluded girls by creating a girls' education evaluation fund that would finance evaluations of initiatives to build the knowledge base for policy.
- Addressing the need for bilingual teachers, books, and instructional materials in lower primary grades in schools serving indigenous populations.

Vouchers will have little effect where demand for education is low. Just building schools is also unlikely to entice families for which the opportunity cost of sending their children to school is high (as it is in many rural areas, where children work in agriculture), families that fear that their daughters will not be safe en route to or in school (as is the case in much of Africa and South Asia), families that expect mistreatment by school administrators and teachers (as the Roma in Eastern Europe do), or families that question the value of schooling or consider it too expensive for their daughters. These groups require more tailored approaches and engagement—and incentives that address these constraints.

Scholarships, which have shown great promise in many settings, may make a difference, but if girls face discrimination within the classroom or have inadequate preparation or study skills, monetary incentives may not be enough to keep them in school. This has been the case among excluded groups in high-income OECD countries, where supplementary investments, engagement of parents, and other targeted initiatives have been required to overcome low demand for education.

Donors have a panoply of investment options that complement government actions, substitute for lack of government funding, or foster collaboration across donor organizations and the multilaterals. Big-ticket items such as a girls' education evaluation fund or a trust fund for multilateral programs permit funding and contracting able organizations to test and implement programs with a high probability of significant impact. This book would not have been possible without similar efforts in the past which are now guiding future investments and actions. Without dedicated investments, the 60 million girls out of school will stay there, to the detriment of their countries and the world.

References

Abadzi, H. 2006. *Efficient Learning for the Poor.* Washington, D.C. World Bank.

Adam, K. 1997. "The Politics of Redress: South African Style Affirmative Action." *Journal of Modern African Studies* 35 (2): 231–49.

Afenyadu, D., and L. Goparaju. 2003. "Adolescent Sexual and Reproductive Health Behavior in Dodowa, Ghana." Centre for Development and Population Activities, Washington, D.C.

Aggarwal, Y. 2001. *Progress towards Universal Access and Retention: Analytical Report, District Report Cards.* New Delhi: National Institute of Educational Planning and Administration.

Aguero, J. M. 2005. "Negative Stereotypes and Willingness to Change: Testing Theories of Discrimination in South Africa." Staff Paper 488, University of Wisconsin-Madison, Department of Agricultural and Applied Economics, Madison, Wis.

Albernaz, A., F. Ferreira, and C. Franco. 2002. "Qualidade e equidade no ensino fundamental Brasileiro." *Pesquisa e Planejamento Economico* 32 (3): 453–76.

Alderman, H., and E. M. King. 1998. "Gender Differences in Parental Investment in Education." *Structural Change and Economic Dynamics* 9 (4): 453–68.

Alesina, A., A. Devleeschauwer, W. Easterly, S. Kurlat, and R. Wacziarg. 2003. "Fractionalization." *Journal of Economic Growth* 8 (2): 155–94.

Al-Samarrai, S., and T. Peasgood. 1998. "Education Attainments and Household Characteristics in Tanzania." *Economics of Education Review* 17 (4): 395–417.

Alva, S., E. Murrugarra, and P. Paci. 2002. "The Hidden Costs of Ethnic Conflict: Decomposing Trends in Educational Outcomes of Young Kosovars." Policy Research Working Paper 2880. World Bank, Washington, D.C.

Amadio, M. 1997. "Primary Education: Length of Studies and Instructional Time." *Educational Innovation and Information* 92: 2–7.

Amir, Y., and S. Sharan, eds. 1984. *School Desegregation: Cross-Cultural Perspectives*. Hillsdale, N.J.: Lawrence Erlbaum Associates.

Anderson, J. 2005. "Improving Latin America's School Quality: Which Special Interventions Work?" *Comparative Education Review* 49 (2): 205–29.

Andrabi, T., J. Das, and I. Asim. 2006. "Students Today, Teachers Tomorrow? The Rise of Affordable Private Schools." Draft Working Paper. Development Economics Group, World Bank, Washington, D.C.

Anzar, U. 1999. "Education Reforms in Balochistan (1990–1998): A Case Study in Improving Management and Gender Equality in Primary Education." Working Paper. World Bank, Education Department of the Human Development Network, Washington, D.C.

Armor, D. J., and C. H. Rossell. 2002. "Desegregation and Resegregation in the Public Schools." In A. Thernstrom and S. Thernstrom, eds., *Beyond the Color Line*. Palo Alto, Calif.: Hoover Institution Press.

Aronson, J., M. J. Lustina, C. Good, K. Keough, C. M. Steele, and J. Brown. 1999. "When White Men Can't Do Math: Necessary and Sufficient Factors in Stereotype Threat." *Journal of Experimental and Social Psychology* 35 (1): 29–46.

Arrow, K. J. 1973. "The Theory of Discrimination." In O. Ashenfelter and A. Rees, eds., *Discrimination in Labor Markets*. Princeton, N.J.: Princeton University Press.

Ausubel, D. 1960. *The Fern and the Tiki: An American View of New Zealand National Character, Social Attitudes, and Race Relations*. London: Angus & Robertson.

Bailey, B. 2004. "Gender and Education in Jamaica: Who Is Achieving and by Whose Standard?" *Prospects* 34 (1): 53–70.

Baker, D., and G. LeTendre. 2005. *National Differences, Global Similarities: World Culture and the Future of Schooling*. Palo Alto, Calif.: Stanford University Press.

Baker, D., R. Fabrega, C. Galindo, and J. Mishook. 2004. "Instructional Time and National Achievement: Cross National Evidence." *Prospects* 34 (3): 311–34.

Banerjee, A., S. Cole, E. Duflo, and L. Linden. 2005. "Remedying Education: Evidence from Two Randomized Experiments in India." Working Paper 109, Bureau for Research in Economic Analysis of Development, Harvard University, Cambridge, Mass.

Barrington, J. 1991. "The New Zealand Experience: Maoris." In M. Gibson and J. Obgu, eds., *Minority Status and Schooling: A Comparative Study of Immigrant and Involuntary Minorities*. New York: Garland Publishing.

Barro, R. J., and J.-W. Lee. 2000. "International Data on Educational Attainment: Updates and Implications." CID Working Paper 42, Center for International Development, Harvard University, Cambridge, Mass.

Bashir, S. 1994. "Public versus Private in Primary Education: A Comparison of School Effectiveness and Costs in Tamil Nadu." PhD dissertation, London School of Economics, Faculty of Economics, London.

Basu, K., and Z. Tzannatos. 2003. "The Global Child Labor Problem: What Do We Know and What Can We Do?" *World Bank Economic Review* 17 (2): 147–74.

Bates, L. M., S. R. Schuler, and F. Islam. 2004. "Socioeconomic Factors and Processes Associated with Domestic Violence in Rural Bangladesh." *International Family Planning Perspectives* 30

(4): 190–99.

Beaton, A., I. Mullis, M. Martin, E. Gonzalez, D. Kelly, and T. Smith. 1996. *Mathematics Achievement in the Middle School Years: IEA's Third International Mathematics and Science Study.* Chestnut Hill, Mass.: Boston College, Center for the Study of Testing, Evaluation and Educational Policy.

Becker, G. S. 1971. *The Economics of Discrimination,* 2nd ed. Chicago, Ill.: University of Chicago Press.

Behrman, J. R., and N. Birdsall. 1985. "The Quality of Schooling: Quantity Alone Is Misleading." *American Economic Review* 73 (5): 928–46.

Behrman, J. R., and A. Deolalikar. 1995. "Are There Differential Returns to Schooling by Gender? The Case of Indonesian Labor Markets." *Oxford Bulletin of Economics and Statistics* 57 (1): 97–117.

Behrman, J. R., and P. Sengupta. 2002. *The Returns to Female Schooling in Developing Countries Revisited.* Philadelphia, Pa.: University of Pennsylvania, Department of Economics.

Behrman, J. R., Y. Cheng, and P. Todd. 2000. "Evaluating Preschool Programs when Length of Exposure to the Program Varies: A Nonparametric Approach." PIER Working Paper 01-034, Penn Institute for Economic Research, University of Pennsylvania, Department of Economics, Philadelphia, Pa. [http://ssrn.com/abstract=286296 or DOI: 10.2139/ssrn.286296].

Behrman, J. R., S. Duryea, and M. Szekely. 1999. *Schooling Investments and Aggregate Conditions: A Household-Survey-Based Approach for Latin America and the Caribbean.* Washington, D.C.: Inter-American Development Bank.

Behrman, J. R., A. Gaviria, and M. Szekely, eds. 2003. *Who's In and Who's Out: Social Exclusion in Latin America.* Washington, D.C.: Inter-American Development Bank.

Behrman, J. R., A. Foster, M. R. Rosenzweig, and P. Vashishtha. 1999. "Women's Schooling, Home Teaching, and Economic Growth." *Journal of Political Economy* 107 (4): 682–719

Benavot, A. 2002. "Educational Globalisation and the Allocation of Instructional Time in National Education Systems." Report submitted to the International Bureau of Education as a contribution to UNESCO's *Education for All Global Monitoring Report 2002.* United Nations Educational, Scientific, and Cultural Organization, Geneva.

———. 2004. "Factors Affecting Actual Instructional Time in Primary Schools: A Literature Review Prepared for the World Bank-IBE Study on Instructional Time." Contract No. ED 871-138-3, International Bureau of Education, Geneva.

———. 2005. "A Global Study of Intended Instructional Time and Official School Curricula, 1980–2000." Background paper for the *EFA Global Monitoring Report 2006: The Quality Imperative, 2005.* United Nations Educational, Scientific, and Cultural Organization, Paris.

Benson, C. 2002. "Real and Potential Benefits of Bilingual Programmes in Developing Countries." *International Journal of Bilingual Education and Bilingualism* 5 (6): 303–17.

———. 2005. *Mother Tongue–Based Teaching and Education for Girls.* Bangkok: United Nations Educational, Scientific, and Cultural Organization.

Berger, J., and M. Zelditch, eds. 1985. *Status, Rewards, and Influence.* San Francisco, Calif.: Jossey-Bass.

Berger, J., M. H. Fisk, R. Norman, and M. Zelditch. 1977. *Status Characteristics and Social Interaction.* New York: Elsevier.

Bieber, F. 1999. "Seminar Report." Paper presented at the Minority Rights and the Freedom of

Religion in Balkan Countries conference, September 24–26, Herceg-Novi, Montenegro.

Bilquees, F., and N. Saqib. 2004. *Dropout Rates and Inter-school Movements: Evidence from Panel Data in Pakistan.* Islamabad: Pakistan Institute of Development Economics.

Binkley, M., J. W. Guthrie, and T. J. Wyatt. 1991. *A Survey of National Assessment and Examination Practices in OECD Countries.* Lugano, Switzerland: Organisation for Economic Co-operation and Development.

Birdsall, N., and R. Sabot. 1996. "The Quality of Schooling and Labor Market Outcomes." In N. Birdsall and R. Sabot, eds., *Opportunity Foregone: Education in Brazil.* Washington, D.C.: Johns Hopkins Press for the Inter-American Development Bank.

Birdsall, N., R. Levine, and A. Ibrahim, eds. 2005. *Towards Universal Primary Education: Investments, Incentives and Institutions.* Sterling, Va.: Stylus Publishing.

Bjorkman, M. 2006. "Income Shocks and Gender Gaps in Education: Evidence from Uganda." Harvard University, Economics Department, Cambridge, Mass.

Bloch, M., J. A. Beoku-Betts, and B. R. Tabachnick. *Women and Education in Sub-Saharan Africa: Power, Opportunities and Constraints.* Boulder, Colo.: Lynne Rienner.

Bodewig, C., and A. Sethi. 2005. "Poverty, Social Exclusion and Ethnicity in Serbia and Montenegro: The Case of the Roma." World Bank, Human Development Department of the East and Central Asia Vice-Presidency, Washington, D.C.

Bosch, A. 1997. "Interactive Radio Instruction: Twenty-Three Years of Improving Educational Quality." World Bank, Human Development Network, Washington, D.C.

Boston, T. D., and U. Nair-Reichert. 2003. "Affirmative Action: Perspectives from the United States, India and Brazil." *Western Journal of Black Studies* 27(1): 3–14.

Bower, B. 2000. "Effects of the Multi-Ability Curriculum in Secondary Social Studies Classrooms." In E. G. Cohen and R. M. Lotan, eds., *Working for Equity in Heterogeneous Classrooms.* New York: Teachers College Press.

Bray, M. 1996. *Counting the Full Cost: Parental and Community Financing of Education in East Asia.* Washington, D.C.: World Bank.

Bruce, J., and C. Lloyd. 1996. "Find the Ties that Bind: Beyond Headship and Household." In L. Haddad, J. Hoddinott, and H. Alderman, eds., *Intra-Household Resource Allocation in Developing Countries: Methods, Models and Policy.* Baltimore, Md.: Johns Hopkins University Press.

Brunnen, B. 2004. "Working towards Parity: Recommendations of the Aboriginal Human Capital Strategies Initiative." Building the New West Report 24, Canada West Foundation, Calgary, Canada. [www.cwf.ca].

Bruns, B., A. Mingat, and R. Rakotomalala. 2003. *Achieving Universal Primary Education by 2015: A Chance for Every Child.* Washington, D.C.: World Bank.

Burnett, N., and M. Lewis. 2005. "Shame in the Heart of Europe: Roma Girls' Education." Draft Policy Brief, Center for Global Development, Washington, D.C.

Caldes, N., D. Coady, and J. Maluccio. 2004. "The Cost of Poverty Alleviation Transfer Programmes: A Comparative Analysis of Three Programmes in Latin America." FCND Discussion Paper 174, International Food Policy Research Institute, Food Consumption and Nutrition Division, Washington, D.C.

Carnoy, M., and J. Marshall. 2005. "Cuba's Academic Performance in Comparative Perspective." *Comparative Education Review* 49 (2): 230–61.

CEA (Canadian Education Association). 2005. "Historical Context." In "Policy Landscape: Aboriginal Peoples." [www.cea-ace.ca].

Chaudhury, N., J. Hammer, M. Kremer, K. Muralidharan, and F. H. Rogers. 2005. "Missing in Action: Teacher and Health Worker Absence in Developing Countries." *Journal of Economic Perspectives* 19 (4): 91–116

Chen, D. H. C., and C. J. Dahlman. 2004. "Knowledge and Development: A Cross-Section Approach." Policy Research Working Paper 3366. World Bank, Washington, D.C.

Clemens, M. 2004. *The Long Walk to School: International Education Goals in Historical Perspective.* Washington, D.C.: Center for Global Development.

Coady, D. 2004. Personal communication. Face-to-face interview. International Food Policy Research Institute. Washington, D.C. August.

Cohen, E. G. 1982. "Expectation States and Interracial Interaction in School Settings." *Annual Review of Sociology* 8: 209–35.

———. 1984. "Talking and Working Together: Status, Interaction and Learning." In P. Peterson, L. C. Wilkinson, and M. Hallinan, eds., *Instructional Groups in the Classroom: Organization and Processes.* Orlando, Fla.: Academic Press.

———. 1986. "On the Sociology of the Classroom." In J. Hannaway and M. Lockheed, eds., *The Contributions of the Social Sciences to Educational Policy and Practice: 1965–1985.* Berkeley, Calif.: McCutchan.

———. 1997. "Equity in Heterogeneous Classrooms: A Challenge for Teachers and Sociologists." In E. G. Cohen and R. M. Lotan, eds., *Working for Equity in Heterogeneous Classrooms: Sociological Theory in Practice.* New York: Teachers College Press.

Cohen, E. G., and R. M. Lotan. 1995. "Producing Equal-Status Interaction in the Heterogeneous Classroom." *American Educational Research Journal* 32 (1): 99–120.

———, eds. 1997. *Working for Equity in Heterogeneous Classrooms: Sociological Theory in Practice.* New York: Teachers College Press.

Cohen, E. G., M. Lockheed, and M. Lohman. 1976. "The Center for Interracial Cooperation: A Field Experiment." *Sociology of Education* 49 (1): 47–58.

Colclough, C. 2004. "Achieving Gender Equality in Education." *Prospects* 34 (1): 3–10.

Conger, D. 2005. "Within-School Segregation in an Urban School District." *Educational Evaluation and Policy Analysis* 27 (3): 225–44.

Conway, J.K. 1989. *The Road from Coorain.* New York: Knopf.

Corson, D. 1993. *Language, Minority Education and Gender: Linking Social Justice and Power.* Clevedon, U.K.: Multilingual Matters.

Crawford, D. 2001. "How 'Berber' Matters in the Middle of Nowhere." *Middle East Report* 219 (Summer): 20–25.

Croizet, J. C., and I. Claire. 1998. "Extending the Concept of Stereotype Threat to Social Class: The Intellectual Underperformance of Students from Low Socioeconomic Backgrounds." *Personality and Social Psychology Bulletin* 24 (6): 588–94.

Crouch, L., and T. Fasih. 2004. "Patterns in Educational Development: Implications for Further Efficiency Analysis." Draft, World Bank, Education Department of the Human Development Network, Washington, D.C.

Cueto, S., and W. Secada. 2004. "Oportunidades de aprendizaje y rendimiento en matemática de niños y niñas Aymará, Quechua y Castellano hablantes en escuelas bilingües y monolingües en Puno, Perú." In D. R. Winkler and S. Cueto, eds., *Etnicidad, raza, género y educación en América Latina.* Washington, D.C.: Inter-American Dialogue, Partnership for Educational Revitalization in the Americas.

Cummins, J. 1997. "Minority Status and Schooling in Canada." *Anthropology and Education Quarterly* 28 (3): 411–30.

Dahlman C., and T. Andersson. 2000. *Korea and the Knowledge-Based Economy: Making the Transition.* Paris: Organisation for Economic Co-operation and Development and World Bank Institute.

Das, J., S. Dercon, J. Habyarimana, and P. Krishnan. 2005. "Teacher Shocks and Student Learning: Evidence from Zambia." Draft, World Bank, Development Economics Vice-Presidency, Washington, D.C.

De, A., and J. Drèze. 1999. *Public Report on Basic Education in India (PROBE Report).* New Delhi: Oxford University Press.

De Ferranti, D., G. Perry, I. Gill, J. L. Guasch, W. Maloney, C. Sanchez-Paramo, and N. Schady. 2003. *Closing the Gap in Education and Technology.* Washington, D.C.: World Bank, Latin American and Caribbean Studies.

De Janvry, A., and E. Sadoulet. 2004. "Conditional Cash Transfer Programs: Are They Really Magic Bullets?" Department of Agricultural and Resource Economics, University of California, Berkeley.

———. 2005. "Conditional Cash Transfer Programs for Child Human Capital Development: Lessons Derived from Experience in Mexico and Brazil." University of California, Berkeley, and World Bank, Development Economics Research Group, Washington, D.C.

———. 2006. "Making Conditional Cash Transfer Programs More Efficient: Designing for Maximum Effect of the Conditionality." *The World Bank Economic Review* 20 (1): 1–30.

de Oliveira Barbosa, M. L. 2004. "Diferencias de género y color en las escuelas de Brasil: Los maestros y la evaluación de los alumnos." In D. R. Winkler and S. Cueto, eds., *Etnicidad, raza, género y educación en América Latina.* Washington, D.C.: Inter-American Dialogue, Partnership for Educational Revitalization in the Americas.

Del Rosso, J. M. 1999. "School Feeding Programs: Improving Effectiveness and Increasing the Benefit to Education. A Guide for Program Managers." London Imperial College, Faculty of Medicine, Department of Infectious Disease Epidemiology, Partnership for Child Development, London.

De Walque, D. 2004. "How Does the Impact of an HIV/AIDS Information Campaign Vary with Educational Attachment? Evidence from Rural Uganda." Policy Research Working Paper 3289. World Bank, Washington, D.C.

De Zwart, F. 2000. "The Logic of Affirmative Action: Caste, Class and Quotas in India." *Acta Sociologica* 43 (3): 235–49.

Deshpande, A. 2005. "Affirmative Action in India and the United States." Background paper for *World Development Report 2006.* World Bank, Development Economics Vice-Presidency, Washington, D.C.

Dock, A., and J. Helwig, eds. 1999. *Interactive Radio Instruction: Impact, Sustainability and Future Directions.* Washington, D.C.: World Bank and United States Agency for International Development.

Dollar, D., and R. Gatti. 1999. "Gender Inequality, Income, and Growth: Are Good Times Good for Women?" Policy Research Report on Gender and Development, Working Paper 1, World Bank, Washington, D.C.

Dowd, A. J. 2001. "The Impact of Community Support for Education on Standard 2 Mathematics Learning in Malawi." Paper presented at the Annual Conference of the Comparative and International Education Society, March, Washington, D.C.

Drèze, J., and G. Gandhi Kingdon. 1999. "School Participation in Rural India." Working Paper 69, Centre for Development Economics, Delhi School of Economics, New Delhi.

Duflo, E. 2000. "Schooling and Labor Market Consequences of School Construction in Indonesia: Evidence from an Unusual Policy Experiment." *American Economic Review* 91 (4): 795–813.

Dureya, S., O. Jaramillo, and C. Pages. 2003. "Latin American Labor Markets in the 1990s: Deciphering the Decade." Working Paper 486, Inter-American Development Bank, Research Department, Washington, D.C.

Eberhardt, J. L., and S. T. Fiske. 1994. "Affirmative Action in Theory and Practice: Issues of Power, Ambiguity, and Gender versus Race." *Basic and Applied Social Psychology* 15 (1–2): 201–20.

Edwards, J., and D. Winkler. 2004. "Capital humano, globalización y asimilación cultural: Un estudio aplicado a los Mayas de Guatemala." In D. R. Winkler and S. Cueto, eds., *Etnicidad, raza, género y educación en América Latina*. Washington, D.C.: Inter-American Dialogue, Partnership for Educational Revitalization in the Americas.

Elley, W., B. Cutting, F. Mangubhai, and C. Hugo. 1996. "Lifting Literacy Levels with Story-Books: Evidence from South Pacific, Singapore, Sri Lanka, and South Africa." Proceedings of the 1996 World Conference on Literacy, March 12–15, Philadelphia, Pa.

Filmer, D. 2000. "The Structure of Social Disparities in Education: Gender and Wealth." Policy Research Working Paper 2268. World Bank, Washington, D.C.

———. 2004. "If You Build It, Will They Come? School Availability and School Enrollment in 21 Poor Countries." Policy Research Working Paper 3340, World Bank, Washington, D.C.

Filmer, D., and L. Pritchett. 1999. "The Effect of Household Wealth on Educational Attainment." *Population and Development Review* 25 (1): 85–120.

Friedman, B. M. 2005. *The Moral Consequences of Economic Growth*. New York: Knopf.

Fryer, Jr., R. G., G. C. Loury, and T. Yuret. 2003. "Color-Blind Affirmative Action." NBER Working Paper 10103. National Bureau of Economic Research, Cambridge, Mass.

Fuller, B., and P. Clark. 1994. "Raising School Effects while Ignoring Culture? Local Conditions and the Influence of Classroom Tools, Rules and Pedagogy." *Review of Educational Research* 64 (1): 119–58.

Gage, A., E. Sommerfelt, and A. Piani. 1997. "Household Structure and Childhood Immunization in Niger and Nigeria." *Demography* 34 (2): 195–309.

Galanter, M. 1991. *Competing Equalities: Law and the Backward Classes in India*. New Delhi: Oxford University Press.

Gamoran, A. 2001. "American Schooling and Educational Inequality: Forecast for the 21st Century." *Sociology of Education* 34 (Extra Issue): 135–53.

Gandara, P., R. Moran, and E. Garcia. 2004. "Legacy of *Brown*: Law and Language Policy in the United States." *Review of Research in Education* 28: 27–46.

Garces, E., D. Thomas, and J. Currie. 2002. "Longer-Term Effects of Head Start." *American Economic Review* 92 (September): 999–1012.

Garcia Aracil, A., and D. R. Winkler. 2004. "Educación y etnicidad en Ecuador" In D. R. Winkler and S. Cueto, eds., *Etnicidad, raza, género y educación en América Latina*. Washington, D.C.: Inter-American Dialogue, Partnership for Educational Revitalization in the Americas.

Gershberg, A. I., and D. R. Winkler. 2004. "Education Decentralization in Africa: A Review of Recent Policy and Practice." In B. Levy and S. Kpundeh, eds., *Building State Capacity in Africa: New Approaches, Emerging Lessons.* Washington, D.C.: World Bank Institute.

Gertler, P., and H. Alderman. 1989. "Family Resources and Gender Differences in Human Capital Investments." Yale University Economic Growth Center, New Haven, Conn.

Gibbs, M. 2005. "The Right to Development and Indigenous Peoples: Lessons from New Zealand." *World Development* 33 (8): 1365–78.

Glenn, C., and E. J. de Jong. 1996. *Educating Immigrant Children: Schools and Language Minorities in Twelve Nations.* New York: Garland Publishing.

Glewwe, P., M. Kremer, and S. Moulin. 2002. "Textbooks and Test Scores: Evidence from a Prospective Evaluation in Kenya." Working Paper. Poverty Action Lab, Massachusettes Institute of Technology, Cambridge, Mass.

Glewwe, P., M. Grosh, H. Jacoby, and M. E. Lockheed. 1995. "An Eclectic Approach to Estimating the Determinants of Achievement in Jamaican Primary Education." *World Bank Economic Review* 9 (2): 231–58.

Glick, P., and D. E. Sahn. 1997. "Gender and Education Impacts on Employment and Earnings in West Africa: Evidence from Guinea." *Economic Development and Cultural Change* 45 (4): 793–823.

Gomes, R. 2004. "Should Communities Succeed Where States Have Not? Community-Based School Management and Girls' Education." Background paper for M. Lewis and M. Lockheed, eds., *Inexcusable Absence: Why 60 Million Girls Still Aren't in School and What to Do About It.* Washington, D.C.: Center for Global Development.

Grissmer, D., A. Flanagan, and S. Williamson. 1998. "Why Did the Black-White Score Gap Narrow in the 1970s and 1980s?" In C. Jencks and M. Phillips, eds., *The Black-White Test Score Gap.* Washington, D.C.: Center for Global Development.

Grutter v. Bollinger et al. 2003 US Supreme Court decision. [www.law.cornell.edu/supct/pdf/02-241P.ZO].

Guillebeau, C. 1999. "Affirmative Action in a Global Perspective: The Cases of South Africa and Brazil." *Sociological Spectrum* 19 (4): 443–65.

Guryan, J. 2004. "Desegregation and Black Dropout Rates." *American Economic Review* 94 (4): 919–43.

Hall, G., and H. Patrinos, eds. 2006. *Indigenous Peoples, Poverty and Human Development in Latin America.* New York: Palgrave.

Hallman, K., and S. Peracca. Forthcoming. "Indigenous Girls in Guatemala: Poverty and Location." In M. Lewis and M. Lockheed, eds., *Exclusion, Gender and Schooling: Case Studies from the Developing World.* Washington, D.C.: Center for Global Development.

Hannum, E. 2002. "Educational Stratification by Ethnicity in China: Enrollment and Attainment in the Early Reform Years." *Demography* 39 (1): 95–117.

Hannum, E., and J. Adams. Forthcoming. "Girls in Gansu, China: Expectations and Aspirations for Secondary Schooling." In M. Lewis and M. Lockheed, eds., *Exclusion, Gender and Schooling: Case Studies from the Developing World.* Washington, D.C.: Center for Global Development.

Hanushek, E. A. 1995. "Interpreting Recent Research on Schooling in Developing Countries." *World Bank Research Observer* 10 (2): 227–46.

———. 2001. "Black-White Achievement Differences and Governmental Interventions." *American Economic Review* 91 (2): 24–28.

———. 2005. *Economic Outcomes and School Quality.* Paris and Brussels: International Institute of Educational Planning and International Academy of Education.

Hanushek, E. A., and D. D. Kimko. 2000. "Schooling, Labor Force Quality, and the Growth of Nations." *American Economic Review* 90 (5): 1184–208.

Hanushek, E. A., and J. A. Luque. 2002. "Efficiency and Equity in Schools around the World." NBER Working Paper 8949. National Bureau of Economic Research, Cambridge, Mass.

Hanushek, E. A., and L. Woessman. 2005. "Does Educational Tracking Affect Performance and Inequality? Differences-in-Differences Evidence across Countries." *Economic Journal* 116 (March): C63–C76.

Hanushek, E. A., J. F. Kain, and S. G. Rivkin. 2002. "New Evidence about Brown v. Board of Education: The Complex Effects of School Racial Composition on Achievement." NBER Working Paper 8741. National Bureau of Economic Research, Cambridge, Mass.

Harbison, R., and E. Hanushek. 1992. *Educational Performance of the Poor: Lessons from Rural Northeast Brazil.* New York: Oxford University Press.

Hendrick, I. G. 1976. "Federal Policy Affecting the Education of Indians in California, 1849–1934." *History of Education Quarterly* 16 (2): 163–85.

Herz, B., and G. B. Sperling. 2004. *What Works in Girls' Education: Evidence and Policies from the Developing World.* New York: Council on Foreign Relations.

Heyneman, S. P. 2000. "From the Party/State to Multiethnic Democracy: Education and Social Cohesion in Europe and Central Asia." *Educational Evaluation and Policy Analysis* 22 (2): 173–92.

Heyneman, S. P., and W. A. Loxley. 1983. "The Effect of Primary School Quality on Academic Achievement across Twenty-Nine High and Low-Income Countries." *American Journal of Sociology* 88 (6): 1162–94.

Hicks, N., and Q. Wodon. 2002. "Reaching the Millennium Development Goals in Latin America: Preliminary Results." *en breve* September 2002 (8): 1–4.

Hill, H., B. Rowan, and D. Ball. 2005. "Effects of Teachers' Mathematical Knowledge for Teaching on Student Achievement." *American Educational Research Journal* 42 (2): 371–406.

Hill, M. A., and E. King. 1995. "Women's Education and Economic Well-Being." *Feminist Economics* 1 (2): 21–46.

Hochschild, J., and N. Scovronick. 2003. *The American Dream and the Public Schools.* New York: Oxford University Press.

Hoddinott, J., and L. Haddad. 1995. "Does Female Income Share Influence Household Expenditures? Evidence from Côte d'Ivoire." *Oxford Bulletin of Economics and Statistics* 57 (1): 77–96.

Hoff, K., and P. Panday. 2005. "Belief Systems and Durable Inequalities: An Experimental Investigation of Indian Caste." Policy Research Working Paper 3351, World Bank, Washington, D.C.

Hopfenberg, W., H. M. Levin, and Associates. 1993. *The Accelerated Schools Resource Guide.* San Francisco: Jossey Bass.

Horowitz, D. 1985. *Ethnic Groups in Conflict.* Berkeley: University of California.

Hovens, M. 2002. "Bilingual Education in West Africa: Does It Work?" *International Journal of Bilingual Education and Bilingualism* 5 (5): 249–66.

Htun, M. 2004. "From 'Racial Democracy' to Affirmative Action: Changing State Policy on Race in Brazil." *Latin American Research Review* 39 (1): 60–89.

Inkeles, A., and D. H. Smith. 1974. *Becoming Modern.* Cambridge, Mass.: Harvard University Press.

International Save the Children Alliance. 2006. *Rewrite the Future: Education for Children in Conflict-affected Countries.* London.

Jacobsen, J., W. Cunningham, L. Siga, and A. Risi. 2004. "Group-Based Inequalities: The Roles of Race, Ethnicity, and Gender." In D. M. De Ferranti, G. E. Perry, F. H. G. Ferreira, and M. Walton, eds., *Inequality in Latin America: Breaking with History?* Washington, D.C.: World Bank.

Jain, S. 2003. "Gender Equality in Education: Community-based Initiatives in India." Background paper for the *EFA Monitoring Report 2003/2004.* United Nations Educational, Scientific, and Cultural Organization, Paris.

Jalan, J., and E. Glinskaya. 2003. "Improving Primary School Edcuation in India: An Impact Assessment of DPEP-Phase 1." World Bank, Washington, D.C.

Janke, C. 1996. "SFPs and Education: Establishing the Context." Backgroud paper for *Catholic Relief Services School Feeding/Education Guidebook.* Baltimore, Md.: Catholic Relief Services.

Jayachandran, U. 2002. "Socio-Economic Determinants of School Attendance in India." Working Paper 103, Centre for Development Economics, Delhi School of Economics, New Delhi.

Jayasundera, T. 2005. "Who Benefits Most from Public Investment in Education: Evidence from Indonesia." Paper presented at the 75th Annual Southern Economic Association Conference, November 18–20, Washington, D.C.

Jejeebhoy, S. J. 1998. "Wife-Beating in Rural India: A Husband's Right? Evidence from Survey Data." *Economic and Political Weekly* 23 (15): 855–62.

Jencks, C., and M. Phillips, eds. *The Black-White Test Score Gap.* Washington, D.C.: Brookings Institution.

Jensen, R. 2003. *Equal Treatment, Unequal Outcomes? Generating Gender Inequality Through Fertility Behavior.* Cambridge, Mass.: Harvard University, John F. Kennedy School of Government.

Jimenez, E., and M. Lockheed. 1989. "Enhancing Girls' Learning through Single-sex Education: Evidence and a Policy Conundrum." *Educational Evaluation and Policy Analysis* 11 (2): 117–42.

Jimenez, W. 2004. "Diferencias de acceso a la educación primarios según condición étnica en Bolivia." In D. R. Winkler and S. Cueto, eds., *Etnicidad, raza, género y educación en América Latina.* Washington, D.C.: Inter-American Dialogue, Partnership for Educational Revitalization in the Americas.

Kağitçibaşi, Ç. 1996. *Family and Human Development across Cultures: A View from the Other Side.* Mahwah, N.J.: Lawrence Erlbaum.

Kağitçibaşi, Ç., D. Sunar, and S. Bekman. 1993. "Long-term Effects of Early Intervention." Unpublished paper. Department of Education, Boğaziçi University, Istanbul, Turkey.

Kattan, R., and N. Burnett. 2004. *User Fees in Primary Education.* Washington, D.C.: World Bank, Human Development Network.

Kauffman, P. 2003. "Diversity and Indigenous Policy Outcomes: Comparisons between Four Nations." In M. Kalantzis and P. James, eds., *International Journal of Diversity in Organisations, Communities and Nations: Cultural Diversity in a Globalising World. Proceedings of the Diversity Conference.* vol. 3. Melbourne, Australia: Common Ground Publishing Pty Ltd.

Kaul, V., C. Ramachandran, and G. C. Upadhyaya. 1993. *Impact of Early Childhood Education on Retention in Primary Grades: A Longitudinal Study.* New Delhi: The National Council of Educational Research and Training.

Kellaghan, T., and V. Greaney. 1992. *Using Examinations to Improve Education: A Study in Fourteen African Countries.* Washington, D.C.: World Bank.

Khalid, H. S., and E. M. Mukhtar. 2002. "The Future of Girls Education in Pakistan: A Study on Policy Measures and Other Factors Determining Girl's Education." United Nations Educational, Scientific and Cultural Organization, Islamabad.

Khandker, S., M. M. Pitt, and N. Fuwa. 2003. "Promoting Girls' Secondary Education: An Evaluation of the Female Secondary School Stipend Programs of Bangladesh." Paper presented at the annual meetings of the Population Association of America, March, Minneapolis.

Kim, J., H. Alderman, and P. F. Orazem. 1998. "Can Private School Subsidies Increase Schooling for the Poor? The Quetta Urban Fellowship Program." *World Bank Economic Review* 13 (3): 443–66.

Kim, J. H., and S. Bailey. 2003. *Unsafe Schools: A Literature Review of School-Related Gender-Based Violence in Developing Countries.* Arlington, Va.: Development and Training Services, Inc.

Kim, K. 1999. "Comparative Study of Instructional Hours in West Africa." Informal Report, World Bank, AFTHR, Washington, D.C.

King, E. 1990. "Does Education Pay in the Labor Market? The Labor Force Participation, Occupation, and Earnings of Peruvian Women." Living Standards Measurement Study, Working Paper 67, World Bank, Washington, D.C.

King, E., and D. van de Walle. Forthcoming. "Girls in Hill Tribes, Lao PDR: Poverty and Isolated Communities." In M. Lewis and M. Lockheed, eds., *Exclusion, Gender and Schooling: Case Studies from the Developing World.* Washington D.C.: Center for Global Development.

King, K., and C. Benson. 2003. "Indigenous Language Education in Bolivia and Ecuador: Contexts, Changes and Challenges." In J. Tollefson and A. Tsui, eds., *Medium of Instruction Policies: Which Agenda? Whose Agenda?* Mahwah, N.J.: Lawrence Erlbaum.

Kingdon, G. 1996. "The Quality and Efficiency of Public and Private Schools: A Case Study of Urban India." *Oxford Bulletin of Economics and Statistics* 58 (1): 55–80.

———. 1998. "Does the Labor Market Explain Lower Female Schooling in India?" *Journal of Development Studies* 35 (1): 39–65.

Klasen, S. 1999. "Does Gender Inequality Reduce Growth and Development? Evidence from Cross-Country Regressions." Policy Research Report on Gender and Development Working Paper 7, World Bank, Washington, D.C.

Klaus, D. 2003. "The Use of Indigenous Languages in Early Basic Education in Papua New Guinea: A Model for Elsewhere?" *Languages and Education* 17 (2): 105–11.

Klein, S. 1985. *Handbook for Achieving Sex Equity through Education.* Baltimore: Johns Hopkins University Press.

Kramer, B. J. 1991. "Education and the American Indians: The Experience of the Ute Indian Tribe." In M. Gibson and J. Obgu, eds., *Minority Status and Schooling: A Comparative Study of Immigrant and Involuntary Minorities.* New York: Garland Publishing.

Kremer, M., E. Miguel, and R. Thornton. 2004. "Incentives to Learn." Massachusetts Institute of Technology Poverty Action Lab, Cambridge, Mass.

Kremer, M., S. Moulin, and R. Namunyu. 2002. "The Political Economy of School in Kenya". Presentation at World Bank, 8 May, Washington, D.C.

Kudó, I. 2004. "La educación indígena en el Perú. Cuando la oportunidad habla una sola lengua." In D. R. Winkler and S. Cueto, eds., *Etnicidad, raza, género y educación en América Latina.* Washington, D.C.: Inter-American Dialogue, Partnership for Educational Revitalization in the Americas.

Lam, D., and L. Marteleto. 2005. "Small Families and Large Cohorts: The Impact of the Demographic Transition on Schooling in Brazil." In Cynthia B. Lloyd, Jere R. Behrman, Nelly P. Stromquist, and Barney Cohen, eds., *The Changing Transitions to Adulthood in Developing Countries: Selected Studies.* Washington, D.C.: National Academies Press.

Lee, H. G. 2005. *Affirmative Action in Malaysia: Southeast Asian Affairs.* Singapore: Institute of Southeast Asian Studies.

Lee, V., and M. Lockheed. 1990. "The Effects of Single-Sex Schools on Student Achievement and Attitudes in Nigeria." *Comparative Education Review* 34 (2): 209–31.

Levin, H., and M. Lockheed, eds. 1993. *Effective Schools in Developing Countries.* New York: Falmer Press.

Levinger, B. 1986. "School Feeding Programs in Developing Countries: An Analysis of Actual and Potential Impact." USAID Evaluation Special Study 30, United States Agency for International Development, Washington, D.C.

Lewis, M. 2005. "Decentralizing Education: Do Communities and Parents Matter?" Unpublished paper. Center for Global Development, Washington, D.C.

Lewis, M. A., and M. E. Lockheed. Forthcoming. "Social Exclusion: The Emerging Challenge in Girls' Education." In M. Lewis and M. Lockheed, eds., *Exclusion, Gender and Schooling: Case Studies from the Developing World.* Washington, D.C.: Center for Global Development.

Lindert, P. 2004. *Growing Public: Social Spending and Economic Growth since the Eighteenth Century.* Cambridge, UK: Cambridge University Press.

Lloyd, C. B. 1994. "Investing in the Next Generation: The Implications of High Fertility at the Level of the Family." In R.Cassen, ed., *Population and Development: Old Debates, New Conclusions.* Washington, D.C.: Overseas Development Council.

———, ed. 2005. *Growing Up Global: The Changing Transitions to Adulthood in Developing Countries.* Washington, D.C.: National Academies Press.

Lloyd, C. B., and A. K. Blanc. 1996. "Children's Schooling in Sub-Saharan Africa: The Role of Fathers, Mothers, and Others." *Population and Development Review* 22 (2): 265–98.

Lloyd, C. B., and A. Gage-Brandon. 1994. "High Fertility and Children's Schooling in Ghana: Sex Differences in Parental Contributions and Educational Outcomes." *Population Studies* 48 (2): 293–306.

Lloyd, C. B., C. E. Kaufman, and P. Hewett. 2000. "The Spread of Primary Schooling in Sub-Saharan Africa: Implications for Fertility Change." *Population and Development Review* 26 (3): 483–515.

Lloyd, C. B., B. S. Mensch, and W. H. Clark. 2000. "The Effects of Primary School Quality on School Dropout among Kenyan Girls and Boys." *Comparative Education Review* 44 (2): 113–47.

Lloyd, C. B., C. Mete, and M. Grant. Forthcoming. "Rural Girls in Pakistan: Constraints of Policy and Culture." In M. Lewis and M. Lockheed, eds., *Exclusion, Gender and Schooling: Case Studies from the Developing World.* Washington, D.C.: Center for Global Development.

Lloyd, C. B., S. El Tawila, W. Clark, and B. Mensch. 2003. "The Impact of Educational Quality on School Exit in Egypt." *Comparative Education Review* 47 (4): 444–67.

Lockheed, M.E. 1993a. "The Condition of Primary Education in Developing Countries." In H. M. Levin and M. E. Lockheed, eds., *Effective Schools in Developing Countries.* New York: Falmer Press.

———. 1993b. "The Development of Sex Typing: Implications for Economic Development." *Monographs of the Society for Research in Child Development* 58 (2): 86–92.

————. 1995. "Educational Assessment in Developing Countries: The Role of the World Bank." In T. Oakland, ed., *International Perspectives on Academic Assessment.* Norwell, Mass.: Kluwer Academic Publishers.

Lockheed, M. E., and B. Bruns. 1990. "School Effects on Achievement in Secondary Mathematics and Portuguese Schools in Brazil." Policy Research Working Paper 525. World Bank, Washington, D.C.

Lockheed, M. E., and A. M. Harris. 2005. "Beneath Education Production Functions: The Case of Primary Education in Jamaica." *Peabody Journal of Education* 80 (1): 6–28.

Lockheed, M. E., and E. Jimenez. 1996. "Public and Private Schools Overseas: Contrasts in Organizations and Effectiveness." In B. Fuller, R. F. Elmore, and G. Orfield, eds., *Who Chooses? Who Loses? Culture, Institutions, and the Unequal Effects of School Choice.* New York: Teachers College Press.

Lockheed, M. E., and H. Levin. 1993. "Creating Effective Schools." In H. M. Levin and M. E. Lockheed, eds., *Effective Schools in Developing Countries.* New York: Falmer Press.

Lockheed, M. E., and C. Mete. Forthcoming. "Tunisia: Strong Central Policies for Gender Equity." In M. Lewis and M. Lockheed, eds., *Exclusion, Gender and Schooling: Case Studies from the Developing World.* Washington, D.C.: Center for Global Development.

Lockheed, M. E., and A. M. Verspoor. 1991. *Improving Primary Education in Developing Countries.* Washington, D.C.: Oxford University Press.

Lockheed, M. E., A. M. Harris, and W. P. Nemceff. 1983. "Sex and Social Influence: Does Sex Function as a Status Characteristic in Mixed-Sex Groups of Children?" *Journal of Educational Psychology* 75 (6) 877–88.

Lockheed, M. E., D. T. Jamison, and L. Lau. 1980. "Farmer Education and Farmer Efficiency." *Economic Development and Cultural Change* 29 (1): 37–76.

Lopez-Acevedo, G. 2004. "Professional Development and Incentives for Teacher Performance in Schools in Mexico." Policy Research Working Paper 3236, World Bank, Washington, D.C.

Loury, G. C. 2000. "Social Exclusion and Ethnic Groups: The Challenge to Economics." In B. Pleskovic and J. E. Stiglitz, eds., *Annual World Bank Conference on Development Economics 1999.* Washington, D.C.: World Bank.

Love, J. M., E. E. Kisker, C. Ross, H. Raikes, J. Constantine, K. Boller, J. Brooks-Gunn, and others. 2005. The Effectiveness of Early Head Start for 3-year-old Children and their Parents: Lessons for Policy and Programs. *Developmental Psychology* 41 (6): 885–901.

Maani, S. A. 2005. Personal communication. Phone call. New Zealand.

Malhotra, A., C. Grown, and R. Pande. 2003. "Impact of Investments in Female Education on Gender Inequality." International Center for Research on Women, Washington, D.C.

Mario, E. G., and M. Woolcock. Forthcoming. "Assessing Social Exclusion and Mobility in Brazil." *Social Exclusion and Mobility in Brazil.* Brasilia: Instituto de Pesquisa Econômica Aplicada and World Bank.

Martin, F. A. 2000. "Roma in Spain." Background paper for D. Ringold, M. A. Orenstein, and E. Wilkens, *Roma in an Expanding Europe: Breaking the Poverty Cycle.* World Bank, Washington, D.C.

Martin, M. O., I. V. S. Mullis, E. J. Gonzalez, and S. J Chrostowski. 2004. *TIMSS 2003 International Science Report: Findings from IEA's Trends in International Mathematics and Science Study at the Fourth and Eighth Grades.* Chestnut Hill, Mass.: Boston College, International Study Center.

Martin, M. O., I. V. S. Mullis, E .J. Gonzalez , K. D. Gregory, T. A. Smith, S. J. Chrostowski, R. A.

Garden, and K. M. O'Connor. 2000. *TIMSS 1999 International Science Report: Findings from IEA's Repeat of the Third International Mathematics and Science Study at the Eighth Grade.* Chestnut Hill, Mass.: Boston College, International Study Center.

Mbassa Menick, D. 2001. "Les abus sexuels en milieu scolaire au Cameroun." Paper presented at the Committee on the Rights of the Child Day of General Discussion on Violence against Children within the Family and in Schools, September 28, Geneva.

McEwan, P. 2004. "La brecha de puntajes obtenidos en las pruebas por los niños indígenas en Sudamerica." In D. R. Winkler and S. Cueto, eds., *Etnicidad, raza, género y educación en América Latina.* Washington, D.C.: Inter-American Dialogue, Partnership for Educational Revitalization in the Americas.

————. 2006. "The Fortuitous Decline of Ethnic Inequality in Chilean Schools." Wellesley College, Wellesley, Mass.

McEwan, P., and M. Trowbridge. 2005. "The Achievements of Indigenous Students in Guatemalan Primary Schools." Unpublished paper. Wellesley College, Wellesley, Mass.

Meerman, J. 2005. "Oppressed People: Economic Mobility of the Socially Excluded." *The Journal of Socio-Economics* 34 (4): 543–67.

Mensch, B. S., J. Bruce, and M. S. Greene. 1998. *The Uncharted Passage: Girls' Adolescence in the Developing World.* New York: The Population Council.

Meyer, J. W., F. O. Ramirez, and Y. N. Soysal. 1992. "World Expansion of Mass Education, 1870-1980." *Sociology of Education* 65 (2): 128–49.

Mgalla, Z., J. T. Boerma, and D. Schapink. 1998. "Protecting School Girls against Sexual Exploitation: A Guardian Program in Mwanza, Tanzania." *Reproductive Health Matters* 7 (12): 19.

Mihajlovic, M. 2004. "Needs Assessment Study for the Roma Education Fund: Serbia (without Kosovo)." World Bank, Washington, D.C.

Miller-Grandvaux, Y., and K. Yoder. 2002. "A Literature Review of Community Schools in Africa." Support for Analysis and Research in Africa (SARA) Project, United States Agency for International Development, Washington, D.C.

Millot, B., and J. Lane. 2002. "The Efficient Use of Time in Education." *Education Economics* 10 (2): 209–28.

Modood, T. 2005. "The Educational Attainments of Ethnic Minorities in Britain." In G. C. Loury, T. Modood, and S. M. Teles, eds., *Ethnicity, Social Mobility, and Public Policy: Comparing the USA and UK.* New York: Cambridge University Press.

Morley, S., and D. Coady. 2003. *From Social Assistance to Social Development.* Washington, D.C.: Center for Global Development and International Food Policy Research Institute.

Motivans, A. 2005. Using Educational Indicators for Policy: School Life Expectancy. *Prospects* 35 (1): 109–16.

Mulkeen, A. 2005. "Teachers for Rural Schools: A Challenge for Africa." Paper presented at FAO, IIEP/UNESCO, ADEA Ministerial Seminar on Education for Rural People in Africa: Policy Lessons, Options and Priorities, September 7–9, Addis Ababa.

Mullens, J. 1993. "The Relationship between Teacher Qualification and Student Learning: Standard One Classrooms in Belize." Unpublished doctoral dissertation. Harvard University, Cambridge, Mass.

Mullens, J., R. Murnane, and J. Willett. 1996. "The Contribution of Training and Subject-Matter Knowledge to Teaching Effectiveness: A Multilevel Analysis of Longitudinal Evidence from Belize." *Comparative Education Review* 40 (2): 139–57.

Muller, C. 2005. "Achievement throughout the Education Pipeline: The Adolescent Years." Presentation at ETS Symposium on the Progress and Challenges of Women and Girls in Education and Work, May 4–5, Princeton, N.J.

Mullis, I. V. S., M. O. Martin, E. J. Gonzalez, and S. J Chrostowski. 2004. *TIMSS 2003 International Mathematics Report: Findings From IEA's Trends in International Mathematics and Science Study at the Fourth and Eighth Grades.* Chestnut Hill, Mass.: Boston College, International Study Center.

Mullis, I. V. S., M. O. Martin, E. J. Gonzalez, and A. M. Kennedy. 2003. *PIRLS 2001 International Report: IEA's Study of Reading Literacy Achievement in Primary Schools in 35 Countries.* Chestnut Hill, Mass.: Boston College, International Study Center.

Mullis, I. V. S., M. O. Martin, E. J. Gonzalez, K. D. Gregory, R. A. Garden, K. M. O'Connor, S. J. Chrostowski, and T. A. Smith. 2000. *TIMSS 1999 International Mathematics Report: Findings From IEA's Repeat of the Third International Mathematics and Science Study at the Eighth Grade.* Chestnut Hill, Mass.: Boston College, International Study Center.

Munshi, K., and M. Rosenzweig. Forthcoming. "Traditional Institutions Meet the Modern World: Caste, Gender, and Schooling Choice in a Globalizing Economy." *American Economic Review.*

Murphy, P., V. Greaney, M. Lockheed, and C. Rojas, eds. 1996. *National Assessment Systems.* Economic Development Institute Seminar Series. Washington D.C.: World Bank.

Mwabu, G., and T. P. Schultz. 1998. "Wage Premia for Education and Location, by Gender and Race in South Africa." Yale University, Economic Growth Center, New Haven, Conn.

Myers, R. 1995. *The Twelve Who Survive: Strengthening Programs of Early Childhood Development in the Third World.* Ypsilanti, Mich.: High/Scope Press.

Nabeshima, K. 2003. "Raising the Quality of Secondary Education in East Asia." Policy Research Working Paper 3140, World Bank, Washington, D.C.

Nambissan, G. B. 1995. "The Social Context of Learning and Schooling of Dalit and Tribal Children." Paper presented at the School Quality in India seminar, November, New Delhi.

Narayan, D. 2000. *Voices of the Poor.* New York: Oxford University Press for the World Bank.

Nath, S., K. Sylva, and J. Grimes. 1999. "Raising Basic Education Levels in Rural Bangladesh: The Impact of a Non-Formal Education Programme." *International Review of Education* 45 (1): 5–26.

Nonoyama, Y. 2005. "Cross-National Study of Multi-Level Effects of Family and School Effects on Achievement." PhD dissertation. Colombia University, New York.

Noorbakhsh, F., and A. Paloni. 2001. "Human Capital and FDI Inflows to Developing Countries: New Empirical Evidence." *World Development* 29 (9): 1593–610.

Nopo, H., J. Saavedera, and M. Torero. 2004. "Ethnicity and Earnings in Urban Peru." Discussion Paper 980, Institute for the Study of Labor, Bonn, Germany.

Ogbu, J. U. 1991. "Immigrant and Involuntary Minorities in Comparative Perspective." In M. Gibson and J. Ogbu, eds., *Minority Status and Schooling: A Comparative Study of Immigrant and Involuntary Minorities.* New York: Garland Publishing.

Ohsako, T., ed. 1997. *Violence at School: Global Issues and Interventions.* Paris: United Nations Educational, Scientific, and Cultural Organization-International Bureau of Education.

Pães de Barros, R., and R. Mendonça. 1999. *Costs and Benefits of Pre-school Education in Brazil.* Rio de Janeiro: Institute of Applied Economic Research.

Pães de Barros, R., R. Mendonça, and M. Soares. 1998. "Uma Avaliação do Impacto do Programa Curumim Sobre o Desempenho Escolar." IPEA Discussion Paper 542. Instituto de Pesquisa

Econōmico Aplicada, Brasilia.

Paqueo, V., and G. Lopez-Acevedo. 2003. "Supply-Side School Improvement and the Learning Achievement of the Poorest Children in Indigenous and Rural Schools: The Case of PARE." Policy Research Working Paper 3172, World Bank, Washington, D.C.

Parker, S. W., L. Rubalcava, and G. Teruel. 2005. "Language Barriers and Schooling Inequality of the Indigenous in Mexico." In J. Behrman, A. Gaviria, and M. Székely, eds., *Who's In and Who's Out: Social Exclusion in Latin America*. Washington, D.C.: Inter-American Development Bank.

Piaget, J. 1926. *Language and Thought of the Child*. New York: Harcourt, Brace.

Postlethwaite, N., and K. Ross. 1992. *Effective Schools in Reading: Implications for Educational Planners*. Amsterdam: International Association for the Evaluation of Educational Achievement.

Pritchett, L. 2004. "Towards a New Consensus for Addressing the Global Challenge of the Lack of Education." Harvard University, John F. Kennedy School of Government, Cambridge, Mass.

Psacharopoulos, G., and H. A. Patrinos. 2002. "Returns to Investment in Education: A Further Update." Policy Research Working Paper 2881, World Bank, Washington, D.C.

Putnam, R. 1993. *Making Democracy Work: Civic Traditions in Modern Italy*. Princeton, N.J.: Princeton University Press.

Quisumbing, A. 1996. "Male-Female Differences in Agricultural Productivity: Methodological Issues and Empirical Evidence." *World Development* 24 (10): 1579–95.

Ravallion, M., and Q. Wodon. 2000. "Does Child Labor Displace Schooling? Evidence on Behavioral Responses to an Enrollment Subsidy." *Economic Journal* 110: C158–C175.

Raymond, M., and E. Sadoulet. 2003. "Educational Grants Closing the Gap in Schooling Attainment between Poor and Non-Poor." University of California, Berkeley, Department of Agricultural and Resource Economics, Berkeley, Calif.

Reber, S. 2003. "Court-Ordered Desegregation: Success and Failures Integrating American Schools Since *Brown*." Unpublished paper. Harvard University, Department of Economics, Cambridge, Mass.

Reinikka, R., and N. Smith. 2004. *Public Expenditure Tracking Surveys in Education*. Paris: UNESCO/International Institute for Educational Planning.

Reinikka, R., and J. Svensson. 2001. "Explaining Leakage of Public Funds." Policy Research Working Paper 2709, World Bank, Washington, D.C.

———. 2004. "Local Capture: Evidence from a Central Government Transfer Program in Uganda." *Quarterly Journal of Economics* 119 (2): 679–705.

Reyhner, J. 1993. "American Indian Language Policy and School Success." *Journal of Educational Issues of Language Minority Students* 12 (Special Issue 3): 35–59.

Riddell, A. 2003. "The Introduction of Free Primary Education in Sub-Saharan Africa." Background paper for *EFA Global Monitoring Report 2003/4: The Leap to Equality*. Paris: United Nations Educational, Scientific and Cultural Organization.

Ridgeway, C. 1997a. "Interaction and the Conservation of Gender Inequality: Considering Employment." *American Sociological Review* 62 (2): 218–35.

———. 1997b. "Where Do Status-Value Beliefs Come From? New Developments." In J. Szmatka, J. Skvoretz and J. Berger, eds., *Status, Network and Structure: Theory Development in Group Processes*. Stanford, Calif.: Stanford University Press.

Ridgeway, C., E. Boyle, K. Kuipers, and D. Robinson. 1998. "Resources and Interaction in the Development of Status Beliefs." *American Sociological Review* 63 (3): 331–50.

Ridker, R. G., ed. 1997. "Determinants of Educational Achievement and Attainment in Africa: Findings from Nine Case Studies." SD Publication Series, Technical Paper 62, United States Agency for International Development, Washington, D.C.

Ringold, D. 2005. "Accounting for Diversity: Policy Design and Maori Development in Aotearoa New Zealand." Fulbright Report, New Zealand.

Ringold, D., M. Orenstein, and E. Wilkens. 2003. *Roma in an Expanding Europe: Breaking the Poverty Cycle*. Washington, D.C.: World Bank.

Rogoff, B. 1990. *Apprenticeship in Thinking: Cognitive Development in Social Context*. New York: Oxford University Press.

Rose, P. 2003. "Communities, Gender and Education: Evidence from Sub-Saharan Africa." Background paper for UNESCO, *Global Monitoring Report 2003*. United Nations Educational, Cultural, and Scientific Organization, Paris.

Rosenberg, F. 2004. "Desigualdades de raza y género en el sistema educacional Brasileño." In D. R. Winkler and S. Cueto, eds., *Etnicidad, raza, género y educación en América Latina*. Washington, D.C.: Inter-American Dialogue, Partnership for Educational Revitalization in the Americas.

Ross, K., and T. N. Postlethwaite. 1989. "Indicators of the Quality of Education: A Summary of a National Study of Primary Schools in Zimbabwe." Report 96, International Institute for Educational Planning and Research, Paris.

Ross, K., M. Saito, S. Dolata, M. Ikeda, and L. Zuze. 2004. Data archive for the SACMEQ I and SACMEQ II Projects. Paris, International Institute for Educational Planning.

Rossetti, S. 2001. *Children in School: A Safe Place*. Gabarone, Botswana: United Nations Educational, Scientific, and Cultural Organization.

Rugh, A., and H. Bossert. 1998. *Involving Communities: Participation in the Delivery of Education Programs*. Washington, D.C.: United States Agency for International Development.

Sadoulet, E. 2006. Personal communication. Face-to-face conversation. Professor, University of California, Berkley. Washington D.C., December.

Sathar, Z. A., C. B. Lloyd, C. Mete, and M. ul Haque. 2003. "Schooling Opportunities for Girls as a Stimulus for Fertility Change in Rural Pakistan." *Economic Development and Cultural Change* 51 (3): 677–98.

Sathar, Z. A., C. B. Lloyd, M. ul Haque, M. J. Grant, and M. Khan. 2005. "Fewer and Better Children: Expanding Choices in Schooling and Fertility in Rural Pakistan." Population Council, Policy Research Division, New York.

Schady, N., and M. C. Araujo. 2006. "Cash Transfers, Conditions, School Enrollment and Child Work: Evidence from a Randomized Experiment in Ecuador." Policy Research Working Paper 3930. World Bank, Washington, D.C.

Scheerens, J. 1999. "School Effectiveness in Developed and Developing Countries: A Review of the Evidence." World Bank, Education Department of the Human Development Network, Washington, D.C.

Schuler, S. R. Forthcoming. "Rural Bangladesh: Sound Policies, Evolving Gender Norms and Family Strategies." In M. Lewis and M. Lockheed, eds., *Exclusion, Gender and Schooling: Case Studies from the Developing World*. Washington, D.C.: Center for Global Development.

Schultz, T. P. 1993. "Returns to Women's Schooling." In E. A. King and M. A. Hill, eds., *Women's Education in Developing Countries: Barriers, Benefits, and Policy*. Baltimore, Md.: Johns Hopkins University Press.

————. 2002. "Why Governments Should Invest More to Educate Girls." *World Development* 30 (2): 207–25.

————. 2004. "School Subsidies for the Poor: Evaluating the Mexican *Progresa* Poverty Program." *Journal of Development Economics* 74 (1): 199–250.

Sen, A. 1997. "Inequality, Unemployment and Contemporary Europe." *International Labour Review* 136 (2): 155–72.

————. 2006. *Identity and Violence.* New York: W.W. Norton.

Shapiro, J., and J. Moreno Trevino. 2004. "Compensatory Education for Disadvantaged Mexican Students: An Impact Evaluation Using Propensity Score Matching." Policy Research Working Paper 3334, World Bank, Washington, D.C.

Sharan, S., P. Kussell, R. Hertz-Lazarowitz, Y. Bejerano, S. Raviv, and Y. Sharan. 1984. *Cooperative Learning in the Classroom: Research in Desegregated Schools.* Hillsdale, N.J.: Lawrence Erlbaum.

Sharan, S., and H. Shachar. 1988. *Language and Learning in the Cooperative Classroom.* New York: Springer-Verlag.

Silva, N. V. 2000. "Extent and Nature of Racial Inequalities in Brazil." In *Beyond Racism, Embracing an Interdependent Future.* Atlanta: Southern Education Foundation.

Sipahimalani-Rao, V., and P. Clarke. 2002. "A Review of Educational Progress and Reform in The District Primary Education Program (DPEP I and II)." DPEP Evaluation Report 1, World Bank, Human Development Department of the South Asia Region, New Delhi.

Skidmore, T. E. 2003. "Racial Mixture and Affirmative Action: The Cases of Brazil and the United States." *American Historical Review* 108 (5): 1391–96.

Smith, L. C., and L. Haddad. 1999. "Explaining Child Malnutrition in Developing Countries: A Cross-Country Analysis." IFPRI Food Consumption and Nutrition Division Discussion Paper 60, International Food Policy Research Institute, Washington, D.C.

Sowell, T. 1994. *Race and Culture: A World View.* New York: Basic Books

————. 2004. *Affirmative Action around the World: An Empirical Study.* New Haven, Conn.: Yale University Press.

Spencer, S. J., C. M. Steele, and D. M. Quinn. 1999. "Stereotype Threat and Women's Math Performance." *Journal of Experimental and Social Psychology* 35 (1): 4–28.

Stash, S., and E. Hannum. 2001. "Who Goes to School? Educational Stratification by Gender, Caste and Ethnicity in Nepal." *Comparative Education Review* 45 (3): 354–78.

Steele, C. M., and J. Aronson. 1995. "Stereotype Threat and the Intellectual Test Performance of African Americans." *Journal of Personality and Social Psychology* 69 (5): 797–811.

Stewart, F., 2001. "Horizontal Inequalities: A Neglected Dimension of Development." Wider Annual Development Lecture, CRISE Working Paper 1, University of Oxford, Oxford, U.K.

Sturrock, F. M. 2004. "Focus on Maori Achievement in Reading Literacy: Results from PISA 2000." Organization for Economic Co-operation and Development, Program for International Student Assessment, Comparative Education Research Unit, Paris.

Sturrock, F. M., and S. May. 2002. *PISA 2000: The New Zealand Context: The Reading, Mathematical and Scientific Literacy of 15-year-olds. Results from the Programme for International Student Assessment.* Wellington, New Zealand: Ministry of Education.

Subbarao, K., and L. Raney. 1995. "Social Gains from Female Education." *Economic Development and Cultural Change* 44 (1): 105–28.

Summers, L. H. 1994. "Investing in All the People: Educating Women in Developing Countries."

Economic Development Institute Seminar Paper 45. World Bank, Washington, D.C.

Suryadarma, D., A. Suryahadi, S. Sumarto, and F. H. Rogers. 2004. "The Determinants of Student Performance in Indonesian Public Primary Schools: The Role of Teachers and Schools." Social Monitoring and Early Response Unit Working Paper, Jakarta.

Swanson, C. 2004. "Who Graduates? Who Doesn't? A Statistical Portrait of Public High School Graduation, Class of 2001." Urban Institute, Education Policy Center, Washington, D.C.

Sweetman, A., and G. Dicks. 1999. "Education and Ethnicity in Canada: An Intergenerational Perspective." *Journal of Human Resources* 24 (4): 668–96.

Tan, J.-P., J. Lane, and P. Coustere. 1997. "Putting Inputs to Work in Elementary Schools: What Can Be Done in the Philippines?" *Economic Development and Cultural Change* 45 (4): 857–79.

Thomas, D. 1990. "Intra-Household Allocation: An Inferential Approach." *Journal of Human Resources* 25 (4): 635–64.

Thomas, V., Y. Wang, and X. Fan. 2001. "Measuring Education Inequality: Gini Coefficients of Education." Policy Research Working Paper 2525, World Bank, Washington, D.C. [http://ssrn.com/abstract=258182].

Tietjen, K., A. Raman, and S. Spaulding. 2004. *Time to Learn: Teachers' and Students' Use of Time in Bangladesh.* Washington, D.C.: Creative Associates.

Tomaschevski, K. 2001. "Annual Report to the UN Commission on Human Rights by the Special Rapporteur on Education." Commission on Human Rights, March, Geneva.

Torero, M., J. Saavedra, H. Ñopo, and J. Escobal. 2003. "The Economics of Social Exclusion in Peru: An Invisible Wall?" Working paper. Group of Analysis for Development, Lima.

UN (United Nations) 2000. *World Population Prospects: The 2000 Revision.* New York.

UNESCO (United Nations Educational, Scientific and Cultural Organization). 2002 *EFA Global Monitoring Report 2002: Education for All: Is the World on Track?* Paris.

———. 2003. *EFA Global Monitoring Report 2003/2004: Gender and Education for All: The Leap to Equality.* Paris.

———. 2004. *EFA Global Monitoring Report 2005: Education for All: The Quality Imperative.* Paris.

———. 2005. *EFA Global Monitoring Report 2006: Literacy for Life.* Paris.

UIS (UNESCO Institute for Statistics) 2005. *Children Out of School: Measuring Exclusion from Primary Education.* Montreal: United Nations Educational, Scientific and Cultural Organization.

U.S. Department of Education. 2006. "National Assessment of Educational Progress." Institute of Education Sciences, National Center for Education Statistics, Washington, D.C. [http://nces.ed.gov/nationsreportcard/].

Van de Walle, D., and D. Gunewardena. 2001. "Sources of Ethnic Inequality in Viet Nam." *Journal of Development Economics* 65 (1): 177–207.

Vermeersch, C., and M. Kremer. 2004. "School Meals, Educational Achievement and School Competition: Evidence from a Randomized Evaluation in Kenya." Harvard University Economics Department, Cambridge, Mass.

Vygotzky, L. 1962. *Thought and Language.* Cambridge, Mass.: Harvard University Press.

Watt, P. 2001. "Community Support for Basic Education in Sub-Saharan Africa." Africa Region Human Development Working Paper. World Bank, Washington, D.C.

Weatherford, M. S. 1980. "The Politics of School Busing: Contextual Effects and Community Polarization." *Journal of Politics* 42 (3): 747–65.

Webster, Jr., M., and S. Hysom. 1998. "Creating Status Characteristics." *American Sociological*

Review 63 (3): 351–78.

Willms, J. D., and M.-A. Somers. 2001. "Family, Classroom, and School Effects on Children's Educational Outcomes in Latin America." *School Effectiveness and School Improvement* 12 (4): 409–45.

Wils, A., B. Carrol, and K. Barrow. 2005. *Educating the World's Children: Patterns of Growth and Inequality.* Washington, D.C.: Academy for Educational Development, Education Policy and Data Center.

Wils, A., Y. Zhao, and A. Hartwell. 2005. "Looking below the Surface: Reaching the Out-of-School Children." Academy for Educational Development, Washington, D.C.

Wilson, D. 2004. "Promoting Gender Equality in and through Education." *Prospects* 34 (1): 11–27

Winkler, D. R., and S. Cueto, eds. 2004. *Etnicidad, raza, género y educación en América Latina.* Washington, D.C.: Inter-American Dialogue, Partnership for Educational Revitalization in the Americas. [www.preal.org/public-lpeLIBROSindex.php]. January 2006.

Woessmann, L. 2000. "Schooling Resources, Educational Institutions, and Student Performance: The International Evidence." Kiel Working Paper 983, Kiel Insitute of World Economics, Kiel, Germany.

———. 2005. "Families, Schools and Primary School Learning: Evidence for Argentina and Colombia in an International Perspective." Policy Research Working Paper 3537, World Bank, Washington, D.C.

World Bank. 1996. "India: Primary Education and Challenges." Report 15756-IN, World Bank, South Asia Country Department, Washington, D.C.

———. 1997. *Primary Education in India.* Washington, D.C.

———. 1999. *PAD for Rajasthan District Primary Education Program.* SASHD, Washington, D.C.

———. 2001. *Engendering Development.* Washington, D.C.: Oxford University Press.

———. 2003. *World Development Report 2004: Making Services Work for Poor People.* Washington, D.C.: Oxford University Press.

———. 2005a. *Lesotho Education Country Status Report.* Washington, D.C.

———. 2005b. *World Development Indicators.* Washington, D.C.

———. 2005c. *World Development Report 2006: Equity and Development.* Washington, D.C.: Oxford University Press.

World Food Programme. 2004. "School Feeding Works - An Annotated Bibliography." Rome.

Wu, K. B., P. Goldschmidt, C. K. Boscardin, and M. Azam. Forthcoming. "Caste and Tribal Girls in India: Residuals of Historic Discrimination." In M. Lewis and M. Lockheed, eds., *Exclusion, Gender and Schooling: Case Studies from the Developing World.* Washington, D.C.: Center for Global Development.

Zoninsein, J. 2002. "The Economic Case for Combating Racial and Ethnic Exclusion in Latin America and Caribbean Countries." Inter-American Development Bank, Research Department, Washington, D.C.

Index

E